W9-AVC-561

THURSDAY

is the

NEW FRIDAY

THURSDAY

is the

NEW FRIDAY

How to Work Fewer Hours, Make More Money,
and Spend Time Doing What You Want

JOE SANOK

HARPERCOLLINS
LEADERSHIP

AN IMPRINT OF HARPERCOLLINS

This book is dedicated to Lucia and Laken, the reason I slow down.
I love seeing you become such bold, brave, and kind women!

Published by HarperCollins Leadership, an imprint of HarperCollins Focus LLC.

Any internet addresses, phone numbers, or company or product information printed in this book are offered as a resource and are not intended in any way to be or to imply an endorsement by HarperCollins Leadership, nor does HarperCollins Leadership vouch for the existence, content, or services of these sites, phone numbers, companies, or products beyond the life of this book.

ISBN 978-1-4002-2604-7 (eBook)

ISBN 978-1-4002-2598-9 (HC)

Library of Congress Control Number: 2021941330

Printed in the United States of America

21 22 23 24 25 LSC 10 9 8 7 6 5 4 3 2 1

CONTENTS

THURSDAY IS THE NEW FRIDAY

1

WORKING LESS IS DANGEROUS

The forty-hour (or more) workweek that spans five days has become an established aspect of society. Out of seven days, we work five and take two off—that's always been the case, right? In fact, the five-day work-week became the norm only after Henry Ford established it in his factories in May 1926. The seven-day week or the five-day workweek are arbitrary and changeable, and so is how we run our businesses. It's "the way it is" for almost no good reason. It is how it is because it is how it has been.

WE MADE IT UP

Bosses, supervisors, and CEOs may say, "You want a four-day workweek because you don't want to work so hard."

Workers may say, "This pace is unsustainable. There's no way I can do everything I need to do as an adult on Saturday and Sunday alone. Plus, I know I could do this more efficiently and work less."

Can this conflict be resolved? It feels like an eternal battle between workers and owners. Even among solopreneurs, overwork is commonplace. It takes the form of emails in the evening, just that one phone call on Saturday, or a never-ending "to-do" list.

We made this all up.

To be sure, discussing labor, work conditions, and progress is dangerous work. In our world, we see our schedules through the lens of our domestic lives: soccer practice, meetings, groceries, and (if we have any time left) life goals.

There are two predominant positions when people approach success. On one side we have the woo-woo folks who say that if we just "will it to the universe" it will happen. This side promotes vision boards, manifesting abundance, and tapping into energy. On the other side, we're told to just "hustle harder." This side pushes working more, fighting against all odds, and steamrolling others.

So, which is it? Does the universe care about how I spend my time? Do I just need to hustle harder? Seriously, most of the time, all I care about is when I'm going to find time to go buy more groceries and maybe watch a movie with my kids.

Is this the best imaginable version of human work-life? How did we get here? What is our system based on? Without a sense of history, we won't have a context for the kind of dangerous work we're discussing. Or why business leaders in the 1800s found this discussion so threatening.

Let's back up a few thousand years to the origin of the seven-day week. The Babylonians who at that time ruled modern-day Iraq could only see seven celestial bodies: Sun, Moon, Mercury, Venus, Mars, Jupiter, and Saturn.

The length of a year is based on the orbit of the earth around the sun. Months are based on moon cycles, but the length of a week is random. Witold Rybczynski wrote in the *Atlantic*, "Seven days is not natural because no natural phenomenon occurs every seven days."[1] We could just as easily have seventy-three weeks a year that are five days. If we still wanted thirty-day months, we would have six five-day weeks in each month. The Babylonians invented the seven-day week. Others followed their example.

Most biblical scholars believe that most of the Jewish Torah (the first five books of the Bible) was brought together from various sources and assembled while the Jews were in exile in Babylon. The book of Genesis, which enshrines the seven-day week, was written while the Jews lived in Babylon.[2] Other cultures had different ways of expressing a "week." In fact, Egyptians had a ten-day week, and Romans had one that lasted eight days. In early history, the number of days in a week didn't matter.

How we dated our calendars varied from culture to culture. In Dr. Vera Rossovskaja's 1936 book, *The Remote Past of the Calendar*, she discussed how Russians began their year on March 1 until the fifteenth century. Their count began at the creation of the world in 5509 BCE. Peter the Great introduced January 1 as the beginning of the year in 1700. Until then, it had been September 1. During that time, they followed the Julian calendar, which has 365-day years and 366-day years. In 1918, the Russians switched from the Julian calendar to the Gregorian calendar. The Julian calendar has three fewer days over a four-hundred-year period, whereas the Gregorian calendar has an added day every four years on February 29. So, when the Russians adopted this calendar, they had to cancel thirteen days to align with the new calendar.[3]

In the summer of 1929, Russia implemented a five-day week. Natasha Frost writes for the History channel, "The ordinary seven-day week now had a new bedfellow: the *nepreryvka*, or 'continuous working week.'" It was five days long, with days of rest staggered across the week. "Now," the Soviet economist and politician Yuri Larin proposed, "the machines need never be idle."[4]

The history of calendars, workweeks, and how we organize our time is not as universal as we might expect. Yes, our way of doing things feels like the only way, but the reality is: We made all of this up! And nothing prevents us from unmaking it.

Once the seven-day week was widely established, numerous manifestations of the workweek morphed. Let's look at a few examples of how cultures and religions have viewed time.

Throughout history people have segregated time for religious observance from ordinary work time. For Judeo-Christians this is a Sabbath, often on Saturday or Sunday. In Islam, this is usually Friday prayers. Theravada Buddhists observe an *uposatha*, which is a day of cleansing the mind. The Cherokee have a rest day, which begins at sunrise the first day of the new moon. Fasting, reflection, and prayer is encouraged for up to four days. In the Bahá'í Faith, Friday is the rest and reflection day.

Having gone to college in west Michigan, I saw this firsthand. West Michigan is home to some of the strongest Dutch Reformed versions of Christianity. Early settlers left the Netherlands because of their liberal leanings. They founded Holland, Michigan, and Calvin College, Christian Reformed Church strongholds. Even today, numerous businesses are closed on Sundays in observance.

What is it about slowing down that is part of every world religion and culture? And what are the implications of a day of rest on how we work? Recent science confirms what humans have intuited for thousands of years: slowing down and reflecting returns dividends. Our DNA said, "This is valuable; we need to keep this."

So, we know certain things are true of our nature. They're a given. Other things we create. A seven-day week is one of those things. We created that. Yes, historically, we inherited it, but humans created it. One day off a week was the standard. Then two days . . . and now maybe three? It's one thing to look backward and define our behavior by evolution, but it's another to look forward to a possible revolution or re-evolution.

Through the stories and research in this book, I will explore three main ideas. The first is the question of how we organize our time. Our schedules, weekly decisions, and ways we choose to work are relatively recent inventions. If we view these schedules as tools, are they serving us? Is the tool doing the job? Or was that tool useful in a past time and place, but now needs to be reconfigured?

The second idea concerns the internal inclinations that drive the most successful people, and how we can develop those within ourselves. What does research show us regarding those inclinations, habits, and actions that can lead to reinventing a new type of schedule and life that is best for us?

The last idea: slowing down leads to innovative businesses that contribute to the world. How can we use the best brain research and apply it to creating a new schedule that builds income, innovation, and impact?

Now some historical context regarding how we got to this point.

THE RISE OF THE FIVE-DAY WORKWEEK

To understand why this is such a charged issue, we must revisit 1886. We often credit Henry Ford with inventing the five-day workweek, but his innovation evolved—slowly—from an explosion in Chicago, Illinois, on May 4, 1886.

On May 3, a large group of workers that included socialists, anarchists, unionists, and reformers gathered in Chicago to support a strike for the eight-hour workday. Nineteenth-century workers were poorly paid and conditions were oppressive. Historical documentation shows that factory workers had at least ten-hour days and worked a minimum of six days a week. Conditions were poor and there was job instability.

Workers were at a breaking point.

Police broke up the demonstration, killing two strikers. On the following day, May 4, the protesters reorganized and returned to Chicago's

Haymarket Square. That evening, after their number had dwindled to some 200 demonstrators, 176 police attacked the protesters as rain came down heavily. Someone, still unknown, threw a bomb that killed eight police officers and injured sixty more. The police killed and injured an unknown number of civilians. On May 5, martial law was declared—not just in Chicago, but nationwide.

Professor William J. Adelman of the University of Illinois-Chicago wrote: "No single event has influenced the history of labor in Illinois, the United States, and even the world, more than the Chicago Haymarket Affair. It began with a rally on May 4, 1886, but the consequences are still being felt today."[5]

One day off per week was the standard until the twentieth century. In 1908, a New England mill became the first American factory to institute a five-day workweek. Conflict between Jewish and Christian workers, not concerns about productivity or workers' rights, forced the decision. The Jewish workers wanted Saturday off to observe their Sabbath and to work half a day on Sunday. The Christian workers wanted to work a half day on Saturday and have Sunday off. So began the first two-day weekend.[6]

The most monumental shift came when Henry Ford instituted the five-day workweek. It started within the company with a handful of male workers. In March 1922, the *New York Times* spoke with Ford's president and Henry's son, Edsel Ford: "Every man needs more than one day a week for rest and recreation. . . . The Ford Company always has sought to promote [an] ideal home life for its employees. We believe that in order to live properly every man should have more time to spend with his family."[7]

With the goal of increasing productivity, Henry Ford announced, "It is high time to rid ourselves of the notion that leisure for workmen is either 'lost time' or a class privilege."[8] The date was exactly forty years after the walkouts that led to the Haymarket Square bombing: May 1, 1926.

We are experiencing another shift. An unplanned-for, worldwide experiment began in early 2020 when COVID-19 started its spread. Almost overnight, the entire world moved to virtual offices. Local nonprofit boards met online, township boards hosted the public's comments virtually, and telemedicine took off.

That mandatory experiment, in which states locked down, children left school, and parents juggled online work, provoked a societal realization.

Maybe we could do this differently? Parents, small business owners, non-essential employees . . . everyone asked the question: Could a different schedule and lifestyle be possible?

THE INDUSTRIALIST FINGERPRINT AND THE PROTESTANT WORK ETHIC

The Industrial Revolution was an important part of society's development, and throughout this book I will make frequent reference to the Industrialists' legacy: productivity and production through optimizing every waking hour. Through the Industrialists' efforts, almost every aspect of society has been automated, producing the maximum amount of goods and services at the lowest cost. But the Industrialist mindset has not solved world hunger, disease, and war. A mechanized view of the world gets us only so far. We can be productive without purpose, or, as the internet, remote work, the gig economy, and the worldwide COVID-19 work-from-home experiment have shown us, we can live differently.

We are in a transitional time.

Although the Industrialists were mainly systematizing business, their mentality determined how school is taught, churches operate, and communities are organized. In the same way, our transition extends beyond business. We see that traditional schedules for home, life, school, and work were significantly disrupted during the 2020 COVID-19 pandemic. Schools and parents had already been reflecting on the mechanical nature of school, with many parents turning away from traditional public school education. Reports show that homeschooling is growing at 2 to 8 percent per year.[9]

In the workplace, a mass reevaluation occurred as both employees and employers saw some businesses carry on with remote workers, often only putting in a few hours of "real" work per day. Research is emerging from the lockdown showing boosts in productivity from working at home, reduction in commutes, and job satisfaction.[10]

I love sleeping in; I'm like a teenager still. I wish I were a morning person, but if I have nothing planned, I could probably sleep in until 11:00 a.m. Recently, our daughters spent the night at my parents' house. We had absolutely nothing planned, and because we were on quarantine lockdown, there was very little in the world to do. I woke up at 9:30 a.m. and lay with my eyes shut, but my inner Industrialist, the voice of our collective sub-conscious, was saying, "Dishes could be washed. There's that book you could read about being a better couple. The yard could use some work."

That damn inner Industrialist kept me awake, but I resisted. I got up and drank tea with my wife and I wasn't "productive." You probably have Industrialist evangelicals in your world: parents, boss, inner critic. When you were a kid, it may have been your parents speaking on behalf of the Industrialists: "Don't be lazy; make your bed." Today it may be seeing all the other moms on Instagram displaying the perfect crafts, schooling, and families. The Industrialist voice manifests incessantly.

The "Protestant Work Ethic"—as it has come to be known—is deeply embedded in the American view of society and religion, but it no longer serves our purposes. It doesn't match what we feel. To ensure productivity, the Industrialists depended on conformity, self-denial, and guilt. Until recently, we didn't have a scientific understanding of the value of sleep for the brain, for example, or that multitasking is terrible, and that meditation can help you achieve more. People are not machines.

So if we're throwing out the Protestant Work Ethic and creating a new Healthy Work Ethic, what is that? Throughout this book, you'll see why slowing down actually speeds things up, how aggressive boundaries in your personal life actually increase productivity, and how shrinking workweeks are being implemented by the most innovative companies. We can get things done without a forty-plus-hour workweek. When we are refreshed and rested, we get more done in a shorter period of time. Working for someone else is not the only way to make a living. In fact, the Industrialist approach is killing us in more ways than we know.

THE INDUSTRIALISTS WANT TO KILL YOU

The Industrialist voice was and is dangerous, but not just for factories. The Haymarket Square protest exposed working conditions and eventually led to improvement in workweeks (thirty years later).[11] But optimizations of every moment, cutting costs, and treating people like machines are the ongoing reincarnation of the Industrialist mindset.

A thirty-two-year study reported in the *Journal of Occupational and Environmental Medicine* showed that working long hours increases the risk of chronic diseases, especially in women.[12] Sleep, stress, and anxiety issues can be tied to the way that we currently live. Maximum productivity, time away from meaningful social relationships, lack of exercise, and poor eating are all part of the symptoms. We're working too damn much!

But change is being tested. Microsoft Japan experimented with a four-day workweek. They saw a 40 percent boost in productivity, but the program was discontinued without explanation.[13]

In Sweden, a Lund University study showed that a thirty-hour workweek built "autonomy, communication, creativity, motivation and commitment, and subjective quality assessment. Our findings suggest that the thirty-hour workweek is a promising concept for knowledge workers and that it helps to counteract some modern challenges related to knowledge work such as work intensification, empty labour and psychological contract building."[14] Researchers are linking positive mood to productivity and creativity.[15] Jason Fried, CEO of Basecamp, implemented a thirty-two-hour workweek for half of the year.[16] Matt Mullinwig, founder of Wordpress, built his company based on work done instead of hours put in.[17]

Despite an overwhelming body of research in a variety of fields, business case studies, and people just plain disliking it, why does the Industrialist mindset persist? Why would Microsoft Japan cancel their program after seeing a 40 percent boost in productivity? It's the fear of the unknown and the undue power of the known. Yet, explorers look beyond the known toward new cultures and experiences. Those who investigate, create, and push the boundaries are the ones who discover new resources to survive.

The Industrialists, as I will refer to them throughout the book, were as much a mindset as a group of men. The Industrialist mindset focused on automation, structure, and an undervaluing of people. Everything was replaceable to make the machine of industry thrive. It was a step forward, as the Industrialists moved toward weekends and safer conditions, but it is no place to remain.

The Industrialists were a step forward in a number of ways, but their fingerprint no longer is helping humanity.

The Industrialists have had their day. The world knows their approach. Farmers needed to move away from the seven-day workweek eventually. The Industrialists paved that path, but there are other routes to forge.

TGIF

The show *Full House* was a hit that ran for 193 episodes from 1987 to 1995. The show was about a single dad raising three girls, after his wife was killed by a drunk driver. He invited his wannabe comedian best friend, Joey, and his rock musician, motorcycle-loving, womanizing, badass brother-in-law to help raise the girls. Three guys, who couldn't be more different from one another, raising three girls.

But the magic of *Full House* wasn't just the story; it was what it represented. It was part of ABC's TGIF lineup. Thank Goodness It's Funny. I still remember the song: "It's Friday night and the mood is right, gonna have some fun, show you how it's done, T-G-I-F!"

When I was a kid, Fridays were a celebration. One of my earliest memories was of my father, a psychologist, coming home on a Friday night. He and my mother would play the *Blues Brothers* soundtrack and we'd dance before dinner. The work for the week was done and now there was the weekend. But before Saturday soccer, raking, cleaning, grocery shopping, and the general reset of middle-American life, there was Friday night.

For my father, having a Friday night was a step forward. His grandparents were farmers, who moved to Michigan from Poland. They had to work every day, feeding animals and tending to farm life.

In 1953, my grandparents, Louis and Jeanette Sanok, moved from Detroit to a small town named Carleton, bought a family house connected to a general store outfitted with gas pumps, and opened Sanok's Market.

My grandfather woke up every Monday through Friday at 4:45 a.m. and quickly put on his clothes. He was in his car by 5:00 a.m. He would drive an hour to the General Motors Cadillac division and work as a metal finisher. My grandmother, Jeanette, would get the five children ready for school. The years between children had been widely spaced, so a baby was often in the mix. She opened Sanok's Market at 9:00 a.m. If she was in the house, an intercom and a drive-over bell alerted her to a customer. During those occasional fifteen-minute breaks between customers, she made dinner, did laundry for seven people, and kept house.

Louis returned at 4:00 p.m. and the family usually had an early dinner around four thirty. Jeanette worked the store while Louis fed the kids, then they switched. Louis then worked the store until 8:30 p.m. He then restocked the beer, sorted cans by hand, swept, and completed the other tasks required to manage a store.

From 9:00 to 10:00 p.m., he sat in his chair and watched two television shows. He then went to bed and woke again the next day at 4:45 a.m. On Saturdays, he worked the store from 9:00 a.m. until 9:00 p.m. and Jeanette would often take some of the children to the closest city, Monroe, to get groceries that could not be delivered, that they would sell in the store. Jeanette and Louis decided they wanted to make a little extra money, so they opened the store for three hours on Sundays. That lasted only three weeks, because the parish priest pressured them to remain closed on Sundays.

But Sundays were not a day of rest. Instead, the family attended 10:00 a.m. Mass, then drove an hour to Detroit to visit family. Once in Detroit, they had to track down where family members had gathered, since cell phones were fifty years in the future.

On any given day my grandparents had an hour of relaxation. Once a week they had a day off and spent it in church or with family. Much of life revolved around work, factory, store, and family obligations.

They were slightly better off than their neighbors, investing in items like a new porch, lawn mower, new cooler, and decent car. Compared to others, they were consumers. Always improving the here and now. For years when they would carpet a room, they would buy a remnant. For most people, that was the norm. No one saw it as unfashionable; it was fine to have carpet end a foot away from the wall. My father remembers when they first installed wall-to-wall carpeting, "It was the most amazing thing; it was so luxurious!"

But a strike in 1970 gave Louis notice that his life was about to change. On September 14, 1970, one of the longest strikes in GM history began. A *New York Times* article from October 3, 1970, reported, "In Detroit, staffs have been increased in the welfare centers after crowds of strikers poured in to apply for food stamps and had to wait for hours or go home without applying because of delays in filling out forms."[18] Then, after sixty-seven days, the strike ended and the UAW "30 and out" pension began. Meaning that a worker who joined at age eighteen could retire at age forty-eight with a full pension. In 1975, Louis retired with his full pension. He and

Jeanette had employees run the store at times so they could take trips to Florida and to their cabin in northern Michigan.

Throughout those years of working, my father never heard his parents gripe about their schedule. He said, "I never heard them complain about work or schedule. They were grateful to have the work and money." It was a step forward from the seven-days-per-week farm life.

Then, six years after retirement in 1981, Jeanette was diagnosed with breast cancer. In less than a year, my grandfather was a widower. Imagine living parallel lives, raising kids, creating a life, only to retire and lose one another?

For much of the World War II generation, shift work and a repeatable schedule was the norm. There was little choice. Time equaled money. Work at GM and get a specific amount of money. Work in a store and make a little more. Opportunities were limited, but their lives were more prosperous than their parents' lives had been.

Baby Boomers, like my father, enjoyed full weekends and TGIF became nearly universal in the 1980s. But even in that generation, many women were encouraged to be teachers or nurses. There were more opportunities, it was a step forward—but still Industrialist in nature.

Now, in my generation, we have to ask, are we still moving forward? I compare my grandparents' rigid schedule to my own comparative freedom and I'm amazed at the time and work they devoted in that generation. But, has enough changed? While writing this book, I've discussed these ideas with numerous friends and clients, and again and again, I've heard, "I need that book, and my boss needs it even more than I do."

Why is this book timely?

I believe that we're sick of productivity development and innovation that doesn't help our bottom-line time or happiness. The newest iPhone helps me to do more in less time, but then I just end up working the same amount of time, or more. Now, instead of being contacted on an answering machine, I can be tracked down on social media, messaging apps, text, and video chat. Others can see what I'm doing in real time as I post on social media.

Something feels off. Deep down, we know that the fingerprints of the Industrialists are everywhere and it's not working. We're sicker, unhappier, and stressed. Something has to change.

GET DISTRACTED FROM YOUR DISTRACTIONS

As we have seen, the forty-hour workweek may feel like something as stable and predictable as the seasons of the year or spending $100 at Target even if you just run in for deodorant, but the reality is that we made it up, so we can change it.

We're stuck with the seven-day week because the Babylonians didn't have telescopes. The eight-hour workday seemed better than twelve to fourteen hours. The weekend came about after a conflict between Christians and Jewish factory workers. What if there had been Muslims and Bahá'í who would have wanted Friday? Would we now have a standard three-day weekend? What if Henry Ford had said a seven-hour day was better? Then a thirty-five-hour workweek would be standard. Or what if we had followed the Romans and their eight-day week? Who knows how the world would be different if we had eight days a week. Would we work an extra day, play an extra day, or create a new form of day?

We are going to talk about how we get to define what we believe is best for ourselves. Humans who came before us created this system. Do we want it to stay that way? The power of Friday is strong, but Thursday is calling us.

We don't know this. At least, it's not top of mind. We often say, "I wish I had more time." But is time the real issue? Intuitively, we know this isn't working. If you're honest, when you were in lockdown in early 2020 due to the COVID-19 pandemic, how did work feel? For some people, it was a busy time juggling the kids' online schedule, work, and trying to wipe down groceries. For others, the lack of socialization gave a break from the unnecessary stresses of life. Some people noticed less overall work, and for others, it was more. During that time, the traditional work structures crumbled. And this reinforces the point that we made this up, and it can change. For many during the pandemic, they began asking questions about their workday, schedule, and started a deep evaluation of how they spend their time.

Working from home created immense stress for those whose jobs demand full time in an office. Was that you? Imagine that your supervisor trusted you to finish your work at your pace and that Friday was another day off. Imagine feeling creatively empowered rather than stressed-out. Instead of needing to sneak time for your childcare and education roles at home, you could be more present for your children and colleagues. Isn't it likely that you would have been satisfied to remain with your company, rather than look for a more flexible organization?

In the coming years, we are sure to learn more about how the worldwide lockdown experiment has challenged our old ways of thinking. Yet, even before the lockdown, there had been ample evidence that our workday is not optimized. The 2018 Workplace Distraction Report included several concerning categories. Chatty coworkers and ambient noise were the top offenders in the office. On average, researchers found it takes around twenty-three minutes to return to concentration after you've been distracted.[19]

When I was organizing my Slow Down School conference, a weeklong event I host on the beaches of northern Michigan, I found that I could approach my tasks in several different ways. I could just start working. I could look at emails about Slow Down School. I could make a checklist. Since I work from home, numerous obstacles could derail any of these approaches.

What do I do? I set a timer so I can focus on the task at hand. I close all other windows on my computer. I put my phone on silent. I tell the family that I'm going into "monk mode." Once I am distraction-free, I can try a variety of tools and can see which ones work better than others.

The problem of distraction and changing tasks goes beyond just coworkers and noise. In that same Workplace Distraction Report, 74 percent of those surveyed said they are distracted, and of that group 46 percent reported this distraction leads to feeling unmotivated.

More than a third of millennials reported spending two or more hours checking their phones throughout a workday. Two-thirds of all employees spend at least an hour a day on their phones while at work, no matter what generation.

On the other hand, 54 percent of people said they would feel more motivated if they were learning more and developing a new role. Our workers are saying something.

It could be:

"I feel a need to stay connected to the world."
"My work doesn't seem important to me."
"I'm not being pushed to be my best."

"I want to work less, but I need the money."

"I'm not inspired here."

This problem may also be that people feel pressured to control all the work that is required even when the workload is not realistic. Many business owners, entrepreneurs, and influencers deal with this problem. I started a podcast in 2012, named *The Practice of the Practice Podcast*. On this show, I focus on interviews and solo shows about how to start, grow, scale, and exit private practices. Mostly counselors, therapists, and coaches listen, but a number of business owners do as well.

For me, it's more about challenging our assumptions about our career, life, and success. I've gone from working a full-time job to running and selling several businesses. After an interview, I frequently talk to my guests for a few minutes. They, too, struggle to appropriately allocate their time. They struggle with mindsets like, "Only I can do this," or "I built this; I can't outsource now." Even top experts get sucked back into the way the Industrialists thought.

The problem is huge: we don't know how to live.

What is the right balance for time spent working, slowing down, optimizing the brain, helping the world, being with our kids, dating our partner, and feeling like we're living a life that matters?

The problem with most books focused on removing distractions or getting more done is that they don't dig into the root cause. Let's look at the way you approach your business life. No matter what you do, there are probably times you don't feel your best.

You may show up to a meeting and think, "This is a total waste of time."

Maybe you're working on a project for a client, but you hate it. "It brings in money for what I love."

You're checking email at night. "No one else will do it and tomorrow will be easier if I do this now."

In all three of these examples, you're doing work you don't want to do, but you believe something on the other side will make it worth it. But is that true?

Tomorrow, won't you go to another stupid meeting? Won't you take another high-paying project you hate? Won't you check email again and again throughout the day?

The entire system is broken and we're not changing it. Instead of pausing and saying, "Should I do this?" we have created a modality for work that we don't buy into, but that we don't feel we can change.

We need to challenge how we spend our time. For your next meeting, ask yourself if it's even necessary. What if not going to that meeting actually helps you level up faster than sitting there for an hour Zoom call? What if saying "no" to bad clients helps you to find work that you love and also pays more? What if letting email pile up is actually a good thing?

When I was the president of the Licensed Professional Counselors of Northern Michigan, we convened a regular panel. During our first hour we networked and talked with our colleagues about how we were getting referrals, what was working in business, and mental health in our communities. It was highly valuable for me.

I remember one meeting that was a turning point for me. Someone who really cared about mental health in the schools had set up a panel of experts. Principals, school counselors, social workers, and school nurses sat behind a table and we heard what they had to say about schools and mental health.

This was shortly after I had left my full-time job at a local community college. I sat there and thought, "I am not interested in learning about mental health in the schools."

Of course the issue matters and I'm glad someone does care. When I worked in schools in Kalamazoo, I cared then. But it wasn't my thing anymore.

"Who is making me come to this meeting . . . on a Friday?" I thought. "I'm my own boss; this is my fault."

I turned to the person next to me and said, "I have to go. Will you wrap up the meeting at the end?" I walked out and started my weekend an hour earlier.

We create the world we live in, whether we are an employee or an entrepreneur. When I worked at the college, I told my boss when I thought a meeting was going to be a waste of time, and usually I wouldn't go. I could then work on projects I thought were beneficial for the department.

For most of us, it's less about removing bad work completely, but figuring out how we best live our lives to impact the world, feel good about what we do, and feel fulfilled. So, whether you find yourself doing a side gig toward a dream, running your own business, or living as an intrapreneur (entrepreneur in a company), this book is for you. We're not talking about just a few productivity hacks or simple things to feel a little less stress. We are talking about reinventing your time to give you more independence, happiness, and innovative ideas that will impact the world.

THIS IS FOR YOU, FIRST AND FOREMOST

If you are ready to challenge the system and reinvent your workweek, this is absolutely for you. This book is for people like yourself, who are open to confronting the system we have inherited, have the power to make change, and will do the inner work to slow down. Then we are going to kill it. By "kill it" I mean do an amazing job—knock it out of the park, totally rock it out.

Maybe you have a full-time job and your side gig is taking off. You could be a coach, counselor, or other entrepreneur in a small business. You may have big ideas that you know will improve the world. You might be an intrapreneur, having an entrepreneurial mindset within a business. Maybe you're a manager, supervisor, or other person in leadership and you want to think differently about time. Later, we discuss your internal inclinations, and what you want to get out of life and work. This book is for you!

But this is not a book that will talk about changing the collective culture in your business. Instead, it is highly focused on the individual. This book will work even in large organizations, but it requires individual buy-in and implementation. That's why we start internally and then look at external habits.

Imagine that a CEO of a large company reads this book and personally implements its insights. Her personal experience of change will revise the company culture through her individual decisions. So, first and foremost, this is a book for you as an individual. Your changes will spill over into your family, business, and society. We're tearing down the expected workweek together and then asking, "Why are there personal blocks in this area?" We're slowing down to experience the changes in the brain and then asking, "Why is this so difficult?" Then we're optimizing our brain to work more efficiently, only to ask, "Why didn't I do this sooner?"

Here's the journey we are going to take. In part one, we will consider the internal inclinations that we find in successful business owners. First, we'll look at how intuition and inclinations work together and in different ways. We will explore core inclinations that lead to success. And we'll ask the fundamental questions: "Why do we do what we do?" and "Can we change our natural inclinations?"

We'll determine whether these inclinations come naturally to us or if they need to be developed. An inclination is the starting place and you may or may not feel those things naturally. Within part one, together we'll assess where you fall. We'll look at your habits, the actions you take, and specific areas that will help you grow.

The most successful people tend to have curiosity and an Outsider Approach, and they act on it. Within each of these chapters, we will meet people who have discovered their internal inclinations and acted upon them. We'll look at research on how curiosity, an Outsider Approach, and action is fostered. Then we'll apply it to your own development.

In part two we will look at the science of slowing down. Why do our brains tend to have breakthroughs in the shower? Why does a long drive allow you to understand a problem differently? And why is it that my "to-do" list only takes shape when Sam Harris's guided meditation starts? In this section we'll look at neuroscience, case studies of how slowing down made a lasting impact, and examine cutting-edge research on the brain's potential.

In part two we will also look at case studies of business owners who have implemented these teachings and grown beyond anything they could have conceived. You'll meet psychologists, an underground oil and gas consultant, a technophobe-turned-SEO consultant, and companies who have thrown the five-day workweek out the window.

It's one thing to understand slowing down, it's another to take steps that will lead to a happier life, more successful business, and a clear plan. I will remind you throughout the book that this is only the springboard into a different life. It is your responsibility to make sure these concepts stick.

Last, in part three we will deconstruct the hustle narrative, whether it's Elon Musk saying, "Work every waking hour," or Gary Vaynerchuk saying, "Hustle harder." We'll also consider specific techniques to get more done in a shorter period of time. Concepts like time blocking, sprints, and boundaries will show you how you've been wasting tons of time and feeling less happy than you could.

As we enter this book together, I want you to take a breath. Whether you are a CEO, mid-level manager, entrepreneur, or student, there's often a baseline anxiety as you jump into a book.

"Does this apply to me?"

"Will this be worth my time?"

"Can I implement this?"

In one sense it's a transaction: you are spending time (and money) on this book and want an ROI for your effort.

I'm going to do my best to give you the clearest and most compelling arguments to make *Thursday the New Friday*. But first I'm going to ask you to make three commitments to get the most out of your time:

1. Be honest about what you want to get from this book.
2. Invite a friend to join you.
3. Pace yourself.

Why are you reading this book? The lens through which you read will determine your outcomes. If I read a marriage book through the lens of wanting to stay married forever, I will be predisposed to acquire the tools needed to do the hard work. Conversely, if I'm looking to justify a divorce, I'll read the recommendations as a comment on the way my marriage is failing. The same is true here.

The Industrialists' fingerprints are all over the world. Together, we will deconstruct that way of thinking. Farming communities worked seven days a week to survive. Cows need to be milked and chickens fed. Industrialists created machines and treated people, schools, and churches like machines. Energy in, product out. But that is no longer our world. Creativity, innovation, technology. These are things that drive us now. We need a software upgrade, a reboot, a rest.

Whether we realize it or not, the patterns of society have already changed. We can watch shows and have a driver pick us up on demand, and we often work outside of a typical workweek schedule. So let's examine how you can get the absolute most out of this book.

Commitment #1: Be honest about what you want to get from this book. The lens through which we approach any situation determines the end. In his Art and Science of Love workshop, researcher Dr. John Gottman reports his finding that the first minutes of a couple's discussion will determine the volatility of the engagement. The same is true when we approach a book. I will limit the amount I take away if I limit the scope in which I allow the book to play. In other words, I will profit from the book to the extent that I approach it with an open mind.

So why are you here? As a CEO, are you considering transitioning your company to a four-day workweek to optimize time and reduce costs? Maybe you have a small business, a growing podcast, or you are a consultant.

Intrapreneurs, how can you instill this more creative work schedule for bigger outcomes? Can you inspire a team to employ these techniques? Can you advocate for the work that you feel will both help the company and your life?

As a small business owner or consultant, how would this help you level up? How will a new type of schedule rearrange your priorities? What would be a game-changing level up for you and your small business?

What do you want personally? Read from the vantage point of your perspective on the world. Examine your inclinations, your slowing down, and your ability to kill it. Do you have innovation inside you that is longing to get out? Ideas that have yet to be given time? Socialization that you want to increase?

You may have immediate goals you want to achieve through this book. Maybe you want to have Fridays off. But what are your long-term goals? Leaving your job? Expanding your business? Having more time with your kids? Exploring creative things that have no financial reward without guilt? Disrupting your market in ways you have yet to realize?

Commitment #2: Invite a friend to join you. Within the Practice of the Practice community (my website/podcast/membership/consulting for business leaders, counselors, and coaches), books frequently make the rounds. For a while it was *The ONE Thing* by Gary Keller and Jay Papasan. That book really helped frame out focus and leveling up. Then it was *The Ideal Team Player* by Patrick Lencioni. My clients were using it to guide growing a group private practice. They were hiring therapists, psychologists, and counselors and wanted people that were perfect for their teams. Then Mike Michalowicz's *Profit First* caught on. It helped my community get their finances in order. Most recently, Donald Miller's *Building a StoryBrand* is having a resurgence.

When a community of people learn together, new ideas, applications, and insights emerge. Their brains start to sync. Innovative research, biofeedback, and brain scans are showing the power of community while learning and taking action. In Steven Kotler and Jamie Wheal's book, *Stealing Fire*, they discuss how groups like the Navy SEALs and Google start to collectively tap into a group consciousness. Close-knit groups and friends can do this too.

It's important to have your foundational books and people that define who you are and who can join you on this journey. It reinforces where you are headed. They are stones across a stream that provide guidance. Even more, they reveal what could be.

A group of accountants will apply this book differently than a group of therapists. CEOs of large companies will find applications that are different from solopreneurs. Finding a few people to join you will help.

Something happens when that hope for your future becomes communal. It's one thing to have hope for *your* future; it's another to have hope for *our* future. When you start imagining reinventing your workweek, pace, and business, that is transformative for you, your family, and your business. But when those around you join in that reinvention, it starts to gain momentum.

Others will share similar ideas, resources, and hacks. You'll become more powerful and strategic because of those around you. We are talking about reinventing something we have been conditioned to see as inevitable, the forty-hour workweek. Together, we are challenging the hustle narrative to be more creative in *less* time.

Doing that with others will make it easier.

Commitment #3: Pace yourself. My hope is that this book is captivating and pulls you in. I intend to make it practical and nuanced in the application. But this is not a quick fix. This is not the blue pill (or was it the red?) from *The Matrix*, that reveals everything. This is a springboard.

Throughout, I will share my own experiments and applications that I have used in my life and in conjunction with my clients.

Just like a springboard in diving, there is much after the initial jump. There will be first rounds of application. You'll test and change your time based on the recommendations here. In your world, some will work and some will not. That is normal.

When I started aggressively placing boundaries on my time, it was clunky at first. There were Fridays I needed to check email or meet an appointment. I hadn't planned ahead or trained my assistant correctly. I accidentally left openings in my schedule where I should not have.

At each step, I put out the fire, examined what caused it, and created a plan to prevent that fire from reigniting. The same is true for longer-term progress. Ideas I had for my business a year ago no longer make sense. As you go through this process individually and within a business or company, your boundaries will change.

The types of clients you see, the ways you spend your time, and where you are willing to allow wiggle room all change. As a result, you'll see what makes sense in this book today through a different lens in six months or a year.

If you start this journey understanding that the process is an evolution, you'll see that pacing yourself and returning to your favorite parts of this book will help you continue in that leveling up.

We are redefining work, productivity, and happiness. But first, we must understand our natural internal inclinations and what needs developing.

Part One

DEVELOPING

INCLINATIONS, HABITS,

AND ACTIONS

In part one we will cover the three internal inclinations: Curiosity, Outsider Approach, and Move on It. We will look at how curiosity research has developed from segmented theories into what I am proposing is an integrated theory. At the core, curiosity forms when we see a gap between what we think we know and what we experience. When that disruption occurs, we get curious, but only if we notice the difference and then take action to resolve it.

An Outsider Approach can help us to see where we have become lazy, what systems or ways of thinking we assume are standard, and what should not be standard. Curiosity is the gap in our mind, whereas an Outsider Approach functionally exposes that difference.

Lastly, we examine how movers are created through the Move on It mindset. In this, we value both thinking and action. We don't get sucked into feeling like an impostor or getting paralyzed by perfection through overthinking and underacting. Nor do we focus so much on speed to have little planning with intense activity. Instead, we seek strong evaluation and strong action, with action being the leader. We need speed with doses of accuracy to give us the best shot at a successful project.

Throughout part one, the research, stories, and application divide these internal inclinations into three distinct beings, but we are describing you. You are not divided. Curiosity is developed from pointing out the cognitive dissonance, Outsider Approach exposes those differences in specific environments, and being a mover allows you to act without fully knowing the outcome.

Once you have very clear activities to develop your inclinations, habits, and actions, it's time to really examine how to move into the world, which will be focus of part two.

2

INTERNAL INCLINATIONS

*"Our first impressions are generated by our experiences
and our environment, which means that we can change our
first impressions . . . by changing the experiences that com-
prise those impressions."*

—Malcolm Gladwell, *Blink*

I remember sitting next to several three-, four-, and five-year-old children: April and Eric from across the street, my brother Pete, and two girls that lived in a house down the road. I was five. All of them were on payroll. Everyone had a role, pouring the Kool-Aid, recruiting new customers, and taking money.

The mailman looked parched. His reflective *Top Gun* sunglasses are burned in my memory as one of the coolest things I had ever seen up until that point in life. Clearly, he would need something to drink on a hot 1980s summer day.

As a five-year-old entrepreneur, I knew the basics. Have a product. Make money. Pay people. Repeat.

What I didn't understand was making a profit. Each night, after I paid the other children, we counted up my money. Then the next day we'd go and buy more Kool-Aid. I imagine this was my parents' way of showing me the direct connection between the product purchase and making Kool-Aid that day.

After a day or two of this, I realized that sitting in the sun, managing other kids, and making almost no money just wasn't worth it. A group of kids were now unemployed.

Fast-forward. I'm now an adult with a successful podcast and small business. My then-six-year-old, Lucia, says she wants a lemonade stand.

I say, "Lucia, do you know there is lemonade people will only pay twenty-five cents for and lemonade they'll pay a few dollars for?"

"Really? Why do they pay more?"

"If you make lemonade with a powder, people only pay a little, but hand-squeezed takes longer and tastes better. It's a lot more work, but you could charge at least a dollar or two for hand-squeezed. It's up to you. What kind of lemonade do you want to make?"

She thought about it a minute and said, "Hand-squeezed."

I'd been looking for a reason to buy a lemon juicer, mostly because my wife had been looking for a reason to buy a lemon juicer.

We started planning. She designed a banner in Canva and had it printed through Vistaprint. We shopped for lemons and learned to make quality simple syrup. We explored how some lemonades have frozen strawberries and basil.

Next, we talked about getting good foot traffic. Our neighborhood has one road that circles around. People walk by, but not with the traffic of a busier street.

"The Bayshore marathon is coming up, and it goes right past Paul and Diane's house. What do you think about that as a spot?" I asked.

"That sounds great. Can you call them?"

"No. You can," I reply.

"But I don't know what to say."

So, we practiced asking if she could use Paul and Diane's front lawn and maybe plug in a power cord. Then she made the call.

Of course they said *yes*.

Next, we discussed how some people will be watching the marathon and they will have been there since early in the morning. "What else could you sell that adults like to drink?"

"Coffee!" she exclaimed.

The day came and Lucia not only served "Lucia's Homemade Lemonade" but she also had coffee, since her table was open from 9:00 a.m. until noon. As a bonus, she sold frozen strawberries and basil. After paying us back for expenses, and paying her little sister and the neighbor boy who helped recruit customers, Lucia averaged more than $30 per hour.

She did it once, but since then she has made and sold slime. On a chilly fall day, she walked around the neighborhood with hot water in a pump pot and sold tea door-to-door. When she and her sister have toys they don't want, they set up a table on the side of the road and sell them.

They are developing into kidpreneurs.

SELLING VACUUMS

That's the word that matters: "developing." Often we think that our internal inclinations are something we are born with. That might be true. Sure, there's research that certain preferences are developed before we have a choice. I remember hearing an NPR story about research in which pregnant mothers drank carrot juice as their babies were developing taste buds. Later in life, those children preferred carrot juice more than other babies.[1]

The way we are raised impacts what feels normal. In my house every now and then we'd have corned beef hash out of a can. It still tastes great. My grandmother would jokingly call it "dog food," which isn't too far from the truth, but it's still delicious. Others would never eat it.

I had a Kool-Aid stand that was a failure according to typical business standards. But what goals did my parents have for me? To occupy time, have fun with friends, practice counting money, and maybe learn to earn something. From that perspective, it was a success.

Another time, my dad brought us a whole bushel of tomatoes and told us he had grown too many. If we wanted, we could sell them by the road and keep the money. Day after day, we sat there with our little brown table under an umbrella. Later as an adult he said, "I bought those tomatoes from the farmers market, the best twenty dollars I've spent to occupy my kids."

I'm not naturally a salesperson. This has been proved over and over. The summer before college, my friends John, Nick, and Brian were all selling "a new technology, where you can make over $500 per sale." Little did I know, I was about to be a lonely door-to-door vacuum salesman. I was terrible at it, despite being shown sales techniques that bordered on unethical. That summer I sold two and a half vacuums. One was to my parents. Another was to a couple they knew. Then after weeks of unsuccessful selling, I asked my friend if she would ride along to keep me company. I told her I would give her half the sale. We sold a vacuum to an elderly couple and split the sale. I was really bad at selling vacuums.

When I was a restaurant server, I was so uncomfortable talking to so many new people that I screwed up orders nonstop. I spilled water on a guest. Within a week, I was moved to banquet catering (which had better tips for less work, so I guess it worked out).

To me, business was all about getting someone to buy something they didn't want, with money they didn't have, at a price they didn't like. That was business and I wanted nothing to do with it.

Yet, when I reflect on the trail that led me to podcasting and consulting, there were clues throughout. I've always had an eye for design and marketing. I was in bands all through college that were C+ on a good night. But we put on a good show, even if the musical talent was lackluster. We'd always make more than the other bands because of our marketing abilities and my brother's awesome swag design.

It was sales and marketing.

When I worked at a runaway shelter, I created programs for youth that were involved in the criminal justice system and foster care. I had to earn trust from referral sources, kids, and foster parents. The promo material had to come across as different, so the teens would want to come, but not so alternative or punk rock that the system would reject it.

It was sales and marketing.

When I started a therapeutic sailing program, I had to work with donors, grants, volunteer board members, nonprofits, and local government. I convinced my boss to pay me to sail all summer from 2009 to 2014.

It was sales and marketing.

Inside each of you, there are natural inclinations and experiences that have molded your abilities. These inclinations are assumed and feel normal. These can come from our culture, family, friends, and experiences. It's what you feel as your natural bent toward something. It is literally from the Latin *inclinare*, *en/in*, meaning "in or upon," and *klei*, meaning "to bend."

In other words, your internal inclination is your natural bent. This can change in specific situations and over a lifetime. Different environments may encourage or suppress your inclinations. For example, if you are stressed, overworked, and tired of people, any expression of creativity may be muted. But if you are on vacation and have the opportunity to take a wine and painting class, it might expand.

Similarly, phases of life may bring out specific inclinations. Your college years, before a serious romantic relationship, may have produced a more social version of you. In early adulthood, working hard in a new job may have entailed less time to read or to engage in thought-provoking activities, despite their interest. Or, later in life, you may have found that with kids at college, you are more willing to take risks in business, because economic failure would not directly hurt as many people.

When we recognize the spectrum of internal inclinations, we begin to realize that they are not about winning some genetic or environmental lottery, but about recognizing our baseline and then deciding if that aligns with the skills needed at this phase of life.

INTUITION RESEARCH AND RICKY GERVAIS

Evaluating, understanding, and growing your curiosity will help speed your success toward a shorter workweek. It's one thing to say, "I want to work less." It's a whole other thing to do it successfully, which may mean making more money, or impressing your boss.

Researchers give us a few clues about how best to do this. Throughout the 1960s, Dr. Douglas Dean and John Mihalsky interviewed 165 company presidents and CEOs. They found that 80 percent of the leaders who scored high on intuitive scales doubled their company profits within five years.[2] In his 1986 book, *The Logic of Intuitive Decision Making*, Weston Agor also contended that top executives relied on intuition. Agor examined 3,000 managers nationwide and categorized the situations in which intuition was most used.

What we now know is that we employ different parts of our brains depending on whether we use logic or intuition. In intuition, our body processes more advanced data points than we are conscious of. Comedian Ricky Gervais humorously noted this regarding toupees and wigs:

> I'd never wear a wig, oh, my god. If you wear a wig or a toupee, and you think you've got away with it . . . you haven't. Everyone knows. Everyone knows immediately. My brain knows a wig has come into the room before I do, right? I could be at a party, it'll go:
>
> "There's a wig in here."
> I go: "Is there?"
> "Yes! There is, yeah!"
> Spidey senses for the wig. It's obvious.[3]

Recognize your latent intuition and determine how to develop it—that's one of the building blocks you'll use to optimize your schedule and reduce your workdays. If you can see how your natural inclinations or "intuition" guide you toward positive or negative choices, that will enable you to make different choices. We need first to understand why our brains nee intuition and inclinations. Then, we can examine which internal inclinations are most helpful for top performers, and finally we'll see what we can do to develop those specific inclinations.

So what is the difference between intuition and an inclination? The word "intuition" comes from the Latin *intueri*, which literally means to "look at or guard."[4] Late-middle English starts to move this toward the spiritual, where it has a meaning of contemplating. Intuition now has moved to mean "independent of a reasoning process."[5]

The word "inclination" comes from the Latin *inclinare*, which literally means "to bend toward." The word is aimed at the personal, currently meaning: "a person's natural tendency or urge to act or feel in a particular way; a disposition or propensity." Intuition tends to be more of a feeling or a sense, whereas an inclination is more what is done with that sense.

In reality, intuition and inclination are different manifestations of what we might call motivation. Why do we do what we do? An inclination has been built. This can come from genetics, our DNA, chemical makeup, hormones, and other factors that we don't control. Or, our environment, experiences, missteps, and behavioral conditioning in the world.

On one side, we have an intuition, a sense, or a gut feeling. For some people this side of the coin is more pronounced. The other side is inclinations. These are the physical manifestations of these intuitions. When in a museum, do I have a tendency to walk clockwise or counterclockwise? It could come from an intuition that most likely I don't realize.

I might believe that I'll have a better experience going in one direction or the other. Maybe intuitively I follow the crowd, so my inclination is to go in the group's direction. Or maybe the inverse is true. For the sake of this discussion, I'll be using the term "inclination" because I think it has less baggage. The word "intuition" still tends to dance in the world of the woo, but for clarity, we're really talking about the side of the coin that leads to action. So how are inclinations developed?

One primary way we develop inclinations is through experiencing, observing, and making meaning of patterns.

Imagine you wake up one morning and something strange has happened. Your phone has a weird bug in it where, instead of seeing your home screen each morning, you see a color. Some mornings it is red and other mornings it is green. Then other mornings, but only once in a while, it is yellow.

Now think about one of the most important people in your life that you see regularly. Maybe it's a partner, a child, a friend, or a coworker. Two phenomena: weird phone thing and person.

At first you don't know if your phone glitch is related to anything. Then you notice that it might be tied to something. Is it how well your workday goes? Maybe the stock market goes up or down based on the color? Are gas prices lower on red days compared to green?

Your brain searches for the meaning of the morning color scheme.

Then you start to notice, when it's red in the morning, you feel a bit off. On green days, it goes better. Yellow days are regular. But it's not with everyone. It seems to be that your day is bad, good, or normal because of one person.

Yes, it's that special person in your life. It seems to be directly tied to their emotions.

If the screen is red, you notice things seem a bit off for that person. Maybe they were tired, cranky, or just didn't act in an expected way. You say something that's funny and they don't laugh. They're in their head about something and you don't know what. They're just a little bit crankier than normal, and the color is revealing that to you.

The next day, you wake up and the screen is green. Today that person buys you your favorite coffee or does something that makes you feel loved. Your partner may initiate something romantic, or a friend may invite you to do something fun you enjoy. Your child may clean her room and offer to help with dinner. They are your dream friend, partner, or child.

Then a yellow day comes. They're similar to how they have always been, somewhere in the middle.

Imagine this continues for months: you get a red, green, or yellow signal, every single day. It's always spot on. Your special person is enjoyable, cranky, or just somewhere in the middle, exactly as your phone predicts. You're now even inclined to treat that person based on their color.

Then one day it stops. This magic glitch stops as mysteriously as it began.

But then, it restarts. But what you don't know is, it is only a color. In the first round, it was true: it could somehow magically tell how your special person was doing. It measured stress levels, hormones, food, virus, gut bacteria, and 99.99 percent of the time could tell what kind of day they would have. But now, it's just a color.

But would your behavior change? Most likely it would not, at least not for a while. You have been conditioned to believe in this, despite no longer having any research to support it. You are looking for patterns that don't exist. Your inclinations to treat your friend a specific way feel real, your actions reflect this intuition, and you create the world you think exists.

When your partner acts cranky, even if it is normal, you'll think about the red you saw in the morning. When your kids pick up their toys without being asked, you'll think with a smile, "Yup, it was green this morning." When your boss acts neither engaged nor disengaged, that yellow will stand out. You will see through the magic app color lens.

That's the danger and delight in being human. We can learn and trust in things so our brains can move on toward something else. If before every single step we had to ask, "Is the ground going to be there?" we'd have a tough time living in the world. It's nice when intentional habit-building moves into automation. That's a good thing.

But what it also does is set in motion a perpetual feedback loop that is harder and harder to break. The original new behavior becomes automated. Then that feels natural as an inclination and moves into feeling like it's the only way; it's an intuition. Then it becomes a core belief about how the world operates. Eventually, it's assumed that is how everything has always been.

As we discuss inclinations, we have to understand the benefits and the hazards.

This mental *Black Mirror*–type world is how the brain creates intuition. It looks for patterns. Red means my special person is having a bad day and attitude. Green means they are in a great mood. Yellow means they are in the middle. When that pattern disappears, the brain is already trained.

When you train a dog to stay in an area by using an electric fence, at some point you can turn off the electricity and most dogs will stay put.

Intuition is developed by real-life patterns. It may be microgestures that you easily understand, so you can sense someone doesn't like you. Maybe it's a tone of voice in a potential client. Or it could be an out-of-the-ordinary phrase in an email. Usually we understand what's happening well before it is clear.

If we are to embrace the *Thursday Is the New Friday* mindset, we must see how those societal norms and internal inclinations that feel unchanging can be challenged and modified. Remember, intuitions and inclinations are feelings and actions that are independent of reason. They are tendencies toward a specific reason. To change, we must know where we are starting.

RATS, LABS, AND ABCS

I had a rat lab in college. To pass the class, you had to train the rat to perform a series of tasks. By the end of the semester, my rat: pushed a lever five times, pulled a chain, pushed a marble, then pushed the lever ten times to turn on a light. When he turned the light on, he received a droplet of water.

All that, for a droplet of water.

The rat was thirsty. Really thirsty. For the twelve hours before our lab, he was not given any water. He would do almost anything for water. The goal of the course was to teach behavioral psychology. Behavioral psychologists believe that positive and negative reinforcers and positive and negative punishers determine most, if not all, behavior, human and animal.

A reinforcer is anything that increases behavior. A punisher is anything that decreases behavior. I could write a whole book on the flaws of this thinking, but there are some basics that provide us truth.

The final task of the lab was to extinguish the behavior. The rat would do almost anything to turn on the light, because that had been paired with the water. So, we were extinguishing the lever pushing to get the light to turn on. Although the original number of lever pushes was five, my rat pushed the lever over three hundred times. At one point, I thought the rat would pass out from exhaustion. Then he gave up. If I had given him a drink of water at that point, three hundred pushes would be the new reinforcer and next time he would have done five hundred. It's very hard to undo a behavior.

From a behavioral perspective, we live much of our lives avoiding pain or seeking pleasure. We drive the speed limit to avoid killing our family or someone else's family, or we don't want a ticket, or we don't want our car insurance to go up. We go out to eat because we feel affluent, or like the taste of the food, or want time with friends. Or it is to avoid doing dishes and working on a meal at home only to have the kids want to eat Cheerios.

One of the most basic and helpful concepts in behavioral psychology is ABC: antecedent, behavior, consequence. Antecedents are anything that push a behavior. The thirst of the rat motivated him to learn to push a marble or pull a lever. Behavior is what the animal or human does in response. In this case, pushing a marble or pulling a lever. The consequence was a drink of water and feeling less thirsty.

We experience the ABCs in life and work:

"Laken, it's time for dinner. Please shut down the iPad."

"Dad, can I have five more minutes?"

"Sure, that's fine." Or, "No, please come now."

When my daughter wants more time on the iPad, the antecedent is her level of enjoyment in the task and that coming into conflict with being told to end her time on the iPad. Her behavior is what she does when I ask her to come for dinner. Her consequence is either coming to dinner or getting more iPad time.

Suppose I noticed that my daughter wasn't coming to dinner when she was asked. I might change ABC where the behavior I wanted was for her to immediately say, "Okay, Dad, here I come." Only when she did that would I give her more time. Changing this behavior shows she's listening and hears me.

Behavioral psychology attempts to make sense of the world and our behavior.

But what it misses is everything else. Why do we think about what we do? How do we ascribe meaning beyond our behavior? Why do we do irrational things?

The main point is that human behavior, habits, beliefs, and points of view can change. But where do we focus this change? Where's the best ROI for our time and energy?

Identifying our fundamental posture toward the world, our internal inclinations, allows us to create a baseline and determine what needs development. But there are three internal inclinations that reflect the largest steps forward in the business world.

NATURAL AND DEVELOPED INTERNAL INCLINATIONS

We all have natural inclinations toward tasks. As a kid, you may have loved art and you still have a bit of an artistic bent. Maybe you were told on every report card, "Joey talks too much," and now you're a podcaster (guilty as charged). Or maybe you were told that you are an "old soul" and really that just meant that you're a deep thinker and a bit introverted.

Our natural inclinations show up in how we engage in business too. We tend to stay about the same unless we have direct and clear intervention. For example, I know that I have a ton of ideas. So, I've had to find ways to capture those ideas, evaluate them, and hand them off so that something happens immediately to move them forward.

The amount we typically change is within a spectrum. But the really great news is that the spectrum of our ability to change is usually much broader than we realize. We can change, but we first need to recognize our natural inclinations, so we know where to grow and develop.

So, how do your inclinations play out in your world? When you think about how you are naturally in the world, what words describe you? Let's consider what you offer to the world.

Here are some questions to get you started:

- When do you feel you are at your best?
- Do you ever feel like you lose track of time on a project? What commonalities do those projects have?
- How do your friends describe you?

In the coming chapters, we'll explore these questions honestly and, one might even say, gently. This approach may initially feel counterintuitive, because the business world typically pushes us to hustle, steamroll, and lead with our strengths/mission/goals/vision board (how many books have been written about that?).

We often think that inclinations are given, not proactively sought. To an extent, that is true. But, when we give time and energy to something, we may discover an undeveloped strength. Maybe a peer points out a skill of yours that you've never noticed, developed, or valued. Or something falls apart and you are forced to reassess all that you have to draw from, often while reevaluating your whole approach to life. While that can be painful and even terrifying if you're forced to do that by some rapid, unexpected, or big change, taking a proactive look at what is shaping your thoughts and actions can be a game changer—in fact, a life changer. The brain is agile: it can adapt if given time and space to create new neural pathways.

INCLINATIONS

Inclinations can be both natural and developed.

Internal inclinations are predominantly just that: internal. They represent how we assess the world, make sense of it, and then react. I've observed three core inclinations in my most successful consulting clients. When I step back and think, "Who are the people that really kill it?" I think of the clients who have these three internal inclinations in a more pronounced way than others.

After working with hundreds of individual clients, interviewing over five hundred business leaders, and helping small businesses to scale, I've noticed three internal inclinations that repeatedly predict success:

1. **Curiosity:** An unrelenting search for knowledge, information, and new processes.
2. **Outsider Approach:** An inclination to question and disrupt the current modality.
3. **Move on It:** A disposition to jump in or leap forward with less information than others, which in turn gives a rapid download of information to assist with refining.

While there are numerous internal inclinations, these are the three I find directly linked to exponential business success. In the next three chapters, you will find exercises designed to help you discover which of the three is your primary inclination—the one that is least in need of development, and is as clear as whether you are left- or right-handed. You will also discover which inclinations may need a radical wake-up or call to action, and where to make your efforts to develop them.

Last, don't take this as hard science but as a guide to help you understand your basic internal inclinations. What we will discover is an XYZ axis. At first, we will look at where you fall regarding curiosity, Outsider Approach, and Move on It. We'll define each of these areas and their subsections. Do they come naturally, or do they need more developing? Are your internal inclinations creating beneficial habits? Are you learning continuously and acting on what you learn?

In the following chapters, you will take the Internal Inclination Test, which will help you identify your specific inclinations and create strategies for success. To take a digital version of this test, just go to www.internalquiz.com and enter the code "TITNF" to take it free as part of this book. There are additional video tips, downloads, and resources there.

3

CURIOSITY

*Curiosity is the most superficial of all affections; it changes
its object perpetually; it has an appetite which is very
sharp, but very easily satisfied: and it has always an appearance of giddiness, restlessness, and anxiety.*

—Edmund Burke

Early one morning at the University of Pittsburgh in 1960, twenty-six male undergraduates walked into a research laboratory to take part in a study. They had been instructed to abstain from alcohol, go to sleep by 11:00 p.m. the night before, and to come to the experiment hungry. What was about to happen would be worth sleeping through, so the experimenters gave the students Dexedrine Spansule, a drug to keep them awake.[1]

The subjects were told that they were going to be part of a study on boredom. But, as is often true in research, that was not the whole truth. They would be in an isolation room, in complete darkness, for ten hours. They would have earplugs and earmuffs to block out any noise. All senses, sight, smell, hearing, and taste, would be deprived. Further, they could not roam the room. They could lay on the bed, eat the food that came every four hours, use the toilet, or press a button.

This study centered on curiosity, part of a new research direction that had been growing since the 1940s. Where does curiosity come from? How can curiosity be enhanced? Was it a drive like hunger or something else?

This was the second experiment of the study. In the first experiment, eight college males had been in sensory deprivation rooms for twelve hours a day for four days in a row. They were paid $12.50 per day, only if they completed the study.

In the original experiment, the button produced colored lights on the ceiling. If the button was pressed, the colors would blink once per second for twenty-four seconds, either red or green. On one day, the colors would be completely randomized. Another day, they would be a third randomized and a solid green or red for the other two-thirds. Another time it would be two-thirds randomized, with the other third a consistent color, and finally, it would be the same color blinking twenty-four times.

For example, on a one-third random day, if R = random (either green or red) and C = consistent (always either green or red) it might go in this order: RCCRCC. So, the colors might be red or green, green, green, red or green, green, green.

The core hypothesis fueling the study was that curiosity was a drive that fed on information gathering. By putting subjects in a low-information environment with no sensory input, and very little movement, they hoped to prove that curiosity was driven by an attempt to gather information. But that was only part of the curiosity puzzle.

MISS MABLE GODFREY LOST HER CAT IN 1916

On March 4, 1916, the headline on page six of the *Washington Post* said, "Curiosity killed the cat."

The story reported that Miss Mable Godfrey lived on the fifth floor in an apartment on 130th Street. She had lived there seven months with her cat, Blackie. He was a normal, homebound cat. On a Tuesday afternoon, Mable was out. Blackie began to explore the fireplace, as he had done numerous times. This time, things were different. He climbed within the chimney and became stuck. When Mable returned, she tried to get the cat to come down. Wednesday, Blackie climbed farther into the chimney. Mable worked with the police, fire, and health departments. She tried to get help from the building management. Their best attempt was lowering a rope to the cat. By Thursday morning, a plumber opened the back of the chimney and the dead cat, Blackie, was taken out.

Curiosity killed the cat. Curiosity is dangerous, so we're told. Pandora was given a box and told not to open it by the Greek gods. When she did, sickness and death were released into the world. Eve was told not to eat the fruit. When she did, knowledge of good, evil, and sin entered the world. Blackie wanted to see what was up the chimney and he died.

Curiosity has killed people on Mount Everest, on the *Challenger* shuttle, and it has killed numerous teenagers who pushed the limit of just about anything they could try. Going into the unknown has been only for the strong, the stupid, and the scientific. Curiosity has been dangerous since time immemorial. That is exactly why curiosity has power. Those who are curious and proceed despite the warnings are the ones that truly make an impact. Curiosity is what sets them apart from the norm.

Think for a moment of the historical impact of curiosity. When Copernicus and Galileo challenged the idea that Earth was not the center of the universe, but revolved around the sun, they were called heretics. Looking backward, it's easy to see the flawed thinking of the elites of that time. We may think that we have evolved and now value curiosity and exploration. Yet, curiosity still challenges systems of thinking, institutions, and power.

Curiosity has also produced unimaginable progress. Curiosity fueled the discovery of penicillin, space travel, and technologies that save lives. Curiosity is deep within our DNA and reinforced by evolution. Most people in the United States need only look back a handful of generations to discover who among their ancestors left their homeland (by choice or not) to come here. The gene pool of those who live in the Americas is marked by curiosity and the impulse to explore. Through immigration, the importation of enslaved people, and the resettlement of refugees, the country has inherited the DNA of the curious who survived.

It's not just in humans. Studies show that rats prefer to explore less familiar arms of a maze.[2] They will go deeper into a maze for no potential reward other than knowing what is there. Inquiry has led to evolutionary progress. There is deep reinforcement when curiosity works. Early humans that were curious found new ways to find food, cook, treat illness, and survive. Whether it is a medical advancement, space or deep sea exploration, or a new math formula, curiosity is good for the world.

The risk involved is what makes the inclination of curiosity stand out among those who are successful. With curiosity, the risk can be high and it stacks. Meaning, if someone goes into an unknown cave, that is a risk, but then diving underwater deeper into the cave, that's another risk. The risks stack on top of one another.

As in a high-stakes spy movie, the risks compound and increase. Uncertainty produces heightened vulnerability and greater reward when successful. The same is true when we look at having an Outsider Approach. As you will see later, the ability to be outside of a group to see its functions and dysfunctions allows for faster growth. Last, being about to Move on It instead of overthinking is key. We will discuss these two other internal inclinations in future chapters. Those internal inclinations have similar levels of risk when failure occurs.

You will see that the three internal inclinations that characterize successful entrepreneurs may also alienate people. This is why so many individuals and companies don't actively pursue risk. The way it has been done has aligned with the Industrialists' point of view. It feels risky to build curiosity, have an Outsider Approach, and move before ready. But businesses that strengthen these inclinations are in a small, successful category. Valuing curiosity is the difference that gives them the leverage to disrupt and create something better.

But as dangerous as curiosity has been made out to be (or actually is), curiosity is part of what drives all of us. It is mystery and suspense that sucks us in. Whether it is a Netflix series that ends each episode with a cliffhanger, a good book, reality show, or a friend telling a story, it is curiosity that keeps our attention. The evolution of our brain has survived and thrived specifically because of curiosity. We want to know what happens and why it happened.

Thousands of years ago, the curious family explored new geographical regions. That led to a diverse diet, learning better ways to complete tasks, and access to medicinal plants. Although curiosity is embedded within us, our society has often devalued it. So it is our call to release curiosity from the shadows and move it to its rightful place at the center of this movement!

THE PSYCHOLOGY OF CURIOSITY

In the sensory deprivation study discussed at the beginning of this chapter, the students pushed the button more at the end of the study than at the beginning. Researchers in this study concluded that there was "support for a drive formulation of information deprivation." In other words, when we don't have information, we crave it. Curiosity is fueled by a drive inside of us, and when we gather information, it feeds that drive for a while. Can you imagine? It took students being in a jail-cell-type experiment for several days for scientists to conclude that when we don't have information we look for it.

There had been earlier studies confirming this. Researchers Dashiell (1925) and Nissen (1930) showed that rats valued answers as rewards. Rats would endure electric shock to explore novel stimuli with no apparent connection to food or water. Harlow (1950) showed monkeys would solve a puzzle for no reward.[3]

Researchers in 1968 defined the behavior of an elementary school child demonstrating curiosity. There were four distinct phases they observed. First, the child would react positively to the new stimuli. For example, they would see a new toy and be excited to explore. Second, they would have a desire to know themselves and/or their environment more. Using the new toy, they would interact with it by themselves or within the setting. Third, they would seek new experiences in relation to those stimuli. They would try new things with the toy to test and understand the limits of that particular toy. Fourth, they persist in exploring.

Both of my daughters are elementary school age. One day during the COVID-19 lockdown, I was in charge of their schooling. I asked them what they wanted to explore. My five-year-old wanted to discover more about the pyramids in Egypt. My eight-year-old wanted to learn about Mayan culture and the cenotes around Tulum, Mexico. We started with Google Street View in Cairo. We looked at how close the pyramids were to the city. Then a question: "Can you go inside the Sphinx?"

We found a video and learned that the Sphinx was dug out of the earth, rather than built up. Also, Egyptian gods typically had human bodies and animal heads, but this pharaoh flipped it to have a powerful lion body and human head. It was a way of taking something known and re-creating it to make a point.

First, my children reacted positively to the new stimuli of learning about Egypt. Next, they pictured themselves at the Sphinx, thinking, "Could I go inside that?" They were imagining themselves within that environment and were interacting with it in a new way.

Next, they asked about the first pyramids. We learned that it started with rock mounds, then each pharaoh made them bigger and was buried with more and more treasure. So they were taking the third step of seeking new experiences. After more discovery, we walked through the streets of Tulum via Google Street View. We learned about the underwater cenotes, caves, and tunnels. Which led to wanting to know more about the Mayan people, who also had pyramids.

The last step, persisting in exploration, came through connecting the dots between Egypt and Mexico. They then did an art project of female Egyptian and Mayan royalty. They wanted to explore larger issues and zoom in to the specifics of the different places we were exploring. There is a rhythm between breadth and depth of knowledge. They were observing the landscape in front of them and then stopping and saying, "Let's stay here for a while." Then they built more understanding of the landscape and stopped again to focus more deeply. That is curiosity. That is what researchers established in 1968 with those elementary kids. A curious person keeps looking at ways to go deeper and wider, while reshaping how they interact with that novel environment.

Although the 1968 definition was derived by observing the curiosity of elementary school children, let's apply the four steps to the business world.

1. Do you react positively to new stimuli, ideas, or experiences? Does this come naturally, or does it need development?
2. How do you better understand yourself and your environment as a result of the new stimuli, ideas, or experiences?
3. Do you seek a wider breadth or depth of stimuli, ideas, or experiences because of this?
4. From this information, do you persist deeper and wider? How are you changed as a result?

Not everything will capture your attention, but when something does, does it produce this process? Before we get to your assessment, let's look at some of the research on curiosity, and some applications of this internal inclination.

THREE THEORIES OF CURIOSITY

The sensory deprivation study examined only one piece of the curiosity puzzle. Three major theories on curiosity emerged: 1. Boredom leads to the seeking of stimuli. 2. The basic human desire to master our environment is provoked by new information. 3. "Incongruent resolution." When we encounter new information that is not congruent with our way of thinking, curiosity awakens. Let's break these down.

Curiosity fueled by boredom occurred when I was in San Diego for a conference. The conference was completed and I was at a hotel close to the airport. I only had the evening to explore because I was leaving early the next morning. I walked from my hotel across the Nimitz Bridge and passed a landlocked navy ship, the USS *Recruit*, that was on display. The autumn night air was crisp. I found a small sports bar, not my usual type, but wanting to stay close to the hotel, I didn't have much choice. The bar was peppered with men watching multiple TVs. Again, not my usual choice.

An important game of some sort was on. The guy sitting next to me appeared to be alone and also uninterested in the games. We struck up a conversation. He worked as a national consultant for stoplights. Stoplights.

I had no idea there were people that consulted on stoplights.

For the next hour, I had the most interesting conversation about the politics, process, and implementation of stoplights. I'm sure this guy was thinking, "Why does he care so much about stoplights?" I learned about how different systems time them differently. I had to know, "Why do some left turns go first, while others blink red and then go after the green light?"

The original fuel for my curiosity was boredom, as analyzed in the 1960s sensory deprivation study. Is curiosity a drive like hunger that needs to be fed?

But then it was fueled by incongruent resolution. I thought it was just a bunch of computer technology that ran stoplights, but there are people behind them!

By the end of the conversation, I was no master of stoplights, nor did I have any desire to be. However, the second leading theory of curiosity is about growing in mastery. Mastery can come in a variety of ways. Our neighbor is a year older than our elementary school age daughter and loves sports, especially baseball. If he learns about a new pitch, he will probably want to master it. When we relieve boredom in the first theory, the positive consequence is that we are escaping the pain of boredom. The mastery theory posits that we're not avoiding a negative, but pursuing a positive, moving toward mastery. This releases chemicals in the brain, allows us to feel more competent than peers, and is self-reinforcing. In other words, our brains love it!

Mastery could be getting better at SEO, rising above your peers in sales, or launching a new e-course that meets your clients' needs. Humans desire to master aspects of their world. I use the word "aspects" because often we feel we aren't curious. But usually it is just a matter of time before we find "aspects" around us. A friend's daughter wasn't really into much. Sometimes she'd draw, try dance, or other sports. Nothing really clicked. Then she started riding her grandparents' horse. Something clicked for her. Our friends sold their house and bought another with room to house the grandparents' horses. Maybe we just haven't discovered what we want to master.

Most kids are only given the options of academics, sports, art, or music. The world is full of possibilities, but the Industrialists were about making people into machines, not creative thinkers. Sometimes the spark of curiosity starts with a new hobby that allows you the chance to master something new.

Incongruent resolution, as the last major theory is called, predicts that curiosity arises when a belief is challenged. For most of my life, my perception of people in business was that they focused on making money first and relationships second. As I noted earlier, in the summer before college, I sold vacuums door-to-door. I was trained to sell a $2,000 vacuum in a trailer park and convince people they were making money by buying it. It was slimy. I had no role models to show me the diversity of people in business. My grandma died when I was three, and my grandfather was a quiet World War II vet who never talked about his business.

Then, in my thirties, I opened a private practice. I read some business books and started listening to podcasts. I wanted to learn how to grow my part-time side-gig counseling private practice (could I add more adjectives in that sentence?). Within the podcasting and writing world, I began to discover content creators like Pat Flynn, Donald Miller, Jaime Masters, Amy Porterfield, Seth Godin, and Daniel Pink, who all made business approachable and true to who I was. My curiosity was fueled by the space between my perceptions and what I thought I knew and what they were teaching that was brand new to me. I had to resolve that incongruence.

When there is a gap between our beliefs and what someone else proposes, assuming it is something we care about, it usually fuels curiosity. The main outcome of this is a reinvention of self, deeper learning, and a curiosity that fuels it all.

While acknowledging that researchers and professors have debated theories of curiosity much longer than I have been alive, I propose that they all describe aspects of the same phenomenon. They are all part of the same process, but describe different aspects. What researchers have been seeing as competing solutions or descriptions are one unified experience.

By the way, if you're curious, the reason some left turn arrows illuminate before the red light and some after is that different consulting groups have different algorithms.

CURIOSITY ASSESSMENT

We all begin as curious creatures, in part because we have a lot to learn when we are young, and we haven't yet developed our own way of doing things. Our brains absorb a significant amount of information as children and then, over time, prune what is less relevant and prioritize the most important. In this way, we develop our version of the "right" way of doing things.

My two young daughters never accept an answer of, "That's just how it is." Any parent knows that statement will be followed up with: "Why?" Why does curiosity seem to disappear over time for most of us? The reasons fall into three major categories:

1. Our brains favor habituation, and like to know what to do next. They favor the familiar.
2. Experiences get cataloged creating a sense of wanting to keep the status quo.
3. Curiosity can be dangerous.

Let's look at a typical dating couple. They start hanging out and are interested in getting to know each other. During this time, they are figuring out whether they want to spend more time together. Each is checking a predetermined list of things that will help them decide if more time will be worth it. Maybe you know you don't want to be with a smoker. You want someone who likes to travel but is also financially wise.

Over time, curiosity starts to answer the question "Should I stay, or should I go?" Curiosity served its purpose: yes, this is the person I want to partner with. But is that the end of curiosity in a relationship?

Curiosity dies when we think that we know.

We think we know our partner, but she's now into the idea of doing a Tough Mudder.

We think we know our kids, but they were just offered pot.

We think we know our career direction, but the business was just downsized.

The death of curiosity is based on a false assumption that the world is stable. That it will remain unchanged. That there is a way that things happen, and we know how to predict it. In actuality, everything is always moving. Life is always dying, pivoting, and reinventing itself. It provides constant incongruent resolution.

When we begin to understand that curiosity entails recognizing that we may be wrong and that things could be better, more interesting, and more joyful, that makes room for a new approach. That's where those three theories from the previous section start to relate to one another. Curiosity has another side, the enjoyment of learning because it is satisfying in itself.

Someone who is naturally curious or develops curiosity is saying: "The 'me' of the past knows less than the 'me' of the present." In doing this, we push back against our natural tendency to maintain the status quo. We're creating space where new information and learning through experience enters our being. Most people lose their natural curiosity because it stands in opposition to satisfaction with their decisions (even when those decisions haven't served us well).

When we consider that we were once wrong—that diet didn't work and it was a waste of time; that investment lost money and I didn't know what I was doing; I wasted years with that friend, who was actually a narcissistic jerk—we open mental space to consider that there might be a better way.

The most successful clients I see are those who start with enough curiosity to keep asking, "Can this be better, different, or improved?" while also asking, "What do I find interesting?"

Curiosity is the first of our three internal inclinations. The first step is to identify what is naturally occurring and what has been or needs to be developed. This assessment will guide you through a process to help you discover your baseline level of curiosity.

Curiosity Assessment

Discovery goals of this self-assessment:

1. Is curiosity naturally occurring in you?
2. Is curiosity a habit?
3. Does curiosity inform decisions and actions in your life?

These are forced-answer questions, meaning there is no "maybe." We want to get to the heart of curiosity in your life. Note your "yes" answers.

Is curiosity naturally occurring in you?

1. I wonder about things.
2. I regularly consume information, podcasts, books, and online content that matters.
3. I've changed a major way of thinking in the last five years (in my spiritual life, in relationships, in work, or in another significant area).
4. I sometimes listen so deeply that I don't think about what to say next.
5. I leave parties knowing more about others (than others know about me).
6. I enjoy new experiences.
7. When I am challenged, I try to figure out what to do differently.
8. I say "I don't know" instead of giving my best answer if I don't know the answer.

9. I have kept my childhood wonder.
10. I self-identify as a curious person.

7+ Naturally curious: for this assessment, you will be an uppercase "C"
4–6 Growing curiosity: for this assessment, you will be a lowercase "c"
0–3 Needs some development, but don't give up; you can develop it! For this assessment, you will be a lowercase "c"

Is curiosity a habit?

1. I add new authors, podcasts, and other content to my library of information.
2. I am learning/experiencing a new skill such as web design, painting, or running.
3. In the last year, I signed up for an event I have never done, such as a triathlon, cooking class, or therapy.
4. I make time to think and wonder.
5. I travel to new places.
6. I take time to slow down.
7. I'm excited to share what I learn with others.
8. I find activities and opportunities to get out of my comfort zone.
9. My schedule has blocks of time dedicated to study and understanding.

7+ Curiosity is a habit: for this assessment, you will be a "+"
4–6 Habits are forming: for this assessment, you will be a "–"
0–3 You need to work toward making curiosity a habit: for this assessment, you will be a "–"

Does curiosity inform decisions and actions in your life?

1. I change directions in my work.
2. I don't pressure myself to get it right the first time and value a process of improvement.

3. I gather information, then make a decision and/or implement what I learned.
4. People close to me (partner, kids, boss, coworkers, etc.) are sometimes frustrated that I switch gears so often.
5. I value other fields of study outside of my own career path or discipline to better inform my own.
6. My business, work, and relationships are better because I gather information.
7. I'm not always sure if the information I gather will be helpful.
8. I enjoy trying new things and having new experiences.

6+ Curiosity informs your actions: for this assessment, you will be a "+"
3–5 You are beginning to inform your actions with curiosity: for this assessment, you will be a "–"
0–2 You need some work here, but you'll get there: for this assessment, you will be a "–"

There are three variables:

1. An uppercase C means you are naturally curious. Lowercase indicates that your curiosity is developing.
2. A + sign means that you have strong information-consuming habits supporting your curiosity. A – sign means your habits need development.
3. A + sign means that you take strong actions to support curiosity. A – sign means your actions need development.

A quick note: I heavily debated the use of uppercase and lowercase, as well as + and –. Because these have negative implications and I want this to be more about developing, I struggled to determine whether this was the best use of these symbols. But my hope for you is that you see them as a shortcut for knowing where you and your peers are honestly assessing yourselves to be. If we are to develop, we need to see where things are incongruent and can be developed.

Types of People | Curiosity

The first exercise was meant to guide you through three areas of curiosity:
Does it come naturally? Has curiosity become habitual? Do you act based
on curiosity? Each area is a guide.

Here are the options:

Naturally curious or developing curiosity
With habits or without habits
With action or without action

Once you have determined your type, below, we'll learn a bit more about
your tendencies, challenges, and next steps.

(C++)	Naturally curious, with habits and with actions. **The Innovator** lives with curiosity. Their schedules make time for curiosity, learning, and experiences, which inform the actions they take.
(C−+)	Naturally curious, without habits and with actions. **The Implementer** was born curious and held on to their curiosity, but they may spend too much time in their heads. They have not made time to habitually create new experiences and learn from them. This could be because of a phase of life (new baby, illness, sick parent), but they desire to develop curiosity. Even though it's not a habit, they do act when they discover something that is new and applicable.
(C+−)	Naturally curious, with habits and without actions. **The Scholar** has also kept their curiosity and makes a habit of consuming information and experiences, but they don't take action. Their new knowledge and experiences sit in their brains. They may share it with others, but it rarely results in major change. They may fear moving out of a community where they no longer fit (church, social, or job) but they stay for several reasons, including fear of consequences.

(C—)	Naturally curious, without habits and without actions. **The Understander** seeks knowledge and experiences, but not habitually, and action is rarely taken. In a social situation they may ask lots of questions, but they don't make major decisions based on this. They may struggle with focus and attention and then feel guilty about their interests internally, while rarely doing anything about it.
(c++)	Developing curiosity, with habits and with actions. **The Fighter** doesn't self-assess as naturally curious, but they make a strong effort toward understanding curiosity's value, engaging it regularly, and implementing the results. They work hard to schedule times to consume new content and make implementation a priority. They work hard and find that curiosity becomes easier to call on over time.
(c−+)	Developing curiosity, without habits and with actions. **The Muse Hunter** also understands the value of building curiosity, but they don't make time for this growth on a regular basis. When they do dig deeper into something, they immediately find value and are happy to apply it. But, because they have not created a habit, those "muse moments" rarely happen.
(c+−)	Developing curiosity, with habits and without actions. **The Planner** is working hard to become more curious. They may force themselves to listen to podcasts, read a book through a book club, or join a class to keep them on track. They want to develop curiosity but know that it does not come naturally, so they have made it a habit. But they still take little action. Only when prompted by a boss, client, or friend do they share or act on all they are learning or experiencing.
(c—)	Developing curiosity, without habits and without actions. **The Newbie** knows they want to develop curiosity, but it's really hard. They are at the beginning of their journey and have not yet created habits to build curiosity or take action, but it will come if they continue the journey.

You're Not Off the Hook, Yet

So, what type are you? Even if you are naturally curious, with habits and action, how are you using this inclination? What stands in the way of you innovating more? What comes to mind as you consider how curiosity has taken a back seat, been kicked out of the car, or even left far behind? As kids, we all had it, but now you have to wonder, where'd it go? Recapturing childhood curiosity is essential for our own development as well as our business goals. What would it look like now to take one step toward curiosity?

We often justify things that we do to feel better. What about you? Later, we're going to talk about mindsets and blocks, how to overcome them, or when to just accept them. In the next section, we'll see how serendipity has fueled curiosity and point out clear steps you can take to develop your curiosity, habits, and action.

WHAT TO DO WITH THIS?

I have learned a few things that allow curiosity to inform the successful launch of a new product or idea. First, I brainstorm: I research, conduct interviews, and consider potential angles. Next, I test the idea or product. Finally, I launch. Later in the book, I'll walk you through exact steps, but for now, I want you to see how this plays out.

About a year ago, I had an idea for an e-course, Podcast Launch School™. Since I launched my podcast in 2012, my primary audience has been counselors, coaches, and other small business owners. Podcasting introduced me to writers, business leaders, and consultants, while also helping me scale to a level I never would have imagined.

My initial hypothesis was that an e-course on starting a podcast would help small businesses. In the brainstorm phase, I wanted to look at the issue of teaching podcasting from multiple angles.

How does this look in practical terms? Starting with the original idea of "podcasting for a small business," I brainstormed some questions:

- Why should/shouldn't someone podcast?
- Why don't people start a podcast?
- What stats are out there about the ROI on podcasting?

- What are the top shows and what are they doing?
- What structures are there for podcasting?
- Where did podcasting come from?
- Is podcasting even a good use of time?
- Aren't there too many podcasts?
- How many podcasts are there?
- What is the average length of an episode? How long does a typical show run?
- What type of podcasts would my clients host, and would that be worth their time?
- What else supports podcasting?
- Do I want to teach editing a podcast, promoting, and other ancillary services?
- How does my audience talk about starting a podcasts? What frustrations come up for them?

After this brainstorm of questions, I seek out just enough information on the idea to see if I like the direction it's taking. If too much time is spent researching and reading others' work, there is a potential it will overly influence your own work or that you may start to experience unnecessary impostor syndrome. At this point, curiosity leads the process, but I need to be clear about how I set aside time for a new project, gather information, and take action.

I focus on the pain and the people before I ever pitch a product. By "pain" I mean all of the frustrations, challenges, and problems that my audience deals with. The main goal of any product is to relieve some pain. So we focus first on getting to know an individual's pain and work toward solutions. My main goals are to see if:

1. I like this direction, because my time should only be spent on things that will build income, influence, innovation, and impact—basically, what I consider enjoyable.
2. There is an audience for this.

After the initial investigation, my curiosity moves toward my audience. Typically, I do twenty-plus phone calls with my ideal clients for fifteen to twenty minutes. In this case, I started with my highest-end clients, representing the top 5 percent of my audience. During these calls, I asked three questions, from the Three Questions to Launch Formula™ I teach in Podcast Launch School™:

1. Pain: Describe the pain. What frustrations, challenges, or pains do you have around this subject, topic, or area?
2. Product: Describe the magic product. If there was a product or service that helped overcome or reduce the pain you just described, what would that look like?
3. Price: How much would you pay for that product you just described?

These clients were all people who had a big idea they were launching. They had moved beyond their private practice and were building something scalable, so I knew they may be receptive to launching a podcast. The first question that prodded for the pain was, "What's it been like to launch a big idea?"

They weren't sure they were investing their time properly. Their business guaranteed income, but was not scalable. They would say things like, "I know this will help the world, but how do I get the word out about it?" During those conversations, I gathered copy for future sales pages.

Next I asked, "If there was a magic product that helped you with these pains, what would it be?" Among their suggested solutions was a ready-made podcasting launch, not an e-course. At their level, they wanted other people to do most of the work.

Lastly: "How much would you pay for that?" Their response was $18,000 to $20,000.

By allowing my curiosity to guide the process, I just went from launching an e-course to creating a done-for-you podcasting arm of my company that brought in $100,000 in the first quarter we launched it. I was simply doing what I had already been doing, but systematizing it for others!

We maintained curiosity and listened to our first podcasting clients. We helped improve their products and learned why people buy.[4]

In the first group, we allowed only four people. Those who were not a fit at a higher tier were a great fit for a lower-priced product. We gathered all of our systems, did a pre-launch opt-in, and then launched the e-course version of our done-for-you services.

By allowing curiosity to drive the process, I didn't fall in love with the product I wanted to launch. Instead, the pain and the people revealed the product to me.

EUREKA VS. THAT'S FUNNY

Science fiction writer Isaac Asimov said, "The most exciting phrase to hear in science, the one that heralds new discoveries, is not 'Eureka,' but 'That's funny.'"

"That's funny." For many scientists, inventors, and revolutionaries, it was noticing the peculiar that spurred their curiosity. To say "That's funny," a few things need to happen:

1. You have to notice, which means you are spending time observing new things.
2. You have to compare what happens in front of you to what you believe.
3. You have to step into that tension.

Before I can notice something, what has to happen? I know what stands in the way. It's attending to our daily to-do list, our kids asking for snacks, or our email at work instead of dreaming up new ways of doing things. It's stress and speed, anxiety and angst, a life so full you are about to burst.

Just think about all that fills the typical adult's life: a job, cleaning, commuting, pandemics, kids, groceries, and the list goes on and on and on. No wonder the term "adulting" has had such a rise in popularity. No one told us it was going to be this hard.

We don't have time for noticing.

The key to unlocking curiosity is time. Remember how the Babylonians invented the seven-day week? How Henry Ford pushed the eight-hour work-day? It was all made up! Will we allow the Industrialist mindset continue to define our week and tell us that we don't have time to notice?

Or, will we reinvent ourselves and our time to say that noticing will actually produce more benefits than the resources it takes?

After we take time to notice, it might strike us as funny. Humor occurs when the expected doesn't happen. I'm in an improv troupe. I began to practice in the fall of 2019. We've done a handful of performances. Lisa, our fearless leader, taught us that when we feel a tension we don't want to step into, stepping in is probably the funnier thing to do. It could be death, sex, or something else that makes us feel awkward.

When the unexpected happens, it's funny.

Imagine any new discovery. At some point, a ship went around Cape Horn, at the tip of Chile. Someone looked down and said, "There's a border between these oceans?!"

What you may not know is that the salt and temperature differences make a distinct visual difference where the Atlantic and Pacific Oceans meet—you should google it, it's crazy! At that moment, someone probably said, "That's funny," and curiosity led people to understand that phenomenon.

What I love about Isaac Asimov's statement is that it takes the pressure off. No longer are we waiting for an invisible muse to push us toward "Eureka!" Instead we can observe, notice, and react. If we do that enough, we're bound to discover something that grows curiosity and transforms our business.

The last action is to step into that tension. It's easy to think about when we're looking at an ocean, but what about when we discover something that doesn't line up in our business? Hmmm, we've never done it that way before.

I remember when I first started working at a community college. The counseling notes were all handwritten. The calendar was handwritten. There was no way to see which students had seen which counselor or to see those notes. Mind you, this was 2010.

As a new staff member, I had new eyes. It's tough when a new employee or intern starts and you need to justify your old patterns. This outsider perspective, which we'll dive into in the next chapter, starts to fuel questions and change.

When I first looked at the systems at the community college, I thought, "That's funny." To be honest, it was more: "That's frustratingly complex and gives me little to no helpful information." That's incongruence speaking. My experience in the counseling world differed from what was expected in my new office. With buy-in from the dean, we updated the records system. Updating the records may seem a minor victory, but in the counseling world, records are everything. Accurate psychological notes are needed for numerous reasons. They may be needed in a lawsuit or government filing. They are the history.

But it was not easy. Front desk staff had to be trained and for some it was too much. One lady quit. For more than a year, instead of looking at the digital calendar, one of the other counselors wanted her schedule printed out in the morning. Past allegiances were challenged, social drama ensued, but in the end, we had more helpful systems for the staff and students that were in line with best practices in the field. Change can be chaotic and curiosity can be dangerous.

HOW TO DEVELOP MORE CURIOSITY

We know that curiosity comes from moving away from the negative feelings of boredom, moving toward the positive feelings of mastery, or addressing incongruent beliefs. Let's walk through how to identify the focus area, create a plan, and take action.

First, when you examine your schedule at work and home, are there times you allow yourself to get bored? Most of us don't. Weekends are scheduled. Every minute is allocated. During the COVID-19 lockdown, over and over my friends would joke, "We have nothing but time."

I'd ask a friend if they wanted to do a Zoom happy hour. "Sure, I've got nothing but time." During that lockdown, I began baking bread, returned to painting (I ran out of canvases so I started painting Amazon boxes), and did deep-dive research for this book.

In her book about homeschooling, Ainsley Arment says this about boredom: "Boredom is the incubator for every great idea, dream, and new creation. Boredom is the wardrobe through which an artist, inventor, and explorer must pass in order to enter new worlds."[5]

Creating more time for boredom spurs curiosity. This is tough in the workplace, since every moment in a business is usually allocated for specific work. For the Industrialists, boredom is the antithesis of productivity. Therefore, it is useless in the work world.

Google is said to have allowed 20 percent of work time to be devoted to special projects, but several articles say this is a bit of a myth. Some say it's "120 percent time"—meaning overtime—and others say only 5 to 10 percent of employees use it.[6]

If the 20 percent time that purportedly spurred the creation of Gmail, AdSense, and Google News ever did exist, it sounds like it has been greatly reduced. The Industrialist mindset has won again. This type of time allocation is exactly what could help grow curiosity and creativity in the business world.

Because the Industrialists have such a stronghold (but not, I hope, after this book), curiosity is more self-driven. Find your own time to be bored. In part two, I will dive deeper into why and how we can slow down more to optimize our brains.

Next, let's look at mastery. Again we come to how we budget our time. Daily tasks are the enemy of mastery. They get in the way of moving the needle forward. Gary Keller and Jay Papasan articulate this in their book *The ONE Thing* as, "What is the one thing I can do, such that by doing it everything else will be easier or unnecessary?"[7]

If I spend all day putting out the fires of my business without ever examining their source, or studying why I am putting them out, or whether I even want to be in the firefighting role, then I am destined to be forever putting out fires.

Mastery allows you to level up and move away from the daily minutiae of your role. In a typical employee situation, this could be skills development or training. Within the 2018 Workplace Distraction Report employees were asked, "What would make you more engaged at work?"[8]

Here are the top answers:

- Fifty-four percent said "Trying new things, expanding my role."
- Forty-two percent said "Being empowered to learn new skills whenever I needed to."
- Thirty-five percent said "Having a clear path for professional growth."
- Twenty-five percent said "Filling my time with education that will advance my career."
- Twenty-two percent said "Participating in workplace training."

Wait, so it says that employees would be more engaged with trying new things, new skills, growth, advancement, and training? Those are all the same thing . . . mastery! Employees are craving an outlet for their curiosity, specifically in the form of mastering something new or enhancing a skill.

In a business, curiosity isn't just for innovation, it is about retention of thinkers. It is allowing staff to expand and adjust roles in a way that breaks the mold. Even though Google, Apple, and Microsoft say they want change, they keep going back to the Industrialists' mindset. Yet workers are saying, "If you want us to stay, give us opportunity for mastery!"

We might even say that there are only two types of organizations, those that have an Industrialist model and those that have an Organism model. Even though this chapter is more about you as an individual, it's important to zoom out for a moment and examine yourself within the context of your business, work environment, or organization.

The Industrialist mindset sees an organization as a machine. There are specific dials, key performance indicators (KPIs), SMART goals, and outcomes that will lead to the optimized machine. We set up the assembly line once and then it just clicks along and makes money until the next model comes out. There is very little room for curiosity, so effort goes toward improving the machine. These types of organizations are finding it hard to adapt to the changing world, because they are machines.

But this change already occurred when we moved away from an agrarian model into an Industrialist model.

But a newer type of organization has been emerging. It is one that behaves more like an organism. When a business acts like an organism, it assumes evolution, creativity, and change. For any organism to adapt, each part has to do its part. My left knee does not get excited if the right knee is getting less blood flow because it will have a larger budget next year. Nor does my left knee hoard blood flow and spend it at year-end so that the next budget of blood is just as great. Organisms look for the most efficient way to protect the organism and obtain or spend resources. In other words, they value creativity.

We'll return to this idea of an Organism model later in the book. For now, we'll stick with the individual, your internal inclinations, and how you will learn to slow down and then kill it.

As you master one area, opportunities to master others often arise. For example, in 2012, I started blogging about the business of private practice. I moved into podcasting in 2013. Over time, I began to master consulting, Mastermind groups, membership communities, and e-courses. This gave rise to more speaking engagements, keynotes, and writing. At each mastery opportunity, I could decide if that was a direction I was curious about and wanted to spend time investigating.

Incongruence, the last of our curiosity generators, had a consequential effect on my early career. I was raised by a school psychologist and a school nurse. My in-laws were a special education teacher and a computer-aided-design teacher. I was surrounded by people who were part of the educational system. One of the main messages I received was, "Work hard and someone will hire you."

Whether it was through the Boy Scouts, church, school, family, or friends, my dominant mindset was "do everything right, then someone will allow me to work for them." I know this was not intentional teaching, but the "security" of a job was taught as better than risk-taking for rewards that are not guaranteed.

My father told me early in my career, "The best way to get a raise is to switch to another company." This is great advice. If you leave, you can often come back at a higher salary. But again, it was about working a job. He was giving the best advice he could within the Industrialist system. I followed the typical counseling script. I worked for nonprofit organizations, then community mental health, and finally a community college with a state pension.

But, I had a side-gig counseling practice and a podcast that was leading to higher-end consulting clients. In 2014, while my wife was pregnant, the college reassessed wages and benefits. Salary increases didn't keep up with inflation, health care costs increased, and job roles changed quickly. I ran the numbers and found that every year I stayed, I made less money.

This was security?

The only way to make more money was to become a supervisor and work more hours. Those of us who were early in our careers during the Great Recession of 2008–2010 realized that job security and opportunity weren't what we thought they would be. My beliefs were incongruent with my new experience.

So, I got curious. I started listening to more podcasts, taking courses on how people make money online, and hired a coach to help me structure my business to scale. Curiosity led to habits of obtaining information, which led to taking action.

So let's get practical here. I want you to be able to:

1. Develop more curiosity.
2. Make it a habit.
3. Take action that fuels your personal curiosity machine (or should I say organism?).

How do you develop more curiosity? We've already seen that when you are bored, seeking mastery, or experiencing incongruent beliefs, those feelings create a buildup of curious energy.

So here are some questions that might get you thinking about this. For an ever-expanding list, go to www.joesanok.com/curiosity:

- Do I allow myself to get bored?
- When am I bored?
- What stress, life activities, or devices get in the way of me experiencing boredom?
- What daily, weekly, or monthly time can I set aside to build space to let my mind roam?
- What reaction do I have to the word "mastery"?
- What areas of my work/business do I want to master?
- What am I mastering in my personal life?
- What stands in the way of "me" time to explore?
- When can I let my guard down?
- What can I begin to master with my partner/friends/children?
- What experiences do I have that challenge my beliefs?
- When something is incongruent, what stops me from taking actions to resolve that incongruence?
- What beliefs feel true from my childhood that I want to challenge?

Spend more time wondering; it will lead to being curious.

Activity: This week I will build curiosity with the following habits and actions:

Curiosity Window:

Habits:

_____
_____
_____
_____
_____
_____
_____
_____
_____
_____
_____
_____
_____
_____

Actions:

-
-
-
-
-
-
-
-
-
-

4

OUTSIDER APPROACH

I am by heritage a Jew, by citizenship a Swiss, and by
makeup a human being, and only a human being, without
any special attachment to any state or national entity
whatsoever.

—Albert Einstein

stood in front of the mirror with a cotton swab that I had just dipped in
black hair dye. The day before, I had cut my hair to about half an inch
long. I had dyed it bleach blond. I slowly took the cotton swab and made
a leopard print pattern in my hair. I was twenty.

I had been waiting a couple weeks for a call from the runaway shelter for
a job interview. At this point, it felt safe to renovate my hair. They weren't
going to call.

You guessed it; they called.

"Can you come in tomorrow for a job interview?"

"Sure."

The cost of re-dying my hair was not in the budget. I went to the interview dressed nicely with leopard print hair. Throughout the interview, the
two interviewers kept looking at the top of my head. "Hello, my eyes are
down here!" I wanted to say. I left, thinking it was probably a waste of time.

Then I got the job.

My hair had been a selling point. They thought my perspective might
help me connect with the teens who had left their homes. This shelter was
a place for kids to stay for up to two weeks, while their families cooled off,
got some counseling, and sorted through their problems. Two weeks was
rarely enough time to fix the situation, but the teens were safe and learned
some life skills.

A runaway shelter needs buttoned-up staff who follow the rules, but
they also need a guy with leopard print hair. The diversity of perspectives

helped the youth feel that we were people like them and people who were not like them.

As we plan for a shorter workweek, the second inclination that will boost our success is an Outsider Approach, a superpower shortcut to growth. When I started the college job and saw how the notes and calendar system were out of line with the world of counseling, that was an outsider perspective.

Albert Einstein lived in Germany, Italy, Switzerland, Austria, Belgium, and the United States. That gave him a distinct advantage. Author Malcolm Gladwell describes his own racial background as: "My mother is not black, but brown. Her father's mother was part Jewish and part black, and her mother's mother had enough Scottish in her that my grandmother was born with straight hair to go with her classically African features."[1] In Gladwell's MasterClass he speaks about his experience as an immigrant from Canada as an advantage. It's something that gave him a different lens.

Most great poets, artists, revolutionaries, and world-shakers have had experiences when they felt they didn't quite fit in. My daughters have been really into the *Little People, Big Dreams* books. They have the Women of Science and Women in Art sets. Also, they have the *Good Night Stories for Rebel Girls* books. It's remarkable how many stories there are of adversity and outsider experiences.

Marie Curie was barred from attending the same university as her brother so she went to France and eventually became the first woman to win the Nobel Prize.

Ada Lovelace spent a lot of time alone as a child and loved math, when other women were not doing math. She was the world's first computer programmer.

Jane Goodall was specifically selected to study chimpanzees because of her lack of formal training. She was a secretary.[2]

Frida Kahlo was very sick as a child. While bedbound, she drew her foot over and over. She became one of the most famous artists in the twentieth century.

Audrey Hepburn was forced from her home in the Netherlands during World War II, became sick, and recovered. Later, she became a defining actress and dancer in the twentieth century. She spent her later years raising awareness and advocating for UNICEF and food, medicine, and clean water for children.

Why does every Disney movie seem to start with parents dying? Why was Luke Skywalker raised by Uncle Owen and Aunt Beru? Why do most great myths start with adversity?

I believe that we actually want an outsider perspective. Deep down, we want disruption and new ideas. Biblical prophets challenged the status quo. Protests in the sixties rewrote laws. Innovators dream of building a greener planet.

An argument could be made that when someone is famous, biographers search for the unique and sensational stories. It makes for a more engaging narrative if someone was sick as a kid, lost a parent, or overcame some adversity. But the truth is, we can all have an outsider perspective. It is not reserved for a special class of sanctioned greats.

The goal is to discover *how* we are an outsider, not *if* we are an outsider.

Within my company, I can get lazy and stop taking an Outsider Approach. For most owners, this comes in the form of the Industrialist mindset creeping back in. Our systems are good and automated; we don't need to try to improve. "We have most of the market share. Let's not innovate for a while. Staff are doing what they should do. Let's not challenge them to evolve into a role they find more satisfying."

It's easy to have an Outsider Approach when you're being rejected. Look at punk rock. In the seventies and eighties, punk was a subculture within a subculture. It was buried deep and had a deeply authentic voice full of angst. It wanted to speak truth to power in a way that power would blow off.

They're not even worth our time. That's where an outsider has their power. But what happens when punk goes mainstream? When, instead of having to go to a biker shop for spikes, you can go to Hot Topic (is that even around anymore?) or a website?

Punk loses something when it's playing in a minivan on SiriusXM on the way to pick up the kids from the robotics club. Or does it? Are we really destined to conform to the world around us? Or can we maintain some level of Outsider Approach?

The next internal inclination is a bit more punk rock. If you never got into punk rock, skateboarding, or the festival scene, you missed out. But that's the point: it was for a sliver of the population because, for a time, it was all the rage. The next internal inclination that we'll explore is that toward disruption.

Being an outsider for the sake of standing out is really just loneliness. That's not what we're talking about. We're not talking about creating situations to be different only to be different. We're not just chaos-making. But being an outsider to improve and expand better ideas, that's something worth pursuing. There are outsiders who are a pain to be around. That is destructive and dysfunctional. But having an Outsider inclination that grows something new keeps you moving constantly forward. It's like those seeds that are only released in a forest fire: a certain amount of pain leads to clarity and sparks the inclination to seek a new way.

Unhealthy disruption is usually fueled by anger, hate, and unresolved hurt. But the kind of Outsider thinking that I focus on here is based on firm and respectful groundedness, which shouts: "It doesn't have to be this way!"

I would argue that, as with curiosity, we must pursue the Outsider perspective intentionally. Curiosity seems to naturally fade away under the stress of being a parent, worker bee, consumer, or [fill in the blank with negative adulting term here]. Sure, we can take the easy path of following the typical script, but what if we could see the world through new eyes?

Sometimes returning to your original childhood Outsider Approach will reveal what you *could* be. I'd like you to meet Jerry.

JERRY HAS A SECRET

Jerry had kept it a secret until third grade. Only his best friends and family knew what was true. He wore pants all the time, despite living in Southern California. Only he knew why he could kick a kickball so far. But everything changed that day.

In the third trimester of her pregnancy, Jerry's mom started spotting. It was the 1970s and Jerry's mom trusted her doctor when she was given Depo-Provera. Depo-Provera is now commonly given in the form of a shot for birth control. In the 1970s, doctors didn't know that late in a pregnancy this could cause birth defects.

Jerry's right foot was born without bones. His left foot was half-size, and missing two toes. Doctors said that Jerry would never walk. At four months of age, Jerry was taken to an amputee center and given orthotics to stabilize the smaller left foot. His right foot was amputated.

As Jerry grew, so did his natural athleticism. He especially excelled in games like kickball and was nicknamed "Bazooka" because of how far he could kick the ball. His prosthetic foot was a secret. "It was like a club," Jerry said.

One day during a game of kickball, Jerry lined himself up. "When I kicked, it felt like it crushed, it didn't feel right," he said. As the ball flew into the air, children looked up. Expressions of horror and disbelief distorted their faces. The ball spun through the air next to Jerry's shoe with his foot inside. Kids started crying and screaming.

A disoriented gym teacher grabbed a dolly and wheeled Jerry over to his foot. He was no longer called "Bazooka" but "pegleg" instead.

Fast-forward to Jerry as an adult. "If Jerry doesn't slow down, he's going to have a heart attack," Jerry's wife, Cara, said to me. It was a pre-consulting call. Cara wanted Jerry to get some help. Dr. Jerry Weichman is a psychologist who takes pride in figuring out how to achieve the unachievable.

Clearly this was more Cara's idea than Jerry's. What I didn't know was that Jerry had a history of heart issues. Eight years before that conversation, he had had a stomach virus. It bothered him for a few days. Then, while he was in a counseling session with a teenager, he started getting chest pains. His left side tightened, he had less breath, and the pain moved through his chest.

He was thinking, "I only have ten minutes until the end of the session." The minutes crept and he called Cara, who was walking at Newport Beach. She wanted him to go to the hospital; he said, "I don't need to go."

Jerry called his doctor, who encouraged him to go to the ER. Tests determined that the virus that had attacked his stomach had moved to his heart, a condition known as myopericarditis, and the heart had been severely damaged.

Jerry felt himself fading away. "I was fading, losing life," he said. After a few days in the hospital, Jerry returned home. He was told to lie low, but he couldn't slow down. While his wife was gone, he pulled his bike out to go for a short, unapproved ride.

"Cara pulled in the driveway and I got caught."

Jerry's follow-up appointments eventually spaced out to every six months, but in the year leading up to our meeting his condition deteriorated. "First my doctor wanted to meet every six months," Jerry says, "then four, then two." His blood pressure was getting worse and his lifestyle wasn't changing.

That's when we met. At that time, Jerry was speaking more, working on a book, running a group private practice, and still doing mostly initial assessments. "I was always motivated; there was no ceiling. I have heard of burnout, but that wasn't me. I was less and less effective in a day."

When the kids were asleep, Jerry would try to work on a page for his book, write some emails, or catch up on work. He'd look up and it would be after midnight. "I only got 5 to 10 percent done of what I should have in three hours."

Between his pre-consulting call and our first meeting, he had another flare-up. It was time for things to change.

JERRY STARTS SNOWBOARDING

"What will really represent change for you?" I asked. When consulting, I want to establish measurable goals that we can use to chart our progress. Clients may suggest financial goals or goals related to time spent working, but we want to find something that means a little bit more.

"Snowboarding every Wednesday," Jerry said.

"Why snowboarding?"

As we examined what snowboarding represented to Jerry, he talked about what it would take to snowboard. He would have to stop returning phone calls. He'd have to train his front desk in more automation. He'd have to rearrange clients. He would have to feel confident in saying "No" to speaking engagements on Wednesdays. His staff would need to be able to put out fires on their own.

For Jerry, snowboarding represented freedom for a day. As we talked, he described what snowboarding on Wednesdays meant to him:

1. Getting out of the house at 6:00 a.m. made him feel different.
2. Driving out of town into the mountains was like "driving out of stress," he said.
3. The mountains were above the smog. The air was clean. It was like a mini vacation every week.
4. He had time to think in short bits while he rode the chair lift.

The act of snowboarding on a Wednesday meant that Jerry had to anticipate both problems and outcomes. To step back and slow down first demands anticipating potential issues. If you are the only one returning emails, calling clients back, and scheduling them, that means the business is reliant on you. Your office should just be closed on a Wednesday.

Instead, shift the mindset to anticipate problems and say, "Why the heck am I doing this?" Jerry is a PhD and licensed psychologist in California. He's probably able to charge $300 to $400 per hour. He could hire an executive assistant that works forty hours a week for $80,000. If we add benefits and taxes, say it was $100,000 per year. If Jerry's rate is $350 per session (this is hypothetical, not his actual rate) that means he would get forty hours a week x forty-eight weeks = 1,920 hours of amazing admin work in exchange for 285.71 hours of his own work.

This is the math that is hard for people who start with a mindset like Jerry:

1. I want to figure it out.
2. I did figure it out.
3. I got praise for figuring it out.
4. I feel good about figuring it out.
5. So I should keep doing it all myself. (Go back to step one.)

This is a dangerous cycle for the Jerrys of the world. Instead, Jerry started snowboarding on Wednesdays. We'd start every session with, "How many times did you go snowboarding?"

THE PROBLEM WITH THE INDUSTRIALISTS' KPIs

In the business world, success and failure are often measured by what are called "key performance indicators," or KPIs. The problem with most KPIs is that they don't have the heart that drives us. Sure, I can say, "I want to make more money."

Why?

This brings us back to the difference between an Industrialist mindset and the Organism approach. A KPI by itself has little meaning or function. It does not compel us. Whereas, seeing how a KPI fuels something new or brings us back to something old or known, that's different. It's a function of something bigger.

Imagine if you were asked by some friends, "How was that family camping trip to Yosemite?" And you answered, "It was great; we had to refill the gas tank five times."

Wait, what? You're saying that your trip was good because you filled the gas tank five times? You may remember two terms from your college research days: qualitative and quantitative. Qualitative research is more about the story, the "why," or a small sample that goes really deep. Whereas quantitative research is about having lots of numbers to be able to show that something is statistically significant. Both approaches are needed for different reasons.

If someone wants to know the quality of my trip, I'll talk about hikes, emotional moments, and connecting with my kids. If someone wants to know about quantity, I might talk about times filling the gas tank, or how many stars I would give restaurants. Both give different kinds of information.

The Industrialist mindset, with its KPIs, business plans, and automation, frequently missed the heart of why we're doing what we're doing. In other words, the story behind it all. What's driving this thing? Is it just profits, or is it avoiding a heart attack and snowboarding more to live a life worth living?

With consulting clients, I ask what making more money and working less would do for them. What would that help you do that you're not doing now? Does it provide a feeling of safety? Maybe a large savings makes you feel better able to take care of your family in tough times. Maybe you want an older parent without much savings to live in an environment they love. Maybe it represents freedom to have a lighter schedule and travel.

Most KPIs end at: to increase profits by 10 percent.

What's the point of increasing profits by 10 percent every year? What if increasing by 5 percent would meet everyone's life goals and create a solid company? When we don't step back from the KPI to dig into how to affect the company and our own lives, we lose all the drive and motivation.

Let's go back to Jerry. In the initial call, the conversation probably went something like this:

"Jerry and Cara, what are some outcomes of consulting you are hoping for?" I ask.

"I just want Jerry to have less stress. He spends so much time working in the evenings and I think he's headed for burnout," says Cara.

"Maybe I am, but I think I can do it," Jerry says.

"I don't doubt you can do it, but at what cost?" Cara answers.

I ask, "So, Cara, what 'costs' are you worried about?"

"If Jerry continues down this path, he might have another heart attack," Cara answers.

At this point, I want to find out what is meaningful to Jerry. It's one thing to have a conversation about what Cara thinks Jerry needs; it's something completely different for Jerry to do the work, set boundaries, and have less stress.

"Jerry, what's something that would really represent moving in a healthier direction?"

"Honestly, if I could just snowboard once a week, I'd be good," he says.

That's usually how it comes out, with something like, "Honestly, I just want to be able to [fill in the blank] and not feel [negative emotion]."

What is that for you? It might be simple: a weekly yoga class, a daily fancy coffee, a call with a friend in the middle of the workday.

For some reason, we have guilt around the true depth of our KPI, but the truth is, that is actually the most powerful fuel for getting more done in a shorter amount of time.

I realized recently that my wife has been asking for a coffee from her favorite spot about five days a week. I thought it through. Her coffee costs $4 to $5. Even if she bought a coffee every single day for a month, that would be $150, max. Sure, that's a big coffee budget. But, if that produces tons of joy, a feeling of freedom, and that she is worth it, why wouldn't I just say, "Whenever you want a coffee, just get it"? Jerry has also adjusted his priorities and found that simple pleasures give him great satisfaction.

Jerry now vigorously defends a handful of activities: workouts, his lunch, and time with his kids and wife at home. Jerry will frequently lose his phone at home. He said this to me, almost like it was on purpose. It's easier for him to disconnect if finding the phone is an extra step to check email or texts.

Structure forces us look at what is right in front of us. Since our work together, Jerry has continued to build structure that creates predictability, reduces stress, and simplifies activities.

Later, we'll talk about exactly what to do to sprint forward. Jerry needed a structure to move forward. This discipline of structure and the vigorous defense of key items is the main point. Jerry had specific key activities that defined success: being able to snowboard, turn off his computer, spend time with his family, and see clients. He eliminated nonessential activities.

As a result of slowing down and stepping back from work, Jerry has more energy and sleeps better. He is more productive and focused. Jerry feels more balanced. Jerry's blood pressure has improved and he's "enjoying not going at 10,000 mph."

OUTSIDER APPROACH ASSESSMENT

You have been an outsider many times in your life. For me, it was when I loved the band Nirvana in ninth grade, wore a flannel shirt, and tied one around my waist. I had a ponytail and was learning guitar. But I went to Catholic school. Not just any Catholic school, but a *Friday Night Lights* sort of school. Kids dressed up as the football coach for Halloween . . . in elementary school!

I was not a part of the "inside" crowd. People who have experienced pain, hurt, and rejection during their teen years often grow up to say, "Never again!" Maybe you found a tribe in college or realized you're an introvert and don't focus on large gatherings. People like you and me tend to overcompensate to ensure we're never outsiders again. But being an outsider and seeing things differently has statistically significant advantages.

If we all have outsider experiences, why do they seem to disappear over time for most of us? The reasons fall into three major categories:

1. The brain wants to avoid pain. The pain of being an outsider may have felt significant. We hide our uniqueness so that we won't be identified as an outsider.
2. Professional life molded us into being like everyone else. We conformed to get ahead. Early in a career, this can be helpful. Experiences get cataloged creating a sense of wanting to keep the status quo (just like with curiosity).
3. Having an Outsider Approach can be dangerous.

Let's look at a typical entrepreneur. They start a side-hustle while keeping a full-time job. That side-hustle grows. They add a few virtual assistants to take care of tasks while they keep their job. At some point they make the decision to start something on their own. There is an increase in pressure to make money, since there is no longer the safety net of the job.

When they had the job, they were working more hours and hustling, but there wasn't the same pressure. They could take risks without worrying about success. They could be different and not care if it worked.

Then, when it became a full-time side gig, something switched. The original fun, inquiry, and uniqueness felt like a bigger risk.

The Outsider Approach starts to die when we think conforming is safer than being unique.

We think established businesses must know what they are doing, so we start to copy their processes.

We hire people who encourage us to follow standard operating procedures.

We become more and more like everyone else.

How many times have you heard the story of a startup that grows? Then they go public and the board wants an established CEO to lead instead of the founders. The new CEO may have business experience, but is missing the original Outsider perspective. Sure, maybe the company expanded at a mind-blowing rate and needs some systems and organization, but what about the original DNA or X Factor that made the company successful in the first place?

The most successful clients I see are those who maintain their Outsider Approach. They walk the line of having operations that maintain growth and keep staff moving toward goals, but they also keep asking, "Are we doing things how we do them because we've always done them this way? How do I explore other ways of doing this? If I'm an Insider now, how do I get more Outsiders to surround me?"

You've already determined your level of curiosity in the previous assessment; now we're going to do the same for your level of Outsider Approach. How much is naturally occurring and what has been or needs to be developed?

Outsider Approach Assessment

Discovery goals of this self-assessment:

1. Do you naturally think like an Outsider?
2. Is Outsider Approach a habit?
3. Does Outsider Approach create openings that inform decisions and actions in your life?

These are forced-answer questions, meaning there is no "maybe." We want to get to the heart of Outsider Approach in your life, so note your "yes" answers.

Is Outsider Approach naturally occurring in you?

1. I regularly think about how to improve systems of government, workplace, or my home.
2. I rarely accept something the first time.
3. When something is mainstream, I avoid it at first.
4. I was not popular in school.
5. Life feels harder than it should be.
6. In a social situation, I notice people that don't fit in.
7. In meetings, I tend to question assumptions more than others.
8. The world needs some revamping socially, politically, or in the business world.
9. I see myself as having an Outsider Approach.

7+ A natural Outsider
4–6 Growing Outsiderness
0–3 Needs some development, but don't give up, you can develop it!

Is Outsider Approach a habit?

1. When given a project or task, I brainstorm multiple solutions.
2. I assume I won't get it right the first time.

3. Just because people approve of something, I don't take it as the best way.
4. I look for unique books, podcasts, and entertainment.
5. Even if I don't agree, I like to learn from quirky or different thinkers than myself.
6. People might call my thoughts "out-of-the-box."
7. I don't always follow directions well.
8. I think through better ways to do things like driving from here to there.
9. I'd say I'm able to think like an Outsider.

7+ Outsider Approach is a habit
4–6 Habits are forming
0–3 You need to work toward making Outsider Approach a habit.

Does Outsider Approach inform decisions and actions in your life?

1. I work on things that challenge the way things are done.
2. I don't attend events just because others are attending.
3. Supervisors did not always appreciate my out-of-the-box thinking.
4. My approaches are unconventional.
5. I try new things.
6. I act in a way that is grounded and unapologetic without hurting others.
7. I'm okay with most of my decisions.
8. I keep reinventing myself.

6+ Outsider Approach informs your actions
3–5 You are beginning to inform your actions with Outsider Approach
0–2 You need some work here, but you'll get there.

There are three variables:

1. An uppercase O means you are naturally curious. Lowercase indicates that your curiosity is developing.

2. A + sign means that you have strong information-consuming habits supporting your curiosity. A – sign means your habits need development.

3. A + sign means that you take strong actions to support curiosity. A – sign means your actions need development.

Types of People / Outsider Approach

This exercise serves to guide you through three areas of Outsiderness: Does it come naturally? Are you making time for it? Do you act on Outsider Thinking? What do you think:

1. Are you naturally an Outsider, or are you developing?
2. Do you have regular habits that make room for you to grow, to think differently?
3. Are you making time to implement what you think and learn?

Here are the options:

Natural Outsider or Growing Outsider
With habits or without habits
With action or without action

Once you have determined your type, we'll learn a bit more about your tendencies, challenges, and next steps.

(O++)	Natural Outsider, with habits and with actions. **The Rockstar** is a natural Outsider who makes time and takes action for new ways to approach the world. Like Tony Hawk, Joey Ramone, or Steve Jobs, you think outside the box and get things done.
(O–+)	Natural Outsider, without habits and with actions. **The Jump-starter** is a natural Outsider but doesn't have a regular habit of thinking outside of the norm or acting to push the boundaries. This person has actions without habits to support them. At times this can be dangerous since there is less to back up the action.

(O+−)	Natural Outsider, with habits and without actions. **The Ponderer** has a natural tendency to think like an Outsider but does not usually act. They may be frustrated with how the world operates, but don't proactively seek to change it.
(O−−)	Natural Outsider, without habits and without actions. **The Go-Alonger** feels like an Outsider, but these feelings do not translate to many of their thoughts or actions. They are actually leaving their superhero skills at home, instead of using their unique perspective to help the world think differently.
(o++)	Developing Outsider, with habits and with actions. **The Reformer** may not have had a life as an Outsider, but they are realizing that their past ways of going along with things may not have been beneficial to them or the people around them. They are growing their thinking and actions to challenge the status quo.
(o−+)	Developing Outsider, without habits and with actions. **The Salesman** is like the Jumpstarter, taking actions without routinely forming habits. They are understanding how approaching things differently is helpful, but not doing the work to make it a regular part of their life and work world.
(o+−)	Developing Outsider, with habits and without actions. **The Conservationist** is working hard to move to the outside. They may push themselves to listen to podcasts, read a book through a book club, or join a class to keep challenging themselves and growing their perspective. They are like someone on the edge of a cliff by a waterfall: they know they want to act, but they haven't taken the plunge yet.
(o−−)	Developing Outsider, without habits and without actions. **The Wide Eyes** has struggled to develop an Outsider Approach. They may fear all that comes with being on the outside while still feeling dissatisfied with the status quo. They aren't taking steps to develop

this perspective and are the most likely to go along with the norms around them, because they have worked for them. Until something disrupts or challenges their comfort zone, they're likely to stay there.

You're Not Off the Hook, Yet

Being an Outsider has tremendous benefit. You can think, evaluate, and act on what you see as the stronger path. But it often comes with consequences. A traditional job may not be for you (or at least a traditional role). You may find that, more times than not, you're disappointed with the world.

Or you notice things others don't seem to notice, like how people will stay in the right lane with twenty cars following each other, when the left is open. Comedians are funny because they exaggerate and bring to light what they notice in the everyday. Their ability to have fun with what we all could see but typically ignore is built on an observer/outsider view.

It's safe to be an insider. In fact, our natural evolution makes it beneficial to stick with our group and the given script. Being in a crowd means that you're less likely to be eaten by a wild animal. But remember that you live with a lifetime of perceived dangers that can keep you stuck.

INACTION AND HAPPINESS

Whether we are considering the primitive social landscape of ten thousand years ago or the party that's happening right now, being in the majority has always had numerous benefits. Being in a group that collectively farmed gave you access to food when your farming didn't turn out so well. Imagine living a few thousand years ago and everyone knew you were bad at farming.

Sometimes I wonder if the diversity of jobs was created when parents got together to discuss their son: "Honestly, Jimbo is incapable of farming. Is there anything else he can do?"

"Maybe we could have him gather wood? Or he could go catch animals in the wild?"

"Honestly, anything would be better than him trying to farm."

Being in a group also spread the risk. It helped to avoid being overtaken by invaders. Even now, being in the majority allows you to pick where you go out to eat, the direction for your business, and to own the direction you want to take.

Just to be clear, we're not talking only ethnic majorities, cultures, or groups. It's any majority. A beneficial trait that we call "rejection sensitivity" arose to preserve our membership in the majority. Understanding social cues, nonverbal cues, and potential rejection helps a person stay in a group or a marriage. It allows an individual to avoid deeper social rejection if they screw up and it allows them to rejoin the group.[3]

Some people just know that something is "off" with those around them. Rejection sensitivity can be viewed as their superpower or sixth sense. Recent studies show that some people feel physical pain when they experience social rejection.[4] Intuitively understanding rejection has had enormous evolutionary and practical benefits.

I've just made the case for the benefits of being in a group, but trust me, you'll soon see why that Outsider Approach is valuable and how to use it for positive change. First, we need to understand that rejection sensitivity prevents us from optimizing our Outsider status.

To be effective, Outsiders need to understand and overcome their sensitivity to rejection. Those who have a natural aversion to rejection will be less likely to speak up or innovate. They may be nearly paralyzed by their perfectionism and fear of failure. Do you recognize this way of thinking? *If I don't try, I won't fail. If I don't fail, I won't be rejected. If I'm not rejected, I will be happier.*

But inaction rarely leads to happiness.

So, instead, we need to work on psychological vulnerability reduction and build rejection opportunities, just like Motown.

YOU COULD LEARN A LOT FROM MOTOWN

I stood next to the candy machine inside the house on West Grand Boulevard in Detroit, Michigan. The house sits where Hitsville USA began, the epicenter of Motown. Strangely, there was always change on the top of the candy machine. The slot for a Baby Ruth bar was always positioned four knobs from the right. The candy bars in other slots may have changed positions over time, but a Hitsville Baby Ruth was always in slot four from the right. Why?

That Baby Ruth was the favorite candy bar of a young, blind, rising star: Stevie Wonder.[5]

Every Friday morning, producers submitted songs for a vote. The Four Tops, The Jackson 5, The Supremes, The Temptations, and more all sat around together expressing their honest opinions. The Motown Museum says, "The competition was fierce––and so was the love. It was survival of the fittest. The artists flourished in that process, as well as the songwriter/producers."[6]

Imagine it was your first day at Motown's Hitsville USA. You move into a house across the street. It's an assembly line of musicians just pumping out music. The doors are always open to the studio, so if you are inspired at 3:00 a.m., you can go play a riff and record a song that you think is the next hit.

It's Friday; you sit down. Some of the greatest musicians of a generation are going to critique your song. Talk about a moment when you may feel some "rejection sensitivity." As you develop and optimize your Outsider Approach, look for opportunities to:

1. Build rejection
2. Engage in psychological vulnerability reduction

Do you remember the first time you gave a big speech? At the beginning of my senior year of high school, I ran for vice president of the student council. I had performed before, participated in band, and read at Mass. But it had never been my speech, my thoughts, my opinions.

I remember nothing about my platform or words. Just the terror of standing in front of the entire student body, teachers, and administration. Public speaking can be terrifying and exhilarating. Over time, the more I did it, the more the positive experiences reinforced the task. It got easier. There were also times I was rejected.

For example, I thought I was good enough to play guitar in the talent show in a "band." We couldn't nail the songs the night before the talent show, so we agreed that playing the music onstage would make it all come together. That was not the case. The best guitarist in our group literally walked off the stage mid-song because we were so bad.

The muscles built by years of alternating positive feedback and rejection supported my comfort in crafting a message and delivering it to large audiences. As entrepreneurs, we may get lazy and fail to push ourselves to levels that make us uncomfortable.

When counseling, I may suggest an exercise I call Comfort-Growth-Panic. I ask the group to imagine a spectrum that spans the room. To your far left is your "comfort zone." This is you at your most comfortable: in your jammies watching Netflix with a glass of wine. In the middle of the room is your "growth zone." These are things that stretch you, maybe make your stomach flip, but you know are good for you. To your far right is your "panic zone." These are the activities that make you freak out, shut down, and go into fight/flight/freeze mode.

"I'm going to name some activities or situations and I want you to physically go to the spot on the spectrum that it represents: your comfort zone, growth zone, or panic zone. So, if I say, 'relaxing on a beach with someone you love,' where would you go?"

After making sure everyone understands the activity, I'll throw out some easy ones: going on vacation, eating sushi, skydiving, driving with a teenager for the first time. People laugh. Then I may throw in some activities appropriate to the organization I'm training. How you feel about your retirement planning, how you felt on your first day here, how you feel now, changing the mission of the company.

What frequently stands out for people are times when they were stranded at one of the extremes of the spectrum, especially if they were not joined by others. They also noticed how many people felt the same as they did after they had predicted they'd be alone; how hard it is to own your feelings if you are different.

We need to spend most of our time in the growth zone. With many of my consulting clients, setting their prices is a big trigger for growth zone activities. I often work with small- to medium-sized businesses who counsel, consult, coach, or create marketing plans.

As they transition from an hourly-based model, in which one hour equals a certain dollar amount, we'll work toward raising their prices. I counseled one highly skilled therapist who was an in-demand keynote speaker, had been featured in top media, and had a group practice of more than twenty clinicians.

"It's not worth my time to see new clients anymore."

He was charging $225 per forty-five-minute session. "Imagine you want to see twenty clients a week. What would that twenty-first cost? What would they have to pay to work with you?[7] Would you do it for $500 per session?"

"Sure, but that's crazy."

"Would you do it for $400 per session?"

"Sure, but no one will—"

"Would you do it for $300?"

"No, I don't think that's worth it for me."

So we set the new price at $350 per session—and new clients didn't blink. Then it was easier to raise his rates with established clients. Soon he was at $450 per session. My client was in the growth zone: he had confronted the possibility that his desire—a higher rate—would be rejected. Test and grow your determination to withstand rejection so that your amazing outsiderness can come out.

But what if you still experience rejection sensitivity? That's when we want to work on psychological vulnerability reduction. That's a fancy way of saying, "Things that make you feel better."

There's a ton of research on how the brain reacts when it feels attacked or the perception of attack. There are two parts to that phrase. First we have "psychological vulnerability" and "reduction."

Everyone's psychological vulnerability is unique, like a fingerprint. I have a collection of experiences that make me more vulnerable to certain attacks. The Adverse Childhood Experiences Study (ACES) considers ten questions about possible childhood experiences.[8]

Before your eighteenth birthday:

1. Did a parent or other adult in the household often or very often: swear at you, insult you, put you down, or humiliate you? or act in a way that made you afraid that you might be physically hurt?

2. Did a parent or other adult in the household often or very often: push, grab, slap, or throw something at you? or ever hit you so hard that you had marks or were injured?

3. Did an adult or person at least five years older than you ever touch or fondle you or have you touch their body in a sexual way?

or attempt or actually have oral, anal, or vaginal intercourse with you?

4. Did you often or very often feel that: no one in your family loved you or thought you were important or special? or your family didn't look out for each other, feel close to each other, or support each other?

5. Did you often or very often feel that: you didn't have enough to eat, had to wear dirty clothes, and had no one to protect you? or your parents were too drunk or high to take care of you or take you to the doctor if you needed it?

6. Were your parents ever separated or divorced?

7. Was your mother or stepmother often or very often: pushed, grabbed, slapped, or had something thrown at her? or sometimes, often, or very often kicked, bitten, hit with a fist, or hit with something hard? or ever repeatedly hit over at least a few minutes or threatened with a gun or knife?

8. Did you live with anyone who was a problem drinker or alcoholic, or who used street drugs?

9. Was a household member depressed or mentally ill, or did a household member attempt suicide?

10. Did a household member go to prison?

This massive research study has found that two-thirds of people have had at least one of these experiences. The incidence of lung disease, depression, hepatitis, jail time, and suicide are significantly higher among people who can answer yes to four or more questions.[9]

If you answered *yes* to some of the above, you may find it helpful to work with a therapist, specifically one trained in EMDR, which is especially helpful with past trauma. Why this is relevant to this discussion is that we all have some level of psychological vulnerability. ACES is one of many research studies looking at childhood trauma. The main point is, we all have vulnerability.

The second part is the reduction. Research shows us that mindfulness practices like meditation reduce vulnerability.[10] Feeling lonely and being lonely have some of the largest risk factors for poor health and early death.[11] Concentration and worker well-being can be improved with specific programs that reduce psychological vulnerability.[12] In chapter six, we're going to dive deep into this research and application so you can genuinely optimize your schedule, business, and brain.

To summarize, evolution has favored being in the majority with more resources and opportunities. We can avoid feeling shut down by developing rejection sensitivity. But this can lead to being paralyzed by perfection to avoid potential failure and rejection. This sets us up for psychological vulnerability that needs to be reduced. Meditation and slowing down will optimize the brain as we increase rejection opportunities to live in the growth zone.

But once we understand that having an Outsider Approach has value, we're grounded in building rejection opportunities, and we're reducing our psychological vulnerability. As an Outsider, how do we move the majority toward our ways of thinking? Also, what are the ongoing habits and actions that we need to employ to be most effective?

THE MINORITY INFLUENCE

In Malcolm Gladwell's book *David and Goliath*, he discusses political scientist Ivan Arreguín-Toft's work. When two countries go to war, if one country has ten times more people and weapons than the other country, how often does the larger country win? It's not 100 percent; they only win two-thirds of the time. Gladwell discusses why the outsider, the minority, and the underdog have advantages over the establishment. The minority or outsider actually has a huge statistical advantage over those that have the seat of power. This isn't just true in war; it's true in business too.

In 1969, Romanian-born French psychologist Serge Moscovici ran a study to see if a minority group could statistically sway the majority. The all-female subjects were given color-blind tests before the experiment, to ensure they could accurately determine shades of colors (you'll see why in a second). The women were randomly assigned to three groups of six people in which four women were subjects and two women—unbeknownst to the others—were part of the research team. So, each group of six included two outsiders.

The groups were told that they were part of a color perception experiment and were shown thirty-six slides of various shades of blue. A participant might see teal, royal blue, cerulean, aqua, or turquoise. The participants were asked to name the color out loud.

Of the three different groups of six women, one was a control group that did not include outsiders—so, since all the slides were blue, all participants named what they saw: blue. But in another group, the two outsiders would name what they saw "green" two-thirds of the time, despite all the slides being a shade of blue. In the last group, the outsiders swore that all the slides were green.

What happened? In the group with no outsiders, a slide was identified as green less than 1 percent of the time. When the outsiders of group two identified blue as green two-thirds of the time, the group as a whole could only be persuaded 1.25 percent of the time. But the group in which outsiders consistently held that the slides were green *agreed* with the outsiders 8.2 percent of the time.[13]

That percentage may seem small, but it's eight times the number of responses in the control group. Researchers concluded that if a person is in the minority (an outsider) within a group, they need to consistently hold their position. In doing this, it builds trust that the outsider is convinced of their approach and this eventually helps sway the insiders/majority.

Moscovici was criticized for his small, single-gender sample, and some critics predicted that the subjects' attitudes about colors were likely different from those they may have cared more about, such as the environment, politics, guns, or any other hot-button issue. In other words, can we really apply this to everyday life?

In a 1986 study, based on a mock jury, a group of four was asked to determine how much compensation should be given in a ski-lift accident.[14] Again, one of the four was secretly part of the research group—an outsider. The outsider argued for very low compensation, and, following the consistency model set forth by Moscovici, refused to compromise. Could the outsider again change the majority's mind by consistently arguing the same point?

In another group, the outsider compromised and moved closer to the majority's thought. The study showed that the outsider influenced the majority more strongly by compromising, compared to the final verdict of the control group.

Research continues to add to this discussion, but we can conclude that just getting people to talk and debate about a topic will give influence to the outsider.

So there appears to be a combination of theories. The outsider needs to be consistent. The outsider needs to be flexible. The outsider needs to raise questions for debate. Is there a central theme?

Consistency may convince us that the person or group feels a position deeply. They are committed. They know what they want. If I'm in the majority, I may not really care as much. I may have a position, but it's not a strong one.

Compromise allows for a human side to the discussion. They have strong opinions and they're willing to wiggle to try to help gain traction. Maybe they aren't all that bad. Then there is research on an outsider raising questions for debate. That could expose what is occurring internally.

It's as if there is the internal opinion that is not spoken and the external actions. With those two variables, someone could be any of the following:

1. An Ally, who believes in the cause and overtly acts to support it.
2. A Closet Supporter, who believes in the cause but behaves neutrally or may even act against it.
3. A Wolf in Sheep's Clothing, who appears to act in support of the cause, but is internally against it.
4. An Enemy, who is against the cause and makes no bones about it.

So, the majority may include those who quietly support or have empathy for the cause of the minority or the outsider. They are our colleagues in business who have long awaited change but who have never spoken up. The wolves may be quietly against the cause, but acting out of duty. Could they flip?

In a sense, a strong outsider creates a place for incongruent values to focus. We learned in the last chapter that curiosity is built when someone notices an incongruent value/thought, attempts to understand it, and then takes action.

Maybe that's why outsiders can be so effective. They see things differently; they are agents of incongruence. They are manifesting the trigger that spurs on curiosity. But none of this matters without the final internal inclination. What do we do with these inclinations? Are we paralyzed by perfection or do we Move on It?

5

MOVE ON IT

You don't have to see the whole staircase,
just take the first step.

—Martin Luther King, Jr.

When Jessica was twelve, she decided she wanted to be a therapist. She's followed a traditional path to early adulthood. She went to grad school, interned, and started a family. After working in a state hospital and a school, Jessica decided to open a private practice when her second child was born. She wanted to be able to help others, but also to be fully present for her family. Jessica is someone who wants to do things correctly. She fears failure and often overthinks decisions. She says it this way: "The biggest struggle was that I was scared to death of failure. I just started my business and was so worried that I would invest all of this time, money, and energy into it only to have it flop. I was worried about not being able to provide for my family or, worse yet, costing us money."

When we started working together, Jessica wanted to grow her business, but not at the expense of her family. Jessica says, "I was worried that I would have to choose between helping people (my business) or being an active part in my family's daily life."

Through our work together, she used just enough of her focus on perfection to create more success. She worked to not overthink. She'd implement and then see how things went.

Jessica says, "You taught me to prioritize. Through our individual conversations over the last couple of years (phone calls and Slow Down School), you challenged my hang-ups around money and helped me realize that being successful would help me meet the needs of my family. That my dreams (taking my kids on vacation, picking my kiddo up from school, getting my son the support he needed) were rational and worth pursuing.

You also helped me stop worrying about doing everything 'right,' so I could instead keep producing and then focus on perfecting later."

Jessica's mindset shifted. For her, it happened while listening to a podcast. "One of my favorite Joe Sanok things was a podcast episode where you were talking about blog posts and you said, 'If you can write it so it's 80 percent good, just put it out there.' I'm certain those weren't your exact words, but that's how I remember it." The biggest shift for Jessica was to move from being paralyzed by perfection to getting things done.

Then Jessica came to Slow Down School.

During Slow Down School, entrepreneurs fly to northern Michigan and sit on the shores of Lake Michigan. We genuinely slow down for the first two days. We go for hikes, I bring in a massage therapist and yoga teacher. We make gourmet s'mores around the fire with all sorts of toppings. We skip stones over the water.

One year, while my eight-year-old daughter was visiting one evening, we started a stone skipping competition. After the competition, we played the game differently. I said, "Find the most unskippable stone for someone else and then we'll see who can skip it."

One of our participants, Michael Glavin, was given a large piece of concrete. It was probably nine inches wide with not a single smooth surface. As you probably know, to skip a stone, you need (or so I thought) at least some smoothness.

My eight-year-old tried her unskippable rock . . . plunk, no skip. I tried mine. No skip. Whitney (another participant) tried hers. No skip. Then came Michael with the concrete.

Michael skipped the unskippable concrete! In fact, last winter he was walking the shores of Lake Michigan near Chicago and sent me a video of him skipping another "unskippable" rock. In my family, Michael is now known as "the man who can skip the unskippable."

Those are the moments of Slow Down School, where high-achieving entrepreneurs skip the unskippable. Or when LaToya Smith went for her first hike and ate a s'more for the first time. Or when Whitney Owens asked me if she could be a consultant with Practice of the Practice. Or the time we had a gourmet chocolate tasting and I tasted cacao juice for the first time. That is Slow Down School and those are the things that take a business from limping along to dominating a market, because it primes the brain for focus.

Then, for the second half of the week, we run full tilt toward their goals. By slowing down, the brain is optimized to kill it. That's what part two is all about.

Let's zoom back in on Jessica. During Slow Down School, she helped fellow Slow Down Schoolers with search engine optimization (SEO) for their websites each evening, rather than just relaxing by the water. As a way to save money for things she needed to outsource, she had been learning SEO and how to rank higher in Google searches.

Jessica is a self-described "technophobe" who says, "I can't even get my smart TV to work most of the time." So she had not expected to be immersed in new technology, and she was surprised to find she was good at it. Each evening at Slow Down School, she shared her skills as her ranking rose on Google. Within the week, her pages had climbed considerably higher.

During our workdays, I said to her, "This is a needed business for professionals, especially therapists." That was all she needed to get to work. Jessica asked fellow participants if they would be interested in SEO service for their website. Ten business owners said they would be interested. In two days, she had sketched out business, marketing, and launch plans. She shared her idea with the group and had her first paying clients before she left Slow Down School!

Now, Simplified SEO Consulting is the leading SEO business for therapists, counselors, and psychologists. It makes more money for Jessica than her counseling practice and she has more time with her family.

PARKINSON'S LAW

British historian Cyril Northcote Parkinson published an essay in the November 19, 1955, *Economist*, which began, "It is a commonplace observation that work expands so as to fill the time available for its completion. Thus, an elderly lady of leisure can spend the entire day in writing and despatching a postcard to her niece at Bognor Regis. An hour will be spent in finding the postcard, another in hunting for spectacles, half-an-hour in a search for the address, an hour and a quarter in composition, and twenty minutes in deciding whether or not to take an umbrella when going to the pillar-box in the next street. The total effort which would occupy a busy man for three minutes all told may in this fashion leave another person prostrate after a day of doubt, anxiety, and toil."[1]

This single sentence in a humorous essay challenged us to understand why work expands to the time given. If a client says to you, "This was due yesterday, I need it in an hour," it doesn't matter what the "it" is, you get it to them. It may not be perfect, but it is done. When friends are coming over, the cleaning and meal always come together just fine in the time allotted. When given a month, it takes a month.

Parkinson made numerous observations about our tendencies to over-think, analyze, and expand unnecessarily. He noticed two laws: The Law of Multiplication of Subordinates and The Law of Multiplication of Work. The basic idea of The Law of Multiplication of Subordinates is that over time an individual may notice that they cannot complete the tasks assigned to them. As this happens, they may ask their employer for people to supervise. Over time, those individuals begin supervising. But, the actual work is not expanding at the same rate as the rate of hiring. This is where the Law of Multiplication of Work comes in. There are additional signatures, memos, emails, meetings, and unnecessary work to keep everyone busy.

We hire more people and we keep them busy. Work not only expands to the time given, but to the people hired. Parkinson gave "scientific proof" of this in his article. He showed that between 1914 and 1928 the number of ships in the Royal Navy declined by 68 percent and crew by 31 percent, but the number of clerks increased by 40 percent and officers increased by 78 percent.[2]

Parkinson called this "orgmanship." Which he says is "the tendency of all administrative departments to increase the number of subordinate staff, irrespective of the amount of work (if any) to be done."

Parkinson's Law became a universal critique of bureaucratization. Of course, these aren't "laws" as much as observations of human behavior. We take a really long time to complete tasks, unnecessarily hire people, and spread work among numerous people to justify our positions.

But a new generation of entrepreneurs is using these inclinations to push back and create the opposite of a fatty organization. Instead, they're getting lean.

I DIDN'T STUDY FOR THE BOARDS

I was in my senior year at my Catholic high school in the wake of Kurt Cobain's death. I had been playing guitar loosely for two years. I had a choice at school: play football or embrace my weirdness. I knew I'd never do well enough in sports. I had tried (unsuccessfully) through middle school, and no one I wanted to impress was impressed. Those who were impressed were my grandmother, parents, and younger siblings.

The night before the talent show, we couldn't nail any of the songs. We thought it would be easier onstage; it was not. As I mentioned before, our songs were so bad that the only guy who could play guitar well walked off the stage in the middle of the worst Foo Fighters cover in the history of St. Francis High School.

The front-row faces showed everything we needed to know. We were not going anywhere musical, anytime soon.

Yet, I gained a tremendous amount of information. I had put myself out there and Moved on It before I was ready. I knew that music would take more time, knowledge, planning, and practice. The internal inclination of jumping before you are ready is about standing up against the predominant narrative that we "practice until perfect." When we Move on It before we're ready, it gives us a download of information that informs our path to action.

In most of our businesses, it makes sense to try something and adjust as we go, rather than have a pass/fail mentality. We need to experiment and gather information. In my consulting, clients who make a move before they are ready typically find the feelings of added pressure motivating and use these to serve as a catalyst to gain confidence in making larger steps forward. Too many of us become paralyzed by perfection, making it incredibly hard to figure out when to best make your move. By moving on it before you're ready, you can better figure out the right steps in the right order to get you to where you want to be.

Nothing is perfect. With any project, the creator sees the flaws. A friend of ours just built a new deck. It's beautiful, but when showing it to us he said, "Over there a few things don't line up, but it's finished." Oftentimes people get paralyzed by perfection instead of getting things done. In school, college, and work, we often are encouraged to "do it right the first time." Or we think we need a project to be polished before we turn it in. This is reinforced in our educational systems and workplaces. But the most effective businesses, people, and projects usually start with a minimum viable product. They get something out there and adjust as they go. This saves time, creates faster innovation, and gets feedback. The same is true for us in our own growth. Just do something, even if it's imperfect, and keep moving forward.

Numerous techniques help overcome this. In lean manufacturing they are plan, do, check, adjust. If work expands to the amount of time given, how do we overcome that? Well, we need to understand why we overthink and get paralyzed by perfection.

So why are we so often paralyzed by perfection? There are good reasons to think carefully about certain things. For example, if you are going to propose to someone and get married, you might want to think that one through. If you want to bring kids into the world, you might want to evaluate that decision a bit first. Even leaving a secure job to do something else requires at least a look at the pros and cons.

But the number of times where it is a big deal with huge consequences when we "fail" is actually far fewer than we fear. The summer I was finishing graduate school, I was working fifty-hour weeks in my internship. That was because my wedding day was the same day as the last day I could complete internship hours. I wanted to be done early so I could be around for wedding prep. On top of the fifty-hour weeks, I was driving back to my hometown three hours each way to help with the wedding planning and it was also the only time I could see my fiancée.

In the middle of this packed schedule, I decided to take the national exam for the National Board for Certified Counselors, the biggest test of a counselor's career. It determines if you get licensed. I decided that I was going to pay the fee and not study. If I failed, I would have to wait a few months to take the test again. I went in on the test day, did my best, and viewed it as information gathering. I knew that if I bombed it, I would need to study really hard. If I just missed passing, I'd only study a bit. Also, maybe, just maybe, I would be able to pass without studying for the exam.

How should we decide to act instead of overthinking? Let's ask ourselves a few questions.

1. Is this a one-shot deal? If there is a failure, are there no other options?
2. What are the consequences of failure? In the case of the board exam, I could take it again a few months later. For others, it may be an annual test.
3. Can the opportunity at hand be viewed as an experiment?
4. What is the reward if under-planning leads to success?

So, let's recap my decision to take the exam without studying:

1. I could take the test a few months later if I didn't pass, so it wasn't a one-shot deal.
2. If I failed, I would have acquired new information.
3. By viewing it as an experiment, I had no shame about failing.
4. If passed, I saved months of study.

I passed by one point. The needed score was 100, and I got 101.

The concept of Moving on It is based on two factors that appear to be in tension with one another: speed and accuracy. I can complete a promo video for my YouTube channel in one hour or one day or one month. If I focus on speed, I can produce significantly more content. Maybe I commit to doing a video per day, four days a week for a month. At the end of the month I have sixteen videos, and I can see which videos did best and replicate those in month two.

In a sense, I am quickly refining my content development through having the audience vote through views. However, if I took a week per video and had four highly produced videos, my accuracy, depth of content, and design would probably be significantly better. This is the trade-off. I can have four times more videos if I focus on speed, but will I have four times more views? If each of my sixteen videos gets 1,000 views, that's 16,000 views in the month. That means that if I took one week per video, they would need 4,000 views per video to make the ROI the same.

Unless I notice that people convert differently based on the higher- or lower-quality video. Before we dive in too deep, we should understand the core differences between speed and accuracy and examine their outcomes. So let's go another layer deeper into the world of psychology.

WHICH IS MORE IMPORTANT: SPEED OR ACCURACY?

Speed and accuracy are manifestations of core conditions. At the extreme, we're talking about two ways of viewing the world: through a world of anxiety or a world of Attention Deficit Hyperactivity Disorder (ADHD). Anxiety can lead to obsessive thoughts, overthinking, and perfectionism. ADHD can lead to sensation-seeking, lack of premeditation, attention issues, and impulsivity.

At one end we have high thought and low action. Individuals that struggle with higher perfectionism often have a level of anxiety. Researcher Dr. Pauline Rose Clance, who with Dr. Suzanne Imes coined the term "impostor phenomenon," notes, "Even though they are often very successful by external standards, they feel their success has been due to some mysterious fluke or luck or great effort; they are afraid their achievements are due to 'breaks' and not the result of their own ability and competence."[3] The core belief of the impostor phenomenon or "syndrome" is "I don't belong here." This manifests when the environment, opportunity, or experience doesn't match our beliefs about ourselves. Rather than this gap leading to curiosity (as we learned in the previous chapters), it leads to self-inflicted pain, judgmental thoughts toward self, and criticism. This internal incongruence can also lead to fear of failure and, consequently, hesitation or failure to act. In other words, you are in your head and not on the move.

Numerous studies have shown how this manifests in the academic world.[4] Imagine you are a student in high school. Throughout your life, you have been praised for your academics.

"You're so smart."

"WOW! Another A, look at you!"

"You're really going to get into a great college with these grades."

Then you have an opportunity to push yourself. Research shows that high-achieving students are more likely to take classes to ensure a high mark than fulfill their fullest potential and fail. It makes sense. If you view your life as praise based on grades, not effort or curiosity or fulfilling potential, you'll stick with the external reinforcer that has worked.

Most researchers, psychologists, and child specialists now recommend emphasizing effort, rather than results:

"Wow, you worked really hard!"

"Dang, what other questions do you now have?"

"Doesn't it feel great to have given this your best?"

See the difference? One is based on a specific outcome, the grade. This locks the student into thinking that is the best reinforcement and goal. Grades at any cost. Whereas the other focuses on what it takes to be a successful adult: curiosity, exploration, growth, and new understandings . . . and how it feels to do something well.

We are trained to think like this. Education says to work on a paper, do a draft, rewrite it, go to the writing center, and submit it when you're done. Overthink and overthink because you only get one shot. One shot? Of course I'm going to feel anxious over that. If I only get one shot, why would I ever move quickly?!

Accuracy is associated with extended thought and slow action.

Speed is the opposite: low thought and high action. In most of the world, symptoms of ADHD interfere greatly with activities of daily living. Hyperactivity, inattention, and moving too quickly are all factors that tend to get in the way of a traditional job.

Imagine sitting in a meeting and Jeff is across the table from you. You're looking at the financials and trying to decide a marketing plan for Q3. Jeff is looking out the window, spinning his pen, and every ten minutes or so, he gets up to get a drink of water. He can't sit still.

Impulsivity doesn't usually serve us in the real world. Submitting incomplete work to a client, disregarding your partner's request to be on time for dinner, and letting your kids down are all impulsive acts most of us seek to avoid.

Sensation-seeking is one of the most common aspects of ADHD. This manifests in numerous ways. Occupational therapists often work with sensory seekers and sensory avoiders. A sensory seeker may need an intervention like a weighted jacket, spinning, or moving. When I think back to my early years, the kids that got in trouble the most probably just needed a little more recess to help their brains chill out.[5] A sensory avoider will find certain types of touch uncomfortable. So occupational therapists will work with them by getting them to play in rice, sand, or to touch Velcro.

The other aspect of ADHD that is worth noting is a lack of premeditation. In people under the age of twenty-five, the frontal lobe has not yet fully developed. The frontal lobe is the section of the brain that helps with decisionmaking, planning, and premeditation. An underdeveloped frontal lobe can lead to less premeditation.

Speed is associated with low thought and high action.

Emerging research is showing that it's not so much the baseline tendency toward speed or accuracy, but the context of the situation that is important. Sensation-seeking and impulsivity are being connected to entrepreneurial success.[6] One aspect to note is that entrepreneurs have a high degree of uncertainty in their lives. In most people, uncertainty causes anxiety, inaction, and worry.[7] But among entrepreneurs, sensation-seeking and impulsivity often help them to overcome these stressors and thrive. In fact, ADHD symptoms are being linked more and more to success in entrepreneurship.

But, of course, a balance is needed. If accuracy at its most extreme is related to anxiety and being paralyzed by perfection, who wants that? If speed at its most extreme is related to ADHD and a lack of thought, who wants that?

That's where this internal inclination brings it together: Moving on It.

Let's break this up into two sections: "Moving" + "on It." First, Moving. By starting with Moving we are putting action above perfection and accuracy. The goal is to move. The "on It" is the thought that goes into the project. How do you know the "It" if you don't do a little bit of planning? Either end of the spectrum is unhelpful, whether it's accuracy or speed.

We want medium thought and accuracy as well as medium- to high-action and speed.

For you, it might be that "Moving" is 70 percent and "on It" is 30 percent. Throughout the coming chapters, we'll be bringing together ways to optimize your brain and action to do this. But first, we need to know where you are.

MOVE ON IT ASSESSMENT

There have been many moments in your life when you have Moved on It. It doesn't always work out, but you sure get some good information. I remember one time when I Moved on It too quickly and the assistant attorney general of Michigan got involved.

Earlier in my career, I noticed that counselors in Michigan that needed supervision in rural areas had very few options. Newly licensed counselors must be under supervision for two years to get a hundred face-to-face hours. In Michigan, those hours must be face-to-face; phone or video supervision doesn't count. I thought, "What if I hosted a conference for newly licensed counselors and they got fifty hours of supervision once a year?"

Typically, counselors pay around $100 per hour of supervision, so fifty hours would often cost $5,000 per year. That's in addition to student loan debt! So, I projected that I could host a conference for $1,000 per attendee, get ten or fifteen people, and bank $10,000 to $15,000. I gave it 30 percent thought and then took action.

I put a page up on my website, emailed counselors in other cities, and promoted the heck out of it. Then I got the call. A local counselor said to me, "Your name came up during the State of Michigan's ethics board meeting today."

My stomach dropped. Was it a past client? What did I do? I couldn't think of anything that came close to any ethical concern. Then he said, "The assistant attorney general said, 'Some guy up in your area is hosting a supervision conference; that's not how the law works.'"

If I refunded the money and canceled the conference, they wouldn't take any action. Of course I did.

Many times, Moving on It fails or, even worse, gets the assistant attorney general's attention. But, as we have seen, entrepreneurs are successful when they can stand in the face of uncertainty that would produce anxiety and paralysis in most other people.

If we all have times that we Move on It before we are ready, why do we tend to play it so safe over time? The reasons fall into three major categories:

1. Thinking feels safer than action, because we can always change our mind, but once an action is out in the world it is less in our control.
2. We are trained to overthink. Education reinforces this and the perfectionism mindset is a leftover fingerprint of the Industrialist's mechanical view of the world.
3. Moving on It can be dangerous.

Let's look at a typical entrepreneur. When they first get going, they try a bunch of new ways to do business. Maybe they are curious and learning quickly. They have strong curiosity and an Outsider Approach. They throw spaghetti at the wall to see what sticks.

They market in ten different ways and have no connection to whether it works or doesn't work. Then their brand and audience starts to grow. They get a following, more customers, and the business does well.

Now there is more on the line. If subpar content is released, more people will be disappointed. Worse, what if an ad has a spelling error or a photo that is culturally insensitive. Action gives way to overthinking. A system, one might say a machine, starts to grow. It's less agile. It can't adapt to new challenges quickly. Instead of Moving on It, the new way of thinking is: "Let's think about it."

The Move on It perspective starts to die when we think accuracy is safer than speed.

We fear speed because inaccuracy and errors turn people away.

We lose sight of small, quick wins rather than larger, spaced-out wins.

We get wrapped up in overthinking and the uncertainty makes us, like everyone else, anxious and actionless.

What would happen if you kept Moving on It? How would business be different? What risks could lead to bigger unforeseen opportunities?

The most successful clients I see are those that maintain their ability to Move on It. They understand that accuracy is needed, but speed of implementation is the main goal.

You've already determined your level of curiosity and Outsider Approach in the previous assessments. Now we're going to do the same for your level of Move on It. How much is naturally occurring and what has been developed or needs to be developed?

Move on It Assessment

Discovery goals of this self-assessment:

1. Do you naturally Move on It?
2. Is Moving on It a habit?
3. Does Moving on It create openings that inform decisions and actions in your life?

These are forced-answer questions, meaning there is no "maybe." We want to get to the heart of Move on It practices in your life. Note your "yes" answers below.

Do you naturally Move on It?

1. I have an easy time letting a project go live or launch even if it isn't completed.
2. Speed is more important than accuracy most of the time.
3. I easily work through perfection.
4. I'm impulsive more than others around me.
5. I'd rather work quickly and go back and fix what's wrong.
6. It takes a lot for me to feel anxious or worried about something.
7. I am a sensation-seeker.
8. I enjoy the process of updating and changing things to make them work better.
9. Friends say I act before I think.
10. I easily try things even if I might fail at them.

7+ Naturally Move on It
4–6 Growing Move on It
0–3 Needs some development, but don't give up, you can develop it!

Is Moving on It thinking a habit?

1. I schedule time to take action.
2. I make action lists.
3. I easily break down larger tasks into steps.
4. I challenge my perfectionistic thinking through reading, podcasts, or therapy.
5. I visualize and plan out how I will do things before I do them, such as in a grocery store.
6. I analyze new ways of organizing and structuring tasks or organization.
7. Even when I am stressed, I am making a plan.
8. I think through plans and strategies better than my peers.

7+ Moving on It practices are habits.
4–6 Moving on It practices are forming.
0–3 You need to work toward making Moving on It practices habits.

Does Moving on It inform decisions and actions in your life?

1. I can take action without all of the information.
2. I can fake my way through almost anything.
3. If I am too prepared, it gets in the way of my success.
4. I've tried something new and failed at it in the last month.
5. I take action quickly when I have an idea like texting someone, making a call, or following up.
6. I sometimes work so fast I make unnecessary mistakes, such as spelling on social media or emailing the wrong person.
7. I'm ready to relax when my workweek is complete.

6+ Moving On It informs your actions.
3–5 You are beginning to inform your actions with Moving on It.
0–2 You need some work here, but we'll get there.

There are three variables:

1. An uppercase M means you are naturally using a Moving on It approach. Lowercase indicates that your Move on It approach is developing.
2. A + sign means that you have strong information-consuming habits supporting your Move on It approach. A – sign means your habits need development.
3. A + sign means that you take strong actions to support a Move on It approach. A – sign means your actions need development.

Types of People | Moving on It Approach

Here are the options:

Natural Mover or Growing Mover
With habits or without habits
With action or without action

Once you have determined your type, we'll learn a bit more about your tendencies, challenges, and next steps.

(M++)	Natural Mover, with habits and with actions. **The Triathlete** is a natural Mover who makes time and takes action for new ways to approach the world. Speed of implementation is the name of the game, but this person also has habits and actions to support success and go the long distance.
(M–+)	Natural Mover, without habits and with actions. **The Sprinter** is naturally a Mover and regularly takes action without first developing plans. This can be dangerous since it brings the benefits of impulsivity without the planning and accuracy of perfectionism.
(M+–)	Natural Mover, with habits and without actions. **The Racehorse** has a natural tendency toward being a Mover and thinks through

	plans. But, they aren't taking strong action to utilize their natural inclinations. They are like a racehorse just waiting for the gate to open, but they don't realize they have the key to the gate.
(M—)	Natural Mover, without habits and without actions. **The Restless** feels like a Mover, but are not forming habits or taking action to support this tendency. They may feel agitated or like a caged animal because they are bursting with ideas with no outlet. This is most common in a typical work or job setting.
(m++)	Developing Mover, with habits and with actions. **The Underdog** may not have led life as a Mover, but like other underdogs, they are put in the world to stand up to natural inclinations like overthinking and stalling.
(m—+)	Developing Mover, without habits and with actions. **The Aspirer** is coming into their own by becoming more of a Mover and is taking action. But, without more habits to develop a plan, they may be like a dog thinking, "Squirrel!" and be less attentive and focused than they should be. This is common of newer Movers, who want to do something, but have yet to develop habits to support the action.
(m+—)	Developing Mover, with habits and without actions. **The Mapmaker** is working hard to become a Mover. They may have realized it's not a natural inclination and they are developing habits to plan. They think, read, and plan, but may be paralyzed by perfectionism. This type is most prone to inaction and focuses on accuracy over speed.
(m—)	Developing Mover, without habits and without actions. **The Employee** is the most common type. They have been trained to think that moving and shaking isn't for them. They overthink, and within their world that may have worked, but this often leads to a job that is below one's abilities. This person should take small steps to improve their way of Moving on It.

You're Not Off the Hook, Yet

Being a Mover has tremendous benefits. You can quickly think, evaluate, and take action on what you see as the stronger path, but it often comes with consequences. A traditional job (or at least a traditional role) may not be for you. You may find that, more times than not, you're disappointed with the world. Or, even worse, you will be harshly judged for innovation, risk, and trying new approaches. Movers often fail, and to the typical Industrialist mindset, that is not okay. For them, the goal is a machine that keeps working until it can be replaced. That is not you.

For most people with an entrepreneurial bent, the context of their inclinations are going to magnify or minimize the appearance and value given to them. If you know you are a Mover and want to try new things without fear of failure, it is important to find or create a job or business where that is valued.

Next, let's look at how to continue to grow as a Mover.

MOVERS AND THE MINDSETS THEY LEAVE BEHIND

Movers are people who know both are necessary but who prioritize acting over thinking. They are unlike those who focus on accuracy and are paralyzed by perfectionism. They don't allow impostor syndrome to creep in. And they are different from those who solely focus on speed, disregard planning, and lead with impulsivity.

Instead, Movers are people who put in enough thought and planning to create a general direction, but ensure that action is the main goal. That's why they're called Movers! The typical business owner frequently conflates self-worth with successfully completing tasks. So each task or project takes on personal meaning. "If the project fails, I have failed," becomes a way of thinking.

This way of thinking may come from imagining that our every move is scrutinized, or that we can't recover from a failure. One helpful psychological technique from Cognitive Behavioral Therapy (CBT) helps clients to see how our thoughts are part of the natural consequences of our actions and to discover how we can modify those thoughts. Researchers have discovered numerous ways we have unhelpful thinking. They call these "thought distortions."

A few distortions that are especially relevant to our conversation are polarized thinking, disqualifying the positive, and magnification.

Polarized thinking is sometimes called "all-or-nothing" thinking. *Either I pass this test or I can never be a business leader.* It stops us from innovating, because we think that everything is riding on this moment. But, in reality, there are very few times this is actually true.

Just today, as I prepared to write this, my eight-year-old daughter returned from an overnight stay with her grandparents. She left her favorite stick at their house. She had mentally prepared for her day; she was going to decorate the stick to make it look like it had flowers. But, to her way of thinking, because she didn't have her favorite stick, there was no way she could be happy. This can also be called "black and white thinking" or "tunnel vision." The focus is the same: if X doesn't happen, Y cannot happen, but the reality is, there are many options between X and Y.

My daughter saw her favorite stick as her only road. Later in the day, after some mindfulness exercises, she was playing with other toys. We talked and I asked, "Did you find other things to make you happy?"

"I did. I'm having fun now."

"What do you think you did that helped you realize that?"

"I opened the windows to get fresh air, looked at my glitter jar, and it calmed me down. Also, I was happy doing something else."

Disqualifying the positive is our next cognitive distortion. We disqualify the positive when we mute the good things that happen and magnify the bad. This is often true when someone starts an eating or exercise program. "You look great!" someone might say, but you reply, "Yeah, but I have a long way to go before I'm ready for that swimsuit." You're disqualifying the positive steps forward and discounting all it took to make the progress already won!

Disqualifying the positive manifests itself in a variety of ways. We disqualify the positive when we attribute positive results to luck rather than our own actions. We say or think: "I just got lucky." The only reason I got that raise/promotion/client/spouse was because I'm lucky. That person disqualifies all the actions that prepared for that success. In a sense, it points back to the fear of failure, being paralyzed by perfectionism, and the impostor syndrome. If you feel like an impostor, wouldn't it tend to reason that you'd also disqualify your successes?

This also emerges when we change the goal over time. Maybe one year you'd be over the moon if a video received one thousand views, but as you grow, now you want ten thousand or fifty thousand views. As our success grows, so do our expectations. But having perspective on that growth helps to stop disqualifying the positive.

Our last cognitive distortion is magnification. Magnification exaggerates the impact of real or imagined results. It's similar to polarized thinking but with some nuances. For example, I may imagine that if I take a risk on a new social media campaign, I'll be criticized and lose clients if it doesn't go exactly as planned.

Other examples of magnification include:

- If I don't get this client, we'll probably go under.
- I have to see 5 percent quarterly growth or the business won't make it.
- If my kid doesn't get into that preschool, they'll never have a shot in life. In fact, that preschool is a feeder to that high school and that Ivy League university. We don't want a kid at a regular state school; those people are never successful!

When we look more closely at what hinders us from Moving on something and identify our cognitive distortions, we're on the path to removing those blocks that are a part of our inner world.

THREE QUESTIONS TO LAUNCH™ ANYTHING

There's a term in the business world popularized within the lean startup community by Eric Ries: MVP, or Minimum Viable Product. The basic idea is, "With an MVP, we build just enough product to learn in-market whether our assumptions about how customers will respond to our venture are correct. Through this learning, we can make adjustments to improve our idea or decide to pivot to a different idea."[8]

An MVP is a way to systematize speed over accuracy. While discussing the Curiosity Internal Inclination, I talked about the Three Questions to Launch™ formula. As a quick refresher:

1. Describe the pain. How would you describe your struggle/launch of this product or service?
2. Describe the magical product. If you have something that helped you overcome the struggle/pain, what would it be?
3. How much would you pay for what you just described?

Let's examine another case study. My Next Level Practice community comprises counselors, coaches, therapists, and thought leaders. Several years ago, I was brainstorming with my team about what was needed to better support practitioners. At the time, we noticed a gap in pricing and support. The gap was between two products, the One Year Practice Plan and the Start a Group Practice Mastermind.[9] The One Year Practice Plan costs a onetime $17 fee. Our clients then receive a weekly email for a year walking them through starting a private practice. In it, the emails cover filing legal paperwork, starting a website, getting insurance, marketing, and how to stand out in competitive markets. It's a lot of support for $17.

For the more advanced product, the Start a Group Practice Mastermind, led by one of my consultants, your practice had to be thriving and established enough to want to add additional clinicians. The cost at the time was around $400 per month for six months.

That's a big jump! $17 to more than $2,000.

What about people starting a practice that want additional support, but don't want a Mastermind or consulting?

We started brainstorming about a membership community. A membership community is based on a monthly or annually recurring fee. In my mind, the jump from $17 would be $20 to $30 per month. So I emailed my list of counselors who were starting a private practice.

I made just under twenty phone calls lasting fifteen to twenty minutes. Before the call, I wrote an email:

"I'm planning to launch a new product to help counselors, coaches, and therapists start a private practice, but I want to get it right. Can I pick your brain for 15–20 minutes? This is not a sales call, I literally just want to hear what you think. Here's a link to schedule a time."

During those calls, I asked:

1. What's it been like to start a private practice?
2. If you could create a product that would make that easier, like an e-course or membership community, what would that look like?
3. How much would you pay per month for that?

The answers to my three questions completely changed my plan. For the first question, I got some great copy for our website and future sales pages. Interviewees said things like:

- It's so confusing.
- Starting a business is stressful; I don't even know if it's worth it.
- It seems like everyone I talk to is so discouraging.
- Why didn't they teach this in grad school?
- I just need a step-by-step plan.

Most of those comments were expected. In the answers to question two, it emerged that potential members wanted three things: access to information, community, and tools of the trade.

Access to information: People are succeeding in private practice all over the country and world—what are the basic steps toward that success? Potential members wanted access to experts, e-courses, webinars, and Q&A. In other words, they wanted to know what's working.

Community: Potential members wanted a community beyond a typical Facebook group. They wanted small groups, accountability partners, and facilitated group discussions.

Tools of the Trade: Potential members wanted necessary paperwork, a logo, images for a blog, and design help for their practice.

At the time, I remember thinking, "Wow, this project is way bigger than I expected. I can't do that for $20 per month!"

Then the final question: "How much would you pay for this?" A few people said they wouldn't pay more than $20 per month. Others said they'd pay $200 per month or more. But the bell curve sat between $50 and $100 per month. I could do it for that price!

Next, I emailed a summary of the discussions to build excitement for the project. I wanted others who were not on the calls to say, "Yes, that's what I want too!" Within that email, I provided a link for first access to the membership community. I said I'd be exploring and building systems, and those on the first access list would get the updates.

About six weeks later, I announced when we'd be opening the doors to the first cohort. We discussed that it would be at a discounted monthly price. They would lock in that price forever. Also, we'd probably screw up a bunch of things.

We launched at $55 per month and limited the first cohort to fifty people. We intentionally kept the first cohort small, so that we could really understand the needs of our first purchasers, which later allowed us to scale much quicker. We sold out on the first day. Then we spent the coming months switching webinar platforms, building courses for this group, and promoting the full launch at $77 per month.

The Three Questions to Launch™ Process

1. Set up twenty calls with your ideal client and use the Three Questions to Launch™ process.
2. Report your findings to your email list of potential clients and offer an early bird/first access list to join.
3. Launch to the initial interest list at a discount, acknowledging that the rollout will probably not be perfect.
4. Refine processes and systems with the first group.
5. Launch to the public at a higher rate with testimonials, case studies, and webinars to publicize member success.
6. Repeat steps 4 and 5.

Here's why this works. If my most connected customers on my email list won't even finish a twenty-minute call with me, that shows me I need to build engagement before I launch a product. If I summarize the calls and those who were on the call and are most invested don't opt-in to an early bird/first access list, I need to craft different messaging. If once they are on that list and I launch and no one buys, I need to reconsider the offer and price. If a small group joins and several members cancel after a month, I need to improve the quality of the product.

At every stage, I'm saving myself time by giving myself the opportunity to kill the project. I'm testing to make sure it works before I put time and money into the new product. Next Level Practice is now the largest paid counselor, coach, and therapist membership community. Members have access to more than thirty e-courses to help with marketing, business, growth, and leveling up. Members get access to live, expert interviews monthly, attend small groups, and have substantially increased access to mental health services.

This project will have brought in over $2 million within three years of launching it with only about ten to twenty total staff hours per month.

Part Two

LAUNCHING INTO

SLOWING DOWN

In part two, we start to move toward realizing the full potential of the *Thursday Is the New Friday* approach. We'll be evaluating the research and application of slowing down and how to slow down. During these discussions, you may experience symptoms that show you are still in the grip of the Industrialist mentality:

- It can't be this way.
- How will this work?
- Can I actually become more successful by working less?

We're going to look at where these feelings come from, as we look at our hustle narratives. Then we will look at how we actually kill it in business (and life) without sacrificing all we have done in the past.

6

SLOW DOWN

The quieter you become, the more you can hear.

—Ram Dass

We only missed a few days of walking during the early 2020 COVID-19 lockdown. Our daily walk with our girls helped us reset and reconnect. Our five-year-old would ride her balance bicycle, a bike without training wheels or pedals. She could clearly balance, but was afraid of trying to ride on two wheels. Then, one day, I dropped the seat on the pedal bike. I said, "Just glide like on the other one and rest your feet on the pedals if you get tired." She pushed to glide and started pedaling in a circle. She never had the moment of me running behind and letting go. She just did it. Now she can almost keep up with her older sister.

During one of our walks, we stopped to talk to our neighbor and fellow entrepreneur, Dan Reynolds. I don't remember the context of exactly what we were discussing. It could have been philosophy, kids, or business; our overlapping topics are vast. I think I asked if he was coming to one of my online improv shows. He said something that had been reiterated several times by others during the pandemic lockdown: "All we have is time."

The topic of the conversation eludes me, but those words really rang true in that moment.

All we have is time.

We always had the time; we had just misappropriated it. I think about school and my kids. They would wake up at 6:45 a.m. We'd have to be leaving by 7:40 to get to school by 8:00. If traffic was light, I'd get back home or to the gym by 8:30. Then, for the 3:00 p.m. pickup, we'd have to leave by 2:40 and typically returned by 3:30. They'd then have homework and maybe be done with that by 4:15. We spent more than three hours getting ready, driving, picking up, and completing homework.

But our homeschooling was an hour of reading and writing, an hour of math, and then several hours of following their curiosity. My work schedule continued to be three days a week during the lockdown. So, unlike many other people, we had plenty of time to find a rhythm with work, schooling, and family time.

But much of this was by design—in fact, years of design. We had been undoing social norms and expectations to ask how we could optimize all our brains and lives within the family.

The conventional view, which has the fingerprints of the Industrialists all over it, looks like this:

Work forty or more hours per week Monday through Friday. In addition to the actual work time, spend two hours before work commuting, getting ready, packing lunches, and getting the kids off to school. After work, commute home, get the kids' homework going, make a healthy meal (or if you're stressed get takeout), spend an hour doing something you enjoy if you are lucky, and then get the kids ready for bed. If you have the energy, watch Netflix and drink some wine and call it a "date night" with someone you love. Repeat until Friday. Then, on the weekend, straighten the house, attend a soccer game, maybe go out with friends. On Sunday, start to feel anxiety and stress about the coming week. Get some groceries and plan the coming week.

You'll feel happy from 4:00 p.m. on Friday while anticipating the weekend until about dinnertime on Saturday when you begin to brace yourself for the coming workweek. That's what you're allowed, twenty-six hours of time that you feel free.

Recently on Sam Harris's *Making Sense* podcast, he was interviewing Daniel Markovits, author of *The Meritocracy Trap*. Markovits noted that the super-rich are now working significantly more hours than the previous generation of wealthy people. Hours worked is the new status symbol of the rich.[1]

If all we have is time, why do many of us feel so busy?

WE GOT THE TORTOISE AND THE HARE ALL WRONG

I remember the story of the race between the tortoise and the hare. The tortoise starts out really slow. The hare almost gets to the finish line but becomes arrogant in his lead and decides to sit next to a tree. The hare falls asleep and the slow and steady tortoise passes the hare to win the race.

The point of this story is to teach perseverance and to see value in other ways of being when the addiction to speed compels us to rush through everything. Our need to do everything quicker, to seamlessly multitask, and to always be "on" to meet growing demand can feel like accomplishment. The approach that I teach certainly values hard work and forward movement, but all while balancing the need to slow down to recover, regroup, and allow for insight about what you should most be engaged in.

I'm rooting for the hare. The hare runs his fastest, but he knows when to stop and relax a bit. He just needed to set a timer to wake up. It's the tortoise that represents the nonstop movement narrative. Be slow and steady, instead of inspired and tired.

I'll take being inspired and tired any day.

It's the difference between playing music in the background all day and intentionally choosing to listen to music. When it's just playing, you tune it out, go in and out of your thoughts, and it's just a layer of your environment. Whereas, when you intentionally listen to dance music with your kids or friends, you jam to every song. Each song is the focus.

The tortoise represents nonstop movement; the hare is inspired and tired.

As professionals set up their practices or as anyone makes the move from a more structured environment in their job to owning their own business, it is easy to stay too busy to notice little things or have any deep thoughts about what you are doing. In other words, you may be living what you thought was your dream, but are you creating the time to take it all in?

Before we can learn to slow down, we need to recognize and deconstruct the barriers blocking our way. These blocks are nonstop access, generational leveling, and unnatural neurosyncing.

We can have almost anything instantly, and as a result, we've created a world where we are available nonstop. Businesses can create profits all day and night, and our natural brain pacing is disrupted.

Consider this question: When was the last time that you were not accessible?

As a mental health counselor, my phone is on silent during sessions. Imagine how disruptive it would be if I were texting my wife while someone was crying about a divorce! But for most people, we are available to our boss, clients, or family at almost any time. The expectation of constant availability makes us feel anxious when we see missed calls, texts, or that little red dot that notifies us of social media updates. That feeling of "what am I missing" and "who is waiting for me" pulls us from our focus and drains our energy. With nonstop availability, we've created an undercurrent of tension. We're not wired for this.

Numerous studies have examined "vigilance decrement," which describes the phenomenon of decreasing attention over time, especially to a task or goal. When we are focused on a goal or task for too long, our attention wanes.

A 2011 study from the University of Illinois found that breaks of as little as a minute can stop vigilance decrement. Students were given a four-digit number to remember and asked to perform an extremely boring task. They sat before a computer screen on which four-digit numbers were flashed. When their number came up, they were to push a button. They did this for fifty minutes. Over time, their vigilance (how well they paid attention) deteriorated (decrement). A second group performed the same task, but were given a one-minute break at the half and two-thirds mark in the study. There was no vigilance decrement. In other words, two minutes of break time helped them do more in the same amount of time.[2]

Our brains are wired less like the tortoise's and more like the hare's. In general, we're better at sprinting toward goals and then resting. Nonstop movement (even if it is slow like the tortoise) is not natural. As a society, we're addicted to nonstop movement forward. We feel like we have to do something, rather than rest. The hare actually got it right.

This attachment to "doing something" is true in how we relax too. Often, it feels like Netflix, social media, and watching the news is relaxing, but slowing down and stepping away from stimulation is usually what our brains need most.

When others have nonstop access to us, we temporarily feel good about our productivity and exploit ourselves while we miss the opportunities to find more happiness in our lives. If you find yourself complaining about your boss, your job, your carpool, and even not having enough time for lunch, it is time to step back and slow down.

In addition to nonstop access, we have generational leveling. Generation leveling is the phenomena of parents wanting better for their children than they had for themselves. This is true with generations of a business as well. We want improvements in profits quarter over quarter.

Generational leveling is also an expectation of societies as a whole. During the summer of 2020, following the first pandemic lockdown of COVID-19, most of the best predictions were that we would see a 10 percent drop in overall GDP once the pandemic was contained. Our economy would shrink by 10 percent.

If we look at average inflation rates of 3.22 percent, that means our spending will be similar to what it was three years ago.[3] Some *Economist* readers may disagree with me. They will say, "The economy must keep growing." But how is this different than asking every generation of kids to be smarter and more successful than their mothers and fathers?

There is nothing inherently wrong with wanting our children to avoid pain and enjoy life. But the idea that this is a mutually exclusive pairing with wealth and happiness is a fallacy.[4]

Humans have a unique capacity to reflect on the past, identify causes or perceived causes of pain, and then plan for different outcomes. For example, my father was raised by hardworking parents who worked all day on their farm and in their general store. Their mindset was to provide opportunities for their five kids, so that entailed a significant amount of work.

My parents were loving and gave lots of hugs, which had not been the norm for much of the World War II generation. My parents also took cues from behavioral science and, again, unlike many in earlier generations, were more present in their children's lives. We had clear boundaries, positive and negative consequences, and generally knew if we would get in trouble for something.

As a parent, I hold on to some of those ideas and let go of others. This is natural. It becomes a blockage when parents begin to revert to those cognitive distortions we covered earlier, like magnification: "If my preschooler doesn't get into this preschool, she'll never be successful!"

That same addiction is true in business. Families don't stop to ask, "Why are we pushing our kids to do all of this?" In the same way, as business owners and leaders, we often push goals, improvement, and changes, without outlining how that increases income, innovation, influence, and impact. But before we go there, we need to understand unnatural neurosyncing.

UNNATURAL NEUROSYNCING

Throughout college, I worked at a runaway shelter. I frequently worked overnights, either 11:00 p.m. to 7:00 a.m. or 12:30 a.m. to 8:30 a.m. As a twenty-something I enjoyed the overnights. I'd clean for a couple hours, make meals for the next day, and then get paid to do homework, watch TV, or read. There was always another staffer there too. Some were more entertaining than others. From 2:30 to 4:30 a.m. was the hardest stretch.

For a while, I heavily drank coffee to stay alert. But over time, I noticed that the mixture of staying awake all night with caffeine made me jittery and gave me acid reflux. I also found that getting sleep after a shift was more difficult when the caffeine was charging through my body. So I started drinking more water and smoothies during overnight shifts.

I also discovered that, after a shift, it was better to do a four-hour sleep cycle. If I was off work at seven, I'd be asleep by 7:30 a.m. and then wake at eleven thirty. Then I'd drink coffee. I was able to jump back on my regular sleep cycle that night.

Either way, this way of living was not in line with my body's natural rhythm.

I was considering why we have the schedule we have. Even back then, I was challenging the Industrialist fingerprint. "Why do I operate on a twenty-four-hour cycle?" Of course it's the Earth's rotation. But there are numerous animals with different sleep patterns. Some are nocturnal, others live at the bottom of the ocean and have schedules that aren't based on light, while others can sense fields we can't. Sea turtles can sense magnetic fields, which can help them to navigate the ocean. Sharks can sense electrical currents, which help them track their prey. Some snakes can thermally image their prey.

So why do I have to sleep just because it is dark? It's just because I was trained that way. My thought was, "What if I could train myself to be on a forty-eight-hour sleep cycle, in which I was awake for forty hours and then slept eight hours?"

Think of all I could get done! Graduate school homework, paintings, I could write more songs, I could read more, or specialize in areas while others were sleeping. I'd be superhuman!

I stayed up all night. I didn't play guitar, because all my roommates were sleeping. I read for a while, paced my room, worked on homework, and started writing the work of fiction I had been dreaming about.

I made it. The next day was terrible. I wanted to sleep, so I drank coffee. I got through it and slept great the next night. I woke up refreshed (because I was twenty-three; if I tried this now, I'd be crabby and have a headache for a week). It was time for the second all-nighter. I couldn't do it. I was so bored with no one around and I felt terrible.

For me, optimizing my time and hustle has been a fascination and struggle since early adulthood. These previous chapters are as much for me as a reminder as it is to share with you. That's how it used to be.

Now, as I leave my slow down weekends, I am ready to get to work when I start work on Tuesday (if I haven't said it yet, I've also made Tuesday the new Monday). The slowing down sparks massive creativity, focus, and attention. But that's not how most people do it. Most people will kill it until they are burned out, then they'll slow down. But we're flipping that here. Instead, we're slowing down and, in that process, making the sprint of work most effective.

Unnatural neurosyncing is a term I coined to describe being out of touch with our natural rhythms with light, seasons, needs of the body, and flow.

It all started with Thomas Edison. It wasn't just his invention of the light bulb but also his point of view. Olga Khazan's 2014 article in the *Atlantic* calls it the "cult of sleep deprivation."[5] Penn State labor history professor Alan Derickson calls it "manly wakefulness." In Derickson's book *Dangerously Sleepy* he says, "Edison spent considerable amounts of his own and his staff's energy on publicizing the idea that success depended in no small part in staying awake to stay ahead of the technological and economic competition."

The Industrialists started treating us like machines. Here are just a few examples of what that now looks like:

- The CDC found that 35.2 percent of adults chronically underslept (average below seven hours of sleep per night).[6] This is highest in people forty-five to fifty-four (39 percent).
- Worry, anxiety, and restlessness make it harder to fall asleep and it is costing businesses billions.[7]
- Yale reported that people are spending significantly less time in nature.[8]
- The General Social Survey, the longest-running public opinion research project, asked Americans to choose whether they are "very happy," "pretty happy," or "not too happy." The survey found that the statement "I am not too happy" jumped 50 percent in thirty years.[9]
- The average American has more than five hours of free time per day and tends to spend that time on screens.[10]
- A recent American Psychological Association and *Journal of Abnormal Psychology* study found that "mental health issues increased significantly in young adults over the last decade: Shift may be due in part to rise of digital media, study suggests."[11]

I could list pages of stats on how we have unnatural neurosyncing. Our brains are responding to the environment in a way we didn't expect. But that's not how some of the greatest minds think and live. Winston Churchill famously had a nonnegotiable afternoon nap.[12] Steve Jobs was a transition between the Industrialists and the next evolutionary phase. He was obsessive and overworked, but integrated numerous aspects beyond the Industrialists. One key change was that he frequently conducted walking meetings, which reduced blood pressure and intense eye contact and made for a better meeting.[13] In Timothy Ferriss's book *Tools of Titans*, he interviewed more than two hundred business executives and found that daily meditation was one of their most common habits.

Jane Goodall, the famous English primatologist and anthropologist, attributes her love of observation to daydreaming as a child.[14] Einstein attributed his late reading and daydreaming to his childlike wonder with the universe.[15] If some of the most influential people of the twentieth and twenty-first centuries made time to slow down, why do we keep going back to the Industrialist's ways of thinking? Maybe if we understood how our brains actually work, we'd see how this secret has been in front of us all along.

What may be most notable is your reaction, or more likely lack of reaction, to these stats. You may have thought, "I know this," or "I hear this all the time." It has become normal to undersleep, have less time in nature, spend time on screens, have more mental health issues, and be unhappy.

It's a problem that this is the norm!

Earlier, we showed that although the eight-hour day and forty-hour workweek feels normal, human beings made it up less than a hundred years ago. What we are now doing with our brains may also feel normal, but it's not helpful for utilizing our brains to create happiness and satisfaction, or to gets things done.

The way we are living stops creativity and increases crankiness. The way we live makes us feel stressed when we could be living in success. We're overwhelmed when we could be optimized.

So let's look at what the brain actually needs to be optimized.

ANCHORING TO SHIFT INTO SLOW DOWN MODE

The big yellow school bus waits outside the airport. Participants from across the United States and Canada meet for the first time while waiting for their luggage. The Traverse City airport is small. It has two gates, one for United and American and one for Delta. Two gates, not wings or terminals. Gates. I almost always see someone I know when I'm flying.

We load the luggage onto the school bus. One year, part of the group landed at noon and was stuck on the tarmac until 4:00 p.m. due to lightning. Another year, a lady flew the red-eye from California, was delayed in Chicago, then her luggage wasn't there. Flying is stressful, and that was before coronavirus!

That's why I make a clear distinction between travel and when Slow Down School starts. Chatter fills the bus. Introductions to one another happen naturally. I hear, "Oh, I've followed your social media forever, so nice to finally meet you."

"You're way taller than I imagined!"

"I can't believe we're here in person!"

"This area is so pretty."

Many of these participants have been in Mastermind groups that have met together online until now. Some have consulted with me or one of my consultants. For many, it feels like a reunion with people they have never met. Some are new, wide-eyed, and unsure what they have signed up for, but quickly get absorbed into the crowd. The great thing about therapists, counselors, and coaches is they want to connect.

"You've been through a lot to get here," I say, standing at the front of the bus like a kindergarten teacher. "Your mind is racing. You have your luggage . . . well, most of you do. You are here. I want you to be here now, in this moment. At most conferences, you hurry to get there, hurry to get to the opening keynote, then rush to breakout sessions. You leave more overwhelmed and with a bigger to-do list than before. That is not what is going to happen here. You are going to leave refreshed and with focus. We'll spend two days really slowing down and then for three days we'll kill it. But first, let's be here with a three-minute meditation. Just breathe and be here. You have nothing more to do."

My Bose speaker rings three bells and the sound of birds and wind quietly sweeps the bus. It quiets my mind too. This conference is beginning. This group will never come together in the same way. I, too, need to be present, aware, and attentive.

Why do I start this way?

A few things are happening in that opening statement:

1. Anchoring
2. Task shifting
3. Forecasting

Anchoring is the act of planting a clear statement in someone's mind. "You are here. You have nothing more to do." How do most people feel after a day or overnight of travel? They feel overwhelmed, relieved, a sense of tension, and maybe anticipation.

The brain is bouncing around asking, "Am I safe?" A new environment, airport, and group of people are all potential triggers for anxiety, worry, and hypervigilance. By saying, "You are here. You have nothing more to do," I'm also saying, "You are safe."

It's similar to a parent in a thunderstorm saying, "I'm here, it's okay to feel these feelings, but know that you are 100 percent safe." Kids want to know that their parent is strong enough to take on the monsters of the world. When we are in new situations, we want the same. Having someone say, "I've got this, you are safe. You can just be present," allows the brain to be optimized during Slow Down School.

Next, humans have trouble shifting tasks. A widely cited University of California, Irvine study shows it takes approximately twenty-three minutes to regain focus after being interrupted.[16] Yet, some people shift faster than others. In that yellow school bus, I employ a number of sensory factors to quickly shift to the next task: being at a conference. We have a clear distinction between travel and starting the conference now (even though we'll be on a bus for about an hour). I shift the mood and experience and insist on the sensory experience of being mindful to underscore that things are different.

Even as I write this book, I do the same thing. I set twenty- to thirty-minute timers to take quick breaks. As we learned earlier, this prevents my vigilance from decreasing. I have a playlist of music without words that I only listen to when writing. I leave the music playing whenever I leave my office. If I go grab a tea or go to the restroom, the music still plays. It keeps the writing energy and mindset going. I change the lighting in my home office from the typical bright video and podcasting light to lower-light desk lamps. These all are triggers that teach my brain that it is specifically writing time. I even sit in a different spot. On the bus, I am deploying similar triggers.

Last, let's talk about forecasting. By framing the Slow Down School week, I am planting the outcome I know they need: to be refreshed and to leave with focus. For two days we are going to slow down and then we will kill it. I'm giving permission.

You can slow down without worry of whether this is a waste of time. At some points, you'll get so excited about the work, but I want you to genuinely slow down. Trust me, it's worth it. I'm helping them move their brains toward their most creative and focused potential.

We go for hikes, skip stones, sit on the beach, throw things in the water, try stand-up paddle boarding, and do yoga. We have campfires and look at the stars.

"I feel like a kid," is one of the most common statements in the first two days of Slow Down School.

That's the point: for us to open the default mode network, which can happen through exercise, being in nature, and allowing our brains to roam freely. Our default mode network is how our brains have been trained; it blocks us. But, at Slow Down School, we seek to turn off that automation using science, brain relaxing activities, and stepping back from daily life.

Someone I know recently bought a farmhouse. The acres behind his house were overgrown. Weeds, trees, and bushes were all blended together. He started trimming but didn't have a plan.

One day while cleaning the basement, he came across a map of the property. Beneath all that overgrowth were heirloom Michigan apples. Over time he found the trees and cut back the other shrubbery that was not allowing the apples to thrive.

Our brains are the same way. When we are young, each element of our brain represents potential. It's highly efficient. What was required of a brain a hundred years ago, or even when I was a kid, is completely different from what my kids need now.

I'm sure you've watched children use technology and considered that they appear to have adapted to its use as "naturally" as if it were an extension of their bodies. Our brains can shift and evolve because of the pruning that happens. Over time specific wires are reinforced. When I was doing therapy with parents, I would use a road analogy. This is particularly helpful when a parent is trying to improve their child's inappropriate behavior.

Imagine the way your child sees that world as being a strong highway, an I-75 or 101 going down the coast. But there's a new road you are developing in their brains. It's a trail now and soon it will be a two-track. Then it becomes a dirt road and maybe it'll get pavement soon. But, we need to let the old road break down, get potholes, and get overgrown.

There will be a moment when the new behavior or road isn't yet trustworthy and the old highway is falling apart. That's when you'll see the biggest behavioral outbursts. That's how you know it's working. They want to go back, but you can't let them. Just keep paving the new road.

Let's take a journey into your brain for a moment. Imagine we jumped on the magic school bus and could dive deep. This is what it looks like in everyday life. We're going to start in the oldest part of the brain and work outward.

So if we were to fly in and go to the center, we would see what is often called the "reptilian brain," with wiring similar to that of lizards and ancient creatures, which regulates body temperature and hormones. Fear, anxiety, sexual desires, and anger all emanate from the limbic system. The cortex, the newest part of the brain, most pronounced in primates and humans, allows us to empathize with others.

In a sense, our brains are fairly automated by the reptilian brain. The emotions of our limbic system help us to feel what's going on, and the cortex helps us choose what to do with those experiences. But what happens in much of our life is living in the limbic system. We are feeling and reacting without planning, identifying, and optimizing the cortex.

As we enter Slow Down School, I want to help participants to clean their brains and slow down before we do the tough work. We want to get back to the natural neurosyncing. So I looked to nature for some examples.

YOU CAN LEARN A LOT FROM AN APEX PREDATOR

Entrepreneurs, business owners, and, frankly, humans in general tend not to sleep as much as they need. According to a Gallup poll, Americans sleep an average of 6.8 hours, down by one hour since 1942. We know that during sleep our brains sort and file information. We optimize our brains for the next day. Hunger hormones like gherlin are released that can make us crave carbs or healthy foods. A lot is on the line when we talk about sleep!

The other night while I was falling asleep, I had an idea.

What do other top animals do for sleep? I was thinking about animals that have no known predators in their environment. Ones that are at the top of the food chain and don't have as much to worry about.

My theory was that if I looked at apex predators, animals with no known predator in their region, I could discover something about thriving and sleeping. So I started to look around at the lifestyle habits of golden eagles, cougars, lions, Eurasian lynx, great whites, and lions, to mention a few.

If these animals are able to be the top animals on their continent and still lounge around, why can't we? My theory was spot on.

Golden Eagles: The North America golden eagle sleeps most of the night (immediately after the sun goes down until the sun comes up). They average anywhere from 8.5 hours on June 21 to 15.2 hours on December 21, and they need to have a comfy bed they can trust. The eagle can teach us that you can be an awesome eagle and sleep fifteen hours. Life has busier times than others. We all need a nest we can trust to get a good night's sleep, so stop looking at your iPhone in bed.

Great White and Killer Whales: In the ocean, a great white is one of the most notorious animals. It has no known natural predators. What's unique about the great white is that it must keep moving to breathe. Scientists from Marine Dynamics think great whites only rest, and don't sleep, due to the makeup of their brain stem. Erasmo Research says that an unconscious shark can still swim and notice divers. Whereas killer whales or orcas do sleep five to eight hours.

Great whites and killer whales can teach us that sometimes a short rest can help us. Great whites are unbelievable and seem like they shouldn't be able to live without sleep, but evolutionary biology informs us that it's helped them be the top predator, so maybe pushing ourselves sometimes is worth it . . . if we can get our brain stem to change.

Crocodiles: The saltwater crocodile is the largest living reptile and hibernates in the winter. It sleeps with one eye open, according to Live Science. But it sleeps around seventeen hours per day!

Crocodiles can teach us that there are times in life when we need to sleep with one eye open if we're worried, but a croc is an apex predator so it shouldn't be worried. Even really old and big animals have weird sleep patterns so maybe we shouldn't be so hard on ourselves. You can be a top animal and sit around seventeen hours a day!

Lions: The African male lion sleeps eighteen to twenty hours per day (83 percent of the day). The female lioness sleeps fifteen to eighteen hours (75 percent of the day).[17] Lions can teach us that there are gender variations even with lions. Four hours of consistent productivity and focus makes you the "king of the jungle."

Komodo Dragon: Like the golden eagle, the Komodo dragon stays up all day and sleeps at night. It is so asleep it can be touched and never responds because it has no known predators. Unlike the crocodile that sleeps with one eye open, the Komodo dragon knows that it can fully relax. Komodo dragons can teach us that we need to get more deep sleep since we have no real predators. A day well worked can lead to very deep sleep, if you give yourself permission.

What I noticed from analyzing the habits of apex predators is that all of them, except the great white, have better sleep patterns than us! Collectively, they get so much more sleep and are able to completely relax.

As a business owner and entrepreneur, there is always more to do. Maybe it is humans' ability to plan into the future and design our decisions that derails healthy sleep habits. Nature has much to teach us about efficiency, rest, and sleeping.

HERE IS YOUR RX FOR SLOWING DOWN

So what happens to our brains when we slow down? At Slow Down School, a few things happen. Early on the first day there is a heightened sense of anxiety. "I could be working on so much!" is a common way people frame it. Participants look around at other high achievers and think, "What a great group. I need to make use of every moment."

After an internal battle, participants tend to start to enjoy the day. We spend almost the entire time outside, so they walk more than they ordinarily do. They sit on the beach. They enjoy a s'more around the campfire. By the end of the first day, participants are starting to enjoy the slow-down time.

The morning of day two is almost always the same. The faces of participants look as if they just had a facial. They are shiny, glowing, and alive. "Why don't I do this more?"

The fresh air, walking, healthy food, and time spent thinking usually has led to some breakthroughs and insights. Participants start to feel more in line with nature. They get more tired when the sun goes down. They naturally wake up earlier. They drink more water. They hit their ten thousand steps by lunchtime.

The worries of the business start to sink into the background, while moving toward the front is the question: "What do I want for my life?"

Frequent questions/thoughts are:

- Why do I keep doing things that make me unhappy?
- The business relies on me so much; what would it look like to step back more?
- Do I have to follow this schedule so much?
- This feels good; I want more of this.
- I'm not around people like this anywhere else; how can I spend more time with people like them?
- What if my life were different? What would that look like?

It's as if the default mode network was also a default mode life. A life that was handed over and not questioned: go to school, get a graduate degree, start a business, and be happy. But participants frequently find themselves dreaming about something more: more income, innovation, influence, and impact.

They feel like a kid who dreams of a future career. Anything is possible. We made this all up. Just like the seven-day week, the eight-hour day, or the forty-plus-hour workweek.

The voice of the Industrialist starts to die; their fingerprints start to fade. That's exactly what happened to Dr. Jeremy Sharp.

Most of Jeremy's conversations with his wife, Carrie, were about negotiating more time to work. Jeremy felt distracted and absent from his kids' lives. Yet there was tremendous demand to keep things moving at his business. As one of the leading testing psychologists in the country, he was in demand, saw the opportunity, and was finally doing the work he had spent his life training for.

After Jeremy completed his PhD at Colorado State University, he was ready to take his skills to the world. After years of education, he envisioned a private practice focused on testing. He launched and it exploded. He was working six long days a week. Jeremy is a self-described "do-it-yourself person." He had shown that when he puts his mind to something, he's usually successful. That's definitely what happened with his practice.

But it wasn't working in his life. While he was working hard in the practice, his wife, Carrie, was at home. She was with their two- and three-year-old children. They were both overwhelmed, burned out, and exhausted. There was professional excitement because the practice was so busy. In fact, it was so busy that he was turning people away. He saw tremendous potential to expand but did not know how to do it.

When I met Jeremy, he was growing in success. He didn't need to learn how to expand his business. Instead, he needed to see how eliminating him from the business would help him grow. It's a counterintuitive strategy that creeps up on new business owners.

Talented people frequently start businesses. It could be consulting, counseling, or some other service-based business. They're really good at their work, but they don't have basic business sense. But they grow. As in Jeremy's case, their businesses might explode.

I often hear, "I'm just amazed this is working!" For much of the world, a six-figure income is a dream. Only 3.1 percent of the world makes more money than a family of four with an income of $100,000.[18] Many people start to feel greedy if they want more.

So the Jeremys of the world are stuck. *I'm making way more money than I expected. The business has tons of opportunity. But I don't want to work more.*

That's usually when the break happens.

"I can't do this anymore," is what I often hear.

When Jeremy and I started working together, we began with organizing his goals into two avenues: expand and optimize the practice to free up time and build his podcast/consulting. It was clear that he needed to remove hats to open time up for more scalable and enjoyable work.

While Jeremy was at Slow Down School, we outlined a new schedule. It was a schedule that focused on his biggest skills and opportunities.

Jeremy says, "I called Carrie. I felt relieved and charged." He realized, "I don't have to do this the way I've been doing this. We can get to a better place in business, family, and marriage; there is a path out of this. I felt relief and direction. Carrie had excitement in her voice and we both were tearful."

For Jeremy, the outside perspective of consulting and stepping back brought a sense of clarity. "I have plenty of ideas and potential; the clarity helped me know what to do next. It also, in a bigger picture, was a turning point for me to become a visionary, to lead others, not just act as a solo person. I turned into a business owner. I took more risks. I had confidence in my decisionmaking with the practice—confidence to take a leap to try something different, which has carried over to other areas of life."

Those original leaps gave confidence to try his messaging in different formats on his podcast, go after bigger interviews, and charge significantly more for his knowledge and services. After Slow Down School, he continued to pull back his time and level up his podcast. Through the process of expanding beyond his own services, he's gone from two offices to ten offices.

Jeremy articulates his shift in this way: "I can do whatever I want to do, just plan it, run some numbers, and make it happen. I'm now working less, adding services, and continue to charge more for consulting services. In my personal life, I'm the healthiest I've been in a long time. I don't work on weekends. I haven't in a while. I'm more present, I pick up the kids three days a week at three, never miss a sporting event, and even more importantly, I don't feel bad about my schedule or choices."

Equally exciting is that his wife, Carrie, has opened her own counseling business. He says, "My own change helped me be more present with my wife's new business and to support her. She loves that I'm home more; it has brought us closer. My business will pass $1 million in gross revenue this year!"

INTENSIVE SLOW DOWN RETREATS

Bill Gates calls it "Think Week."[19] Some call it a retreat or reflection time. The name and exact modality is not important. The goal is to have time away to reflect on how business is going. Jeremy says it this way, "Without my twice-a-year retreat, I would just tread water."

Twice a year, Jeremy flies from Colorado over the Rocky Mountains to Los Angeles. But it doesn't begin with the flight. In the lead-up to the three-day retreat, Jeremy selects a vacation rental that has very clear specifications:

1. Everything is walkable, including meals.
2. There is an outdoor space to work; a pool is a bonus.
3. Places close by to walk or run.

Once Jeremy selects his rental, he plans each meal ahead of time. In fact, he only goes to three restaurants. The same coffee shop for breakfast, a lunch place, and dinner. He will examine the menu and pre-select what meals look good.

"It limits decision fatigue, so I don't screw around with what to eat," Jeremy said.

Jeremy is a psychologist who loves optimizing his time and energy. The idea of "decision fatigue" is based on the idea that we should use our best energy on what matters most. It is why Barack Obama, Steve Jobs, and Mark Zuckerberg famously wear a small selection of clothing.[20]

The opposite is when we check email first thing in the morning or read the news. Instead, spending time on the best items is one approach to staying hyper-focused.

Jeremy boards the plane and spends the two-hour flight working on a Thought Map. This process is something Jeremy had not formalized until our conversation. It's something he now does reflexively. I asked, "If you were to systematize this for someone, what would be the steps?"

Thought Map

Goal: To identify key areas of time, work, and thought during a retreat.

1. Brain-dump stress, ideas, directions, and time-sucks.
2. Divide items into his private practice work and his consulting work.

3. Examine where the focus will get the strongest ROI. In other words, what's the one thing that will move the needle forward.[21]
4. Create an order of importance for the tasks.

The first morning, Jeremy takes a big walk or run. Being outside helps him to prime his brain for the day ahead. He treats each day like a workday.

Retreat Schedule

During the morning block, Jeremy does the heavy lifting. During one retreat, he identified that he needed to free up more time for work on the podcast and consulting, but to do that, he needed to be able to rely on his staff more. For him to trust that delegating would work and mirror the culture he had created at the business, he had to impart clear instructions and training.

During the first block, he worked on building a training manual to delegate tasks. This in turn allowed him to free up more time for the scalable work. If Jeremy is missing needed puzzle pieces, he will spend time texting other consultants and set up times to talk on day two or three.

Jeremy then walks to lunch and orders a pre-selected meal.

In the afternoon, he does his afternoon block. During this time, he focuses on fun, creative, and enjoyable tasks. For example, researching and learning a new automation app, building out Zaps to automate tasks in Zapier, or brainstorming how to level up *The Testing Psychologist* podcast.

When asked why he wants to learn these tasks, he says, "If I don't know it first and try to outsource it, it doesn't usually go well. I'll do 80 to 90 percent and have an expert polish the end product."

In the evenings he usually watches a movie or goes to a movie. For Jeremy, movies transport him out of his world and refresh him.

When Jeremy reflects on outcomes of his twice-a-year retreat, he says that it gives him time to think and build internal clarity. One year, he was planning to launch a membership community for his podcast listeners. Instead, he realized that he needed to eliminate that idea.

For you, it may not be this same structure. But what are the core elements that you can build to personalize a retreat? Reduce decisionmaking fatigue. Plan ahead for an optimal environment. Formalize a Thought Map to have a clear plan. Be open to new ideas and eliminate tasks.

YOUR BRAIN NEEDS TO SLOW DOWN

Slowing down reflects acceptance of self. Most entrepreneurs have been living someone else's dream, building someone else's business, and living someone else's schedule.

The business benefits of slowing down are overwhelming. Research shows that mindfulness training and slowing down reduces stress at work.[22] People who spend more time outdoors have more fulfilling lives.[23] A UCLA study looked at how long-term meditation practitioners' brains look different than the average population.[24] The study looked at cortical gyrification, the folds in the cortex, the decisionmaking and thought area of the brain. The more folds in that area, the more overall cognitive function.

In fact, a University of Chicago study in 2019 evaluated a two-week mindfulness training program administered via smartphone.[25] This intervention decreased loneliness and increased socialization among stressed adults. In the next chapter, we will cover exactly how to slow down, but to prepare, I've identified three core principles to be mastered:

1. Stop, eliminate, reduce
2. Growth over reaction
3. 24/7 profits

Stop, Eliminate, Reduce: A central support of slowing down will be creating boundaries that allow us to have the most energy, creativity, and time to work on important tasks. First we identify what can be stopped. These are tasks that don't need to be outsourced or handed off. They just need to be stopped. Examples are double-checks of reports, unnecessary methods that have been inherited from previous owners/bosses, or maybe even your kids' multiple sports. Sometimes you just have to say, "We're not doing another after-school activity."

Central to this phase of our growth is asking, "Why am I doing what I'm doing?"

Next, we might eliminate tasks that are just filling space and taking away from a healthier and happier life. Eliminating comes in a variety of forms. It's not stopping; it's eliminating it from your list. Some of these items could be passed to another team member, automated through technology, or outsourced to a company outside of yours. Examples include handing off most of your email correspondence, stopping phone calls and initial follow-up with clients, or handing off social media marketing to another team or company.

Last, we want to reduce what you do. In the next chapter, we'll demonstrate exactly how boundaries open up possibilities, but for now, let's focus on reducing. Earlier, we discussed how work expands to the time allotted (Parkinson's Law). If you reduce time, it forces you to reduce activity. Then it frees up your best energy for what matters most.

We can effectively reduce some of our tasks and involvements. Maybe an answer will be to send out our laundry or stop taking on other tasks that we dread.

Growth Over Reaction: When we don't have a specific focus in life, it's easy to live in a responsive and reactive manner instead of a planned-growth approach. We must constantly reply to that email, run to that soccer practice, make that homemade meal, or meet that family obligation. But we don't ask ourselves, "Why are we committing to soccer every single Saturday? Is that good for our family and relationships?"

Intentionally slowing down is about deciding what we can do to take clear steps toward a healthier life that intentionally starts with betterment of self for those around us and our communities.

Within my business, there are occasional fires that need to be taken care of. It could be a consulting client issue, a podcast that doesn't launch correctly, or something last minute at Slow Down School or Killin' It Camp.

Fires will happen.

Here is the process that my team now knows by heart:

1. **Proceed Until Apprehended:** There is a fire. Can I take care of it? If not, who else on the team can help? I involve Joe only if necessary. We have a phrase we use on our teams: "Proceed until

apprehended." I want my team to do their best to act; we'll discuss why it worked or didn't later. They are encouraged to fail. As a result, they problem-solve and create without me putting time or energy into the fires.

2. **Gather Information:** If Joe needs to be involved, what information does he need to make a quick decision? For example, my Director of Details may need to gather a receipt, email correspondence, or brief someone on what has already occurred. This makes problem-solving meetings quick and efficient.

3. **Look up the River:** After the fire is put out, we evaluate if there are systems that need to be developed, information clients need, or other preventive measures that could be implemented. Then whoever is the point person for that client interaction will develop the plan and present it. The person most involved should be most invested in the plan implementation. If they create it instead of me, they're more likely to follow it.

Within this model, fires are expected, team members can make decisions, and long-term growth is valued over reacting in the present moment.

24/7 Profits: In 1930, economist John Maynard Keynes wrote an essay called "Economic Possibilities for Our Grandchildren." In it, he predicted that people of the future would be so productive that they would hardly need to work.

Despite being more productive, getting more done, and doing it with less, we have just expected more out of ourselves. We've raised the bar to such an extent that there is no way we can meet it, and it increasingly makes us feel like crap. Instead of celebrating all that we do and feeling magnificent about all that is accomplished, we stress and distress. If each year we expect to see a specific percentage growth beyond the previous year's growth, that means that we need to produce more. When we used to write letters in response to requests or had to send something by "next day," we had a reasonable cushion and knew no one was expecting an immediate response. Our expectations are all over the place now, often making us feel edgy, and we don't have a handle on what is considered "urgent," "reasonable," or "it can wait." And if it can wait, for how long? And are we then thinking about it waiting for us, wishing it was already done? Our "piles" cry out to us constantly.

When I think about slowing down, I think about stopping and sitting on a hill. The sun is rising (I'm like, *How the heck did I get up this early; obviously this* is *a dream!*) and crisp air hits my face as I sit in a peaceful meditative pose.

The reality is, I'm probably never going to meditate on a mountain at sunrise. Even when I'm hiking in beautiful and exotic locations, the crisp air never calls to me as strongly as my warm sleeping bag.

In our mind's eye, we equate slowing down with stopping. Sure, it can be that. We know the pull to unplug and think we'll get restored on vacation. But the positive effects of one concentrated getaway are hard to sustain. Sometimes you're just beginning to reconnect with yourself when it is time to jump back in. We all know that feeling when the stress begins to creep back in even before we return to our demands. When I talk about slowing down, I'm talking about reducing, eliminating, and stopping. In my version of slowing down, we're building habits and setting boundaries to open the way for true elimination of mental fatigue and squandered spirit.

My approach alternates structured slow down with times of focused and compressed work. Throughout my work with thousands, I see the ability to alternate periods of sprinting and periods of pausing to be one of the greatest determinants of success. Sometimes it's working sixty-plus hours per week to make a success of a dream business. Sometimes it is building a side-hustle to ease your transition from being an employee to owning your own business. Sometimes the rhythm is about phases of parenting or taking care of another family commitment, such as when you're sandwiched between taking care of both parents and kids.

The reality is, life isn't really a marathon where we never stop. Instead, it's a bunch of sprints and rests; it's like a pause button and a fast-forward button. What I teach clears the way and shows you how you can create a viable rhythm between work and relaxation that:

1. Reduces stress
2. Makes you more productive

3. Ignites creativity
4. Adds structure
5. Supports action followed by enjoyment and rest
6. Creates a sustainable system

You may recall that in the story that opens this chapter, the hare is arrogant and thinks he has the race easily won so he takes a break too soon. In my process, I teach how to pulse your time and effort between slowing down and killin' it. Creating a symbiotic rhythm between these two is the answer to creating a whole new life.

Deep down, we know this to be true; we don't want to work all the time and we want our work to matter. No matter how much research or application I send your way, you have to experience it—just as we do on morning two of Slow Down School. That is exactly what we're going to do in the next chapter.

7

HOW TO SLOW DOWN

Silence is not simply calmness or quietude. Over all words
and thoughts it implies transcendence. A state of beyond, a
state of pervasive peace, it denotes.

—Yoda

My favorite holiday season is Christmas. My birthday is right before it and my mom always made sure my birthday was its own distinct holiday. Numerous relatives were scolded when asked if they could combine birthday and Christmas presents. "Would you do that to his brother, Pete, who's born in June?"

The week before Christmas, our family gets together to make pierogi for the Polish Christmas Eve, Wigilia. Then there's my niece's birthday, my birthday, a day off, Christmas Eve, and then Christmas morning with my wife and daughters. My wife's brother has a birthday shortly thereafter, and then there is New Year's. It's ten days of parties, and I love it.

"I'm going to be gone for four weeks," I said to my assistant last year.

She was four months into her position with me. We scheduled one phone call during the four weeks to deal with any fires that needed to be put out. In preparation for that time, I gave a few instructions:

1. No texts with me.
2. Check my email and try to have it down to thirty by the time I return (I get two-hundred-plus emails per day).
3. Proceed until apprehended; do your best and we'll figure it out when I get back.
4. Refund anyone that you feel we need to refund, keep a list, and we'll discuss them when I return.
5. Create a to-do list in my calendar based on important emails or things that come up.

6. Don't contact me unless it is a fire that must be put out.

After New Year's, my wife and I left the country with our friends Paul and Diane. I didn't hear from my assistant the entire time. When I returned, I had only thirty emails to attend to, and I had a robust, yet focused, list of what I needed to complete in the first week after returning.

For a couple days into the break, I had podcast ideas, consulting thoughts, and product launch systems. I wrote them down. But through the pierogi and presents, restaurants and scuba diving, and board games with friends, I forgot I even had a business. In fact, for the first time in a while, it felt hard to go back to work. I was an object not in motion that wanted to stay not in motion.

But that's not how most people vacation.

HOW TO INCREASE WORKLOAD AND BE LESS PRODUCTIVE

Our access to technology has helped us make unprecedented progress as a society. As a kid, I remember fighting over the TV remote. When we got a second TV, things got better. If someone had told me that when I had kids they would carry around a TV and watch any show on demand (without having to record it live), my mind would have exploded.

For all the benefits, there are a plethora of challenges and negatives to technology, especially related to this conversation about optimizing our brains through slowing down. Let's just look at vacation and leisure time. An American Psychological Association study found: "More than half of employed adults said they check work messages at least once a day over the weekend (53 percent), before or after work during the week (52 percent), and even when they are home sick (54 percent). More than 4 in 10 workers (44 percent) reported doing the same while on vacation. . . . More than one-third of employed Americans said communication technology increases their workload (36 percent) and makes it more difficult to stop thinking about work (34 percent) and take a break from work (35 percent)."[1]

A 2019 joint research study from the University of Hong Kong and University of Illinois at Urbana-Champaign found that screens also leave us cognitively depleted, reduce work performance and attention, and increase mental health issues.[2] In that same paper, they found that even if you are in nature, which research shows should rejuvenate you, a screen will counteract that positive value.

In other words, don't take a break with a screen; it won't help!

But this is only part of the problem of slowing down. One of the most common things I hear from my clients is a feeling of guilt. Some call it "mommy guilt"; others talk about "adulting" as being really tough. Here are the core aspects of this guilt:

- If I don't do it [fill in the blank for the "it"—it could be dishes, sports, cleaning the house, bailing out a coworker, or marketing your business], who will?
- It takes so much money to keep up with life; if I slow down, how will I afford [fill in the blank: summer camp, tutoring, nice things, etc.]?
- I'm so stressed; my social media time is the only time when I can get away.

Those plaints are mostly from home; what about work? Will things fall apart if I leave, go silent, or vacation for more than a day or two?

There's a Mastercard commercial that starts with a little girl saying, "We've heard that over 400 million vacation days go unused every year."[3]

Then it cuts to a little boy. "That's the stupidest thing I've ever heard."

The commercial is encouraging people to take one more vacation day a year (and use their Mastercard). But it's true. In this chapter, we will examine why we don't slow down and the internal changes that need to happen so we can. Then we'll explore research on what happens to the body when we don't slow down and when we do. Next, we'll show how establishing boundaries unlocks the ability to slow down. Last, we'll look at a menu of options to start a slow-down plan for yourself.

GET YOUR ACT TOGETHER

What is your single biggest obstacle to slowing down? Your time? Your family? Your work? Your to-do list?

I would argue that all these reflect how well you accept yourself. Let's take time. How often have I heard, "I don't have time"? Yet, the average

American has around five hours of free time per day and spends most of that time on screens.[4] So why don't we focus our time on slowing down?

We don't accept our world as it is. Now, I'm not saying that you should never clean, do yard work, or market your business. But, if you feel heightened anxiety when things are undone, you'll keep working. You will toil away at work forgetting about your family and friends. You'll do yard work, when your kids really want to play. You'll spend time working on everything that is needed in a business, only to find that your checklist grows faster than you can complete it.

That is the secret right there. Adulthood is about accepting that things are left undone. Sometimes a basket of clothes will sit next to the bed for a week and sometimes it will be put away sooner.

We are always mentally figuring out the ROI on our time. How much anxiety or frustration will I have on the other side of not doing this task?

In the psychological world, there is a form of therapy named ACT: Acceptance and Commitment Therapy. The Association for Contextual Behavioral Science (ACBS) defines ACT as: "a unique empirically based psychological intervention that uses acceptance and mindfulness strategies, together with commitment and behavior change strategies, to increase psychological flexibility." ACT also helps people to embrace their thoughts and feelings, instead of judging, fighting, or feeling guilty about them.

A typical way a therapist would use this would be if a client said, "I want to change, but I'm anxious about it." The therapist would respond, "You want to change and you are anxious about it."[5]

The goal is to take action without having to change the feelings about the action.

Let's break some of that down. ACT has three major parts:

1. Acceptance and mindfulness strategies
2. Commitment and behavior change strategies
3. Goal to increase psychological flexibility

The goal of acceptance and mindfulness strategies is to begin to observe what is happening in our bodies and minds without judgment. Some activities incorporate breathing, body scans, and acceptance of past negative emotions.

The next area of ACT worth noting is the commitment and behavior change strategies. Just today, my therapist, Steve McLeary, challenged me to think through expectations vs. intentions. We discussed how expectations are very black and white. They're clear cut. You are successful or a failure.

But intentions are more about what you are becoming. Steve encouraged me to keep a "to-become" list rather than "to-do" list. Instead of framing my goals around specific actions, I should instead work on my self development to become the person I want to be.

I shared with him how I feel compelled to fulfill my potential and become the best version of myself. "What if you have no potential?" he asked. He meant that focusing on my potential and fulfilling it was causing me unnecessary pain. Rather, I should seek to build my intentions.

The last part of ACT is increasing psychological flexibility. According to The Association for Contextual Behavioral Science, psychological flexibility is "the ability to contact the present moment more fully as a conscious human being, and to change or persist in behavior when doing so serves valued ends."[6]

In other words, we are able to be here and now and then make changes to serve our values. Back to the therapy session: I talked through a fight I recently had with my wife about putting things back where they belong. My line of thinking was that if she saves fifteen seconds by not putting something away and then I spend five minutes looking for that thing, that's being a bad roommate and partner. It's valuing her time and not mine. It's not courteous.

From her perspective, she has a lot on her plate as a mom, wife, and fellow adult. There should be more flexibility by realizing people sometimes screw up. Who cares?

My therapist challenged me, "How else is she courteous and helpful to the family? How is she a good roommate?"

I listed the ways she goes nonstop to keep the kids organized, how she rarely gives herself a break, and how during quarantine she has looked after homeschooling, groceries, and our safety.

My therapist was building my psychological flexibility.

Through decades of research and practice, ACT has developed six core processes that help to build psychological flexibility.[7]

1. **Acceptance:** Instead of avoiding experiences and past thoughts, one works to accept them. Instead of avoiding the negative feelings of anger or anxiety, clients are taught to feel and struggle through those emotions.
2. **Cognitive Defusion:** This technique focuses on helping an individual to separate from their thoughts. Instead of being intertwined with them, they can evaluate how a thought may be unhelpful and depersonalize the thought.
3. **Being Present:** When you can experience the world directly, it allows you to do less predicting and judging. Then you can experience what therapists call "self as process" in a way that is less judgmental.
4. **Self as Context:** This idea reveals that because we are the "I," it is hard for us to understand our context in the greater world, because it is coming from our own perspectives. Through exercises, "defusion and acceptance is fostered."
5. **Values:** The focus on values is huge in ACT. It allows for choices to be made based on one's own determination instead of what their family of origin, society, or current social culture encourages.
6. **Committed Action:** Through working on behavior change, you'll probably run into your own psychological barriers or lack of flexibility. Committed action works to enact larger patterns of what is working.

You, too, can build psychological flexibility. This is one of the core building blocks of slowing down. We all have things in our businesses that feel essential, but we ought to run them through the stop, eliminate, reduce filters.

Allowing for intentions to grow and expectations to minimize is essential to optimizing our brains through slowing down.

I SHOULD HAVE ASKED A FOLLOW-UP QUESTION

I was at about sea level in Chitwan National Park of Nepal. Days earlier, we had finished climbing the 17,575-foot mountain Gokyo Ri. We had what most people call the most beautiful view of Mount Everest in the world. Now at sea level, we were drinking oxygen.

Next to me stood my friend Todd. Also present were a Peace Corps volunteer on holiday and a guy who had flown across the globe to be with her, only to be clearly rejected in front of us.

"If you get chased by a rhinoceros, climb a tree," our guide said.

There are times in life you should ask a follow-up question, or two, or three, like:

"How often do rhinos chase people?"

"Is there a specific kind of tree we should climb?"

"Can we practice climbing trees?"

But I did not ask any follow-up questions. We walked through the jungle. I heard birds sing scales I had never heard. A few small monkeys and critters pounced. But for the most part, it felt like a hike in Michigan. Todd and I began to wonder if the rhino thing was more to create a sense of adventure.

Then we saw her, an enormous rhino. She stood about fifty feet away, only a few small bushes between us. I pulled out my camera. The year was 2001, so I had a film camera. I took a picture. Not knowing how it turned out, I zipped ahead to the next exposure and stepped forward. I didn't fully trust Todd's digital camera. I took a photo and another step.

The rhino charged. I took off running. I knew in the first few yards I could beat Todd. I was a sprinter and could beat him for the first hundred yards, but his long-distance skills were much better than mine. The peace corps volunteer and the sucker that flew around the globe were behind us.

I swatted leaves out of my face as I ran. Faster and faster. Then, the charging stopped.

I turned around. No rhino. We all walked back to our guides. The two of them slid down trees.

"Why you no run up tree?" our guide yelled.

Why didn't I run up a tree? When you're being chased by a rhino, that's not the time to try something new. Imagine if I tried to climb a tree and awkwardly slid back down. What if I couldn't choose a tree that looked good?

I knew I could outrun at least one person from our crew. When you're chased by a rhino, you go with what you know. It's not a time to experiment with climbing trees. But what was happening inside of my body?

When fear is triggered, whether by a rhino, fire alarm, or a near-miss car accident, our sympathetic nervous system takes over. It releases hormones and neurotransmitters to alert our body. Epinephrine and norepinephrine, for example, are released to both inhibit and propel at the same time. When those chemicals hit smooth muscles, they touch what are called alpha receptors, which constrict blood flow. The stomach is a smooth muscle, and when you're being chased by a rhino, there's no need to keep digesting breakfast. When epinephrine and norepinephrine hit beta receptors, they expand. The most important organs get an increase in blood flow, and the adrenal glands kick out more adrenaline.

As I walked back to the group, that's when my parasympathetic system started to take over. As if it were a traffic cop saying to the sympathetic system, "Nothing to see here, keep moving," it helps to bring a body back to baseline. That system works to get you back into the business of living.

It then triggers the vagus nerve to assist by increasing communication between the brain and other parts of the body such as the heart, lungs, liver, and digestive organs. A team at UC Berkley found that "activation of the vagus nerve is associated with feelings of caretaking and the ethical intuition that humans from different social groups (even adversarial ones) share a common humanity."[8] Dr. Stephen W. Porges, professor emeritus of the University of Illinois at Chicago, called the vagus nerve the nerve of compassion. He believes that human social interaction, motivations, and behaviors are positively or negatively changed by the intervention of the vagal system. Stimulation of the vagus may lead to increased trust, affection, and cooperation.[9]

When our lives are in danger, the sympathetic system takes over to protect the body and increases the likelihood of survival. Then the parasympathetic system takes over to get back to baseline using the vagus nerve and numerous other chemicals. In that situation, stress and the body's response is completely justified; it is saving me from a rhino!

But our brains can't decipher the stress of a rhino from a stressful client situation. Even more, the research is showing that nonstop access to email, texting, social media, screens, and working doesn't allow our nervous system to reset. So all those positive things that the parasympathetic system and vagus nerve offer is muted. We have less compassion, creativity, and cooperation. Instead, we are flooded and reactionary.

Earlier, we talked about vigilance decrement, the idea that the quality of our attention goes down over time. Remember the one-minute breaks that they discovered at the University of Illinois? They disrupted the decrement.

By now you should be seeing the pattern emerge: Engagement and disengagement. React and then retreat. Slow down and kill it.

But the Industrialists were creating perpetual motion machines. They were the tortoise: slow and steady. This mindset was captured when Elon Musk was asked at the World Government Summit about the keys to success. He said, "Work every waking hour. There need to be reasons to get up in the morning. Life can't just be about solving problems; otherwise, what's the point? There's got to be things that they find inspiring and there need to be reasons to get up in the morning."[10]

The Industrialists had their purpose and time. Now let us move into the next phase of humanity.

BOUNDARIES AND BREAKS

Boundaries and breaks do something that the Industrialists missed: dropping the ball. The very first step in slowing down is to establish nonnegotiable boundaries. Why nonnegotiable? Creating firm boundaries stops creep. You know the creep. I'll work an extra fifteen minutes. Then it grows, maybe not today, but it grows. Soon enough, you're back to your present-day mentality.

By determining the best use of time, it forces you to go through the stop, eliminate, and reduce lenses, because you no longer are trying to do everything within a time period that is not defined.

We want to look at boundaries and breaks in relationship to your day, week, month, and year.

Daily boundaries come in a variety of forms. Here are a few of mine and some questions:

- I take Mondays and Fridays off.
- I write in twenty- to forty-minute increments and force myself to move so that my brain is optimized.
- Almost everything is in my schedule for the day.
- I start the day by 9:30 a.m. at the latest.
- I don't check email before writing.

- I end at 4:30 p.m. at the latest.
- We go on a daily family walk.
- I return phone calls that might be stressful at the end of the day (so I'm not pissed off the rest of the day).
- I eat a healthy lunch.
- I start with a cup of tea and limit myself to two cups of coffee a day.
- On Fridays and Mondays, I only check email for a maximum of thirty minutes.
- When do you have the most energy in a day?
- What do you hate doing?
- If you could add one thing that brought more innovation and creativity into your world, what would that be?

A handful of nonnegotiable boundaries help to distinguish between the environment I work in and everything else. Mondays and Fridays means helping around the house, errands, homeschooling, and roadschooling. Saturdays and Sundays are focused on rejuvenating. My workdays are focused on getting a lot done in a short period of time.

Weekly boundaries set the rhythm for the week: three days of work, two days of household maintenance, and two days of rejuvenation. Here are examples of weekly boundaries and some questions:

- Specific days and times for work.
- A balance of social and alone time.
- A sense of the direction of the business, family, and self, based on the weekly rhythm.
- When you look at the pacing of your week, does it sound draining or invigorating?
- If you reined in your time, how would you do that?

I establish monthly boundaries as I look at longer-term projects within Practice of the Practice. For example, if one of my consultants comes to me with a new idea for a Mastermind group, I would set time for us to talk about it and then have her sketch out more of the idea, test it, and then we'd meet again. I want to have a clear idea of my own use of time and energy for any new project. I'd also look at how that will impact other aspects of our work with Practice of the Practice.

Similarly, we look at our schedule as a family. This is a less formal process and has become routine. We can tell if we're in need of more social time, time away from the kids, family visits, or an adventure out of town. By setting boundaries around our children's activities, it allows us to have a better sense of pacing for everyone in the family.

Here are some examples and questions to help with monthly boundaries:

- We don't want our weekends to be taken up with one child's activities.
- We enjoy freedom to plan things last minute.
- I don't take on projects that distract from whatever big project I'm working on.
- We designate a time to evaluate new ideas.
- What do you love and hate about each month's pacing?
- If you gave a few words to your month, what comes to mind? Do you like those words?
- A year from now, what tasks do you hope you are not doing at work and home? How can you eliminate those next month?

In other words, we're asking over and over, "What do we want out of life?"

Lastly, yearly boundaries are important. How do the seasons, activities, and time out-of-town look on an annual basis? Here are a few questions.

- What adventures do I want this year?
- What time do we need away individually, as a couple, and as a family?
- If each quarter had themes, what would they be?

Later in the book, we will discuss how Kalamazoo Valley Community College has used this same structure to move into a four-day workweek, to save millions, to increase staff optimization, and to increase happiness. Clear boundaries are the first step to freeing up time to slow down. But once you have that time, how do you actually slow down?

ACTIONS TO SHIFT YOUR SLOW-DOWN HABITS

The trap of adulting is believing that this is the way it has to be. My wife and I have two short-term rentals. We love hosting people visiting northern Michigan.

We are part of an advocacy group for short-term rentals. We are people that want to preserve the neighborhood feel, think through the issues, and find a way to have short-term rentals without hurting our area. Northern Michigan has a long history of cabins, vacation rentals, and visitors; we want to be a part of that.

Recently, the group met online to talk about a county commission meeting, planning, and advocacy. No one had sent an agenda out. Fifteen minutes into the meeting, it was clear that there was no clear purpose for the meeting. People gave "updates," ranted about the issues, and shared what the governor's office was doing. There was very little focus.

The trap of adulting is that we have to be polite, respectful, and suck up what other people give us. Instead, I sent the facilitator a private message and said, "I have to go help with the kids; do you need anything else from me?" She said "no" and I was free thirty-five minutes early. If someone in home life or business is going to ask for my time, I'm thinking that that time is best spent there. But when it becomes clear that playing and feeding my kids, joining my wife in parenting, and getting away from a screen early are all better options, I need to have the chutzpah to say it.

Making your own life decisions over and over will help you to find more time than you know what to do with. Once you start observing how much of your time is taken by others, you'll be best positioned to then decide how you want to slow down. One of the best ways to both stop the unhelpful habits and grow the optimization of our brains is in nature.

The power of nature is significant. In a 2010 study looking at 101 Michigan schools, those with greener views from the classroom and cafeteria had higher graduation rates, standardized test scores, students attending four-year schools, and lower criminal behavior.[11] Study after study shows that even nature pictures can be effective in helping employees slow down and have useful breaks.

There are two major categories of slowing down:

1. Reducing tasks and activities that trigger the sympathetic system.
2. Increasing activities that amplify the parasympathetic system.

In Category One, we are stopping doing things that are unhelpful. In Category Two, we are doing more healthy activities. For example, we stop checking email at night or on the weekend and we start meditating ten minutes each morning. One is reducing the negative and the other amplifies the positive.

This is a menu of changes for you to consider. I highly recommend you view this as you would an actual menu. Even if everything at a restaurant looks delicious, you only have enough room for an appetizer, main course, and dessert. Only start a few of these activities. To download this full menu as a printout, go to joesanok.com/menu.

STOP THE UNHELPFUL

So let's start by looking at the types of activities that are most frequently cited in the reduction category: technology, obligations, and stressful interactions.

Technology

- Set a clear beginning and end time to work on a project. For example, I will work twenty-five minutes on this and then go for a short walk.
- Don't check texts, emails, or the news before your workday starts.
- Set a clear beginning and end time for your day.
- Monitor how refreshed you feel when looking at technology before bed.
- Reduce apps that trigger "work mode" by disabling notifications on your phone for those apps.
- Have tech detox days where you only use a photo for coordinating that day's events.
- Schedule your own Slow Down School (or come to mine, www. slowdownschool.com) and spend a week free from technology.

- Stop and breathe more. Realize that you are a human being, not a human doing.[12]

Obligations

- Eliminate any obligations that don't meet your personal, family, or business goals. These could include serving on a board of directors that you no longer enjoy.
- Set boundaries with your family or friends. For example, if someone asks you to do something, either tell them you can't or just wait to text for twelve hours; it usually sorts itself out.
- Identify professional tasks that no longer serve your big goals.
- Create boundaries to give yourself an additional eight hours off per week. Watch what falls apart and outsource that to someone else.
- Outsource obligations you no longer need such as mowing the lawn, folding laundry, or cleaning your house.
- Stop thinking about work when you are not at work.
- Make a list of things you hate doing and see if a system or person could do them for you.
- Stop and breathe more. Realize that you are a human being, not a human doing.

Stressful Interactions

- Evaluate which clients are the most difficult to handle, consider raising their prices, handing them off to another staff member, or eliminating them from your workload.
- Communicate with others in the way you want to. If they want to "jump on a quick call" and you think it can be solved with a voice memo, do what you think is best.
- Consider leaving friendships or relationships in which the other person is needy and not making you feel good about yourself.
- Reduce the amount of time you are with family members who are toxic; no one said you have to be at Thanksgiving all day (or if they did, that's their issue).

- Set boundaries with unhealthy coworkers or supervisors to limit communication, after-hours email/text, and expectations.
- Put yourself first.
- Stop and breathe more. Realize that you are a human being, not a human doing.

INCREASE HEALTH

Let's start by looking at the types of activities that are most frequently cited in the increase category: rejuvenation, satisfaction pursuits, and relationship cultivation.

Rejuvenation

- Spend more time in nature, even if it is only a few extra minutes per day.
- Schedule longer amounts of time in nature weekly and annually.
- Move more with yoga, walking, or hiking.
- Invest in new wellness approaches you have not tried.
- Listen to podcasts that are not related to your business.
- Build friendships outside of work. Try new things together like restaurants, board games, or an improv show.
- Start therapy.
- Get meditation training.
- Explore your default mode network through working with a trained psychedelic guide.[13]
- Get a massage.
- Plan things on days off or in the evening that promote rejuvenation so you're not drawn to work.
- Spend time with your kids, partner, or friends brainstorming new activities that will rejuvenate you.
- Stop and breathe more. Realize that you are a human being, not a human doing.

Satisfaction Pursuits

- Create a process to capture good ideas so you can let them go from your brain. This could be a list on your phone or something like Trello. When you're not at work and have an idea, you can capture it and move on.
- Create triggers to remind you of what you want to do; this could be as simple as putting out exercise clothes the night before, journaling in the evening/morning about intentions for the day, or writing it on your mirror.
- Cultivate next steps for your internal inclinations.
- Block out time in your schedule for slowing down and insert hobbies or experiences that challenge you. Remember that curiosity grows out of the known and out of experiences that challenge that known.
- Take a class on something interesting. I joined an improv troupe and love it!
- Cook something new.
- Listen to music that is different from what you are used to.
- Make an "I'm going to" list of experiences you have longed to do.
- Listen to a book about something that will ground you. Recently, I loved *Taming the Tiger Within: Meditations on Transforming Difficult Emotions* by Thich Nhat Hanh.
- Volunteer in a way that addresses an issue you care about.
- Stop and breathe more. Realize that you are a human being, not a human doing.
- Books that can help: Ram Dass's *Polishing the Mirror,* Rachel Hollis's *Girl, Wash Your Face,* Rob Bell's *How to Be Here,* Glennon Doyle's *Untamed,* and Sam Harris's *Waking Up.*

Relationship Cultivation

- Remember that all old friends start as new friends. Observe who you're drawn to now.
- Evaluate your romantic relationship/s. What's working and what needs work?
- Join groups where you have a common interest.

- Set aside time to call or text friends to keep the relationships alive.
- Plan a weekend away with old friends.
- Plan a vacation with other friends.
- Host a gathering where friends can meet other friends.
- Invite a small group of people who don't know one another to enjoy a discussion, documentary viewing, or game night.
- Have adventures with friends and family like biking, hiking, or scuba lessons.
- Follow up with people after you have an enjoyable time.
- Have times of the week and month that are blocked for socialization and fun with other people.
- Work on your own emotional hang-ups with a coach or therapist.
- If you are in a relationship, go through the Gottman Art & Science of Love Workshop or read through their book *Eight Dates* with your partner.
- Set goals for yourself and others you enjoy spending time with.
- Stop and breathe more. Realize that you are a human being, not a human doing.

CONVERSATION STARTERS

Often, our overworking comes from having little that brings us deeper joy. Sure, we run the kids around town for all of their activities or we go on date nights. But do we ever stop and really ask, "What do I want to be spending my time on?"

Conversations of significance with others build intimacy, a sense of belonging, and are just plain interesting. Here are some conversation starters in no particular order. For more, go to joesanok.com/discussion.

- What's one of the weirdest things that has happened at work?
- How are your spiritual beliefs now different from those you were raised with?
- How are your spiritual beliefs different from five years ago?
- When did you change your mind about something important?
- Would you ever do a guided psychedelic journey?
- What friends do you miss?

- How did you get one of your scars?
- What would be one issue, if solved, that would give us a better society?
- If you had to watch one movie for the rest of your life, what would it be?
- What are you self-conscious about?
- What are you learning right now?
- What books have influenced you?
- If you, all your friends, and family had to move because your town was disappearing, but everyone you loved would go with you, where would you relocate?
- If you had to start over and switch to another career, what other directions would you consider, if you kept all the knowledge you have now?
- What books do you intend to read but haven't?
- How do you feel about technological advancement?
- What are the pros and cons of more advanced AI?
- Would you ever do a ten-day silent meditation retreat?
- What do you want to cut out of your life?
- How's your relationship with your parents? Is it complicated or easy? How would you describe it?
- Do you get along with your siblings?
- Who is your favorite relative?
- Where have you traveled? What adventures have you had?
- What's a crazy story from your twenties?
- How have you shifted politically? What caused that?
- Are there areas of your spiritual perspective that differ from the teachings of your spiritual leaders?
- Who do you wish you could meet?
- What would you do with an extra ten hours a week?

When written like this, it can feel like a checklist. As a fellow achiever and self-growth junkie, I see questions like these, and I want to answer them all. In fact, I might even feel a little like a failure if I don't try them all. But, again, it's a menu. It's not even a comprehensive menu. It's encouraging you to stop doing things that don't help your brain and start doing things that do. It's a guide to help you have deeper and more fulfilling conversations.

BRAIN FACTS

At Slow Down School, we usually start in small groups of four to six. These are the "families" for the week. They are people who are at a similar phase in business with similar goals. Within the counseling world, we say that when teams are effective they form, norm, storm, and perform.[14] So, after we've formed, the goal is to "norm," to discover what we have in common.

I want to get beyond, "I want more time and money." Rather, I want to get to the heart of it. Why is that important? What stories or experiences make time more valuable? What would an extra $100,000 per year give you? How would stress look if you controlled your time and money?

Mind you, this is the same afternoon these people just met. They were picked up in a big yellow school bus at 4:30 p.m. at the airport, ate dinner, and now we are about two hours into these relationships. What happens sets the tone for the week. We're sitting in the woods, with a stream running past. Lake Michigan is creating a techno beat of waves in the background. Birds sing. Instead of just talking about KPIs, goals, and time, people tell stories.

"My mom died last year, and I realized that I can't keep working this much."

"My kids are headed off to college in a few years and I realized this part is almost over."

"I just got a divorce . . . and it's been so hard."

"I can't live in the poverty I saw as a child."

"My dad was a drug-dealing gang lord and I'm setting a new future for my family."

The stories are incredible. They give the depth that is needed to remind us that we're not just talking money and time, we're talking about something much, much deeper.

Brain Fact #1: When we feel safe and connected to others' stories, neuro-mirroring occurs. That means the part of your brain that lights up when telling a story is the part that lights up in the listener. This helps the brain prime for learning, creativity, and openness. This is key to expanding beyond the typical way of thinking.

Slow Down School occurs at a boarding school property on Lake Michigan. The first few days are spent mostly outside. We spend time eating indoors, but even that space has floor-to-ceiling windows looking out at a beautiful forest. The responsibilities to cook, think about the day, and make decisions are removed. The environment primes the brain for optimization.

The mornings of days one and two are hikes along the Sleeping Bear Sand Dunes National Lakeshore. These are places with special meaning to me. The hike to the peak of Pyramid Point takes approximately thirty minutes. The week of our wedding, when we were stressed, Christina and I went there to remind ourselves why we were getting married.

When we arrive, we unload from the yellow school bus and partner up. I give questions to prompt conversation, again with the intention to build connections, friendships, and depth beyond business. The hike is through a wooded area, typical of northern Michigan. In the final steps, you crest and see a sweeping view of Lake Michigan.

"I had no idea Lake Michigan was this big; it's like an ocean!" is a very common reaction to those new to Michigan. Having 20 percent of the world's fresh water, the Great Lakes are a sight to be seen.

The view has North and South Manitou Island directly in front of Pyramid Point. We spend an hour exploring the terrain. Some people run down the dune to the water. They spend the remaining time climbing back up a sand dune—with each step, they slide back down approximately three quarters of a step. I've done it once. I don't need to do it again. Sometimes we go wild raspberry picking on the dune. Others escape from the group and meditate.

"I feel like a kid."

"This is amazing!"

"Why don't I do this more?"

Instead of facilitating and directing emotions, we allow reactions to spontaneously occur. One year a group wanted to take an alternate path to the top. They got lost for an hour and couldn't get a cell phone signal. Other years, people ran to the bottom and had a workout that was more than they bargained for. Other times people sat and had wildlife join them.

I don't need to ask facilitating questions. Nature teaches through experience and the metaphors participants create.

That afternoon, I brought in massage therapists and a Thai body worker. When not getting massages, we hung out on the beach playing games, swimming, or reading. It's fun, it's social, it's being human. That night, we had a fire and looked at the stars after the sunset. One year we had a silent disco, and another we did improv. Other years, we just skipped stones.

On day two, we hike Empire Bluffs, another hike with a view of the dunes from another angle. We do yoga and again spend time on the beach. As on day one, people socialize, but with less facilitation. It's as if it shifts from being "Joe-led" to "self-led." That's the whole point, right? For them to see they have all they need inside of themselves.

Brain Fact #2: The people, experiences, and environment you surround yourself with will create the outcomes. Reduce time on decisions so that you can allow for natural optimization to occur. Nature teaches and metaphors naturally arise, but we are usually too busy to see them.

So stop right now and breathe. You are fine how you are. This modality is about enjoying now and living now. You are okay. But you're not just "okay" or "fine," you have big things inside you that need to be released. We need to erase the fingerprint of the Industrialists, because we are not machines; we are complex organisms that will take humanity to the next level. But not if we are stressed and maxed out . . . that's for machines. Instead, we are going to slow down to let the best ideas come to the surface and then kill it.

Now that we know why and how to slow down, let's look at the other side of the equation: killin' it. It always goes in this order. We don't kill it only to be exhausted and have to slow down; that's the Industrialists talking. That's a machine taking a break. No, we're talking about slowing down and then with ideas, creativity, and innovation, spending our time on the very best ideas for the world. Then we slow down before we are out of energy to rejuvenate again.

So let's talk about your hustle narrative and why it's failing.

HOW THE

FOUR-DAY WEEK WORKS

In part three, we examine how first slowing down can allow us to get more done in a shorter period of time. We'll be evaluating the research and application of productivity, expanding ideas, and leveling up. During these discussions, you may feel some jolts—that's the Industrialist mind-set trying to keep its grip on you.

- But I have to work more, don't I?
- How do I allow myself to drop the ball on the unimportant, to focus on the best?
- Can I really become more successful by working less?

We're going to look at where these feelings come from, as we look at ways to bring all of this together into one plan for you.

8

YOUR HUSTLE NARRATIVE

Type in "hustle" into any search engine or social media and you'll get entrepreneurs saying that everyone needs to work harder, be everywhere, and never set their phone down for fear of missing a selfie moment. The hustle narrative is dangerous. It goes against what research shows us about how the brain thinks, encourages us to create more instead of better products, and doesn't see time as a currency.

Step back for a minute and do some simple math with me. Let's say the average hustling, hopeful Instagram influencer spends two hours a day snapping pictures, networking, and thinking about how to build a business. Let's just say those two hours don't have a clear or strong return on investment for that time. It's all speculative.

Over a year, that is 730 hours or 18.25 forty-hour workweeks. Said another way, that's 35 percent of a year's work! Hustle without clear intention is a waste of time and energy. When we leave things undone, it allows us time to scale beyond our own work.

That pretty much captures how many entrepreneurs and leaders talk about business, entrepreneurship, and making it in the world. Why wouldn't we think this way with the Industrialist's fingerprint all over our world and icons like Elon Musk or Steve Jobs as the aspirational figures for business?

When speaking to the World Government Summit and in subsequent speeches, Elon Musk has told the story of when he and his brother first began their startup, which later became PayPal. They rented a small office, showered at the YMCA, and slept under their desks. He even noted how he had a girlfriend at the time and if she wanted to see him, she had to come to the office.

His advice to future generations of startup founders is, "Work every waking hour . . . work like hell, put in eighty- to one-hundred-hour weeks, every week."[1]

Walter Isaacson's biography of Steve Jobs reveals the many unique qualities of Jobs. According to Isaacson, it took Jobs from 1991 to 1999 to furnish his house, due to his extreme aesthetic design. For years he didn't have furniture for guests to sit on, because nothing suited his taste.

Further, Isaacson noted Jobs's way of interacting with people. Colleagues noted that Jobs had a way of interacting, which they named the "reality distortion field." This was from a *Star Trek* episode in which aliens created their own version of reality. Andy Hertzfeld, one of the original Apple team members, said this in Isaacson's book: "The reality distortion field was a confounding mélange of charismatic rhetorical style, indomitable will, and eagerness to bend any fact to fit the purpose at hand."

Isaacson quotes Bill Atkinson, another early Apple engineer, saying, "He can deceive himself, it allowed him to con people into believing his vision, because he has personally embraced and internalized it."[2]

Jobs's reality distortion field came down to one defining characteristic, Isaacson concludes, that the "rules didn't apply to him. He had some evidence for this; in his childhood, he had often been able to bend reality to his desires."[3]

No one doubts that Musk and Jobs have been successful in some ways. Of course we'd all love to be visionaries that change the course of human history. No one is attacking that record for these two innovators. But the problem, I propose, is that both of these models are representative of the Industrialists' mindset.

Jobs and Musk subscribe to the narrative that the world continues to push: hustle is the key to success.

1. Work and vision should be the #1 priority, even if it takes over your life. For these two, this became obsessive and ruined many of their relationships.
2. Those that work with you are machines to output a product.

On any given day, you can search your favorite social media for the hashtag #hustle and find that this narrative is strong. It has even moved from just hustling as an action to a "side-hustle," as in a "side gig" or just a hustle as a side project.

Here's an example of what I found on Instagram today:

- Twenty-four million posts with #hustle.
- @thebossyempire: "Not every closed door is locked. You've just got to push, babe. @bossbabe.inc."
- @aimeelouisefit: "It's hustle time. Watch this space."
- @annieee_d: "Worked 27 hours straight, smashed 1 Pole Class and surviving on 3 hours of sleep."
- @sheconquers: "And then one day, I discovered my own light, my own inner-gangster. I snatched my power back and the game changed."
- @_boys.attitude_: "Bro, don't forget the lifestyle you have promised to yourself."
- @thegrowinginvestor: "The harder the journey, the stronger you will become. @successpictures."
- @newage_visuals: "Entrepreneurs waking up at 5 am."

On the surface, nothing appears wrong with these statements. In fact, many of them can be inspiring to people that need a kick in the pants. Also, I don't know their lives. Maybe the twenty-seven-hour person is a nurse helping in a hospital and still found time to work out. In the next chapter, we'll talk about how to sprint.

The main difference between the Industrialists' way and this new way of thinking is that Industrialists move nonstop. Whereas this new modality is about genuinely disconnecting, slowing down, and doing things to allow the best, most creative brain to emerge—then running full tilt and killin' it in the best areas possible.

The Industrialists, the hustlers, the Steve Jobses and Elon Musks of the world work hundred-hour weeks, without examining why that is needed. They sacrifice relationships for "the hustle"; they are obsessive about their work, and their identity and personal value is wrapped in that work.

A healthier mindset, one that moves away from the damaging Industrialists, is to fully value, love, and interact with the work we're called to do *and* to have clear boundaries as to when that work pauses.

But why is this so difficult? In this chapter, we will examine three reasons we get pulled back into hustle: the overdeveloped worth, the underdeveloped fun, and the biochemical addiction. We'll also look at an effect that researchers have discovered as to why and when we have more or less confidence in our work. After that, we'll explore the conundrum businesses are in to fix this problem and how one oil and gas consultant changed that. Then we'll explore a few techniques employed by *Frozen II* and my consulting clients.

OVER AND UNDERDEVELOPMENT MESSES THINGS UP

If companies like Microsoft see increased productivity during a four-day workweek and don't permanently adopt that schedule, how do we even stand a chance? If Google's 20 percent time is a myth or overstated, how are we to move away from the Industrialists' grip? Why is the Industrialists' model so compelling, even when we know we have worse health outcomes, employees are more unhappy, and they want a three-day weekend?

There are three primary reasons that we keep getting drawn back to the old Industrialist Model: the overdeveloped worth, the underdeveloped fun, and the biochemical addiction.

Through education, early jobs, and media, society continues to perpetuate the lie that our worth is tied to our work. The Protestant work ethic tied it to religion. Graduating high schoolers are asked, "What are you going to do with your life?" And one of the first questions socially is: "What do you do?"

Much of our worth comes from what we do for work.

Quickly, we mentally classify how we compare to others based on what they "do" and what we "do." The first tractor beam that pulls us back toward the Death Star of the Industrialists is that of overdeveloped worth. In psychology, we know that a sense of self is important. Children need to understand how they fit in a family, and how they fit in their neighborhood, school, church, or sports team. From there, they gain perspective on who they are within a culture, race, and sexual identity. Ideally, children feel safe, accepted, and free to become the best version of who they are.

That's the healthy version of worth. Overdeveloped worth puts too much stock into what is detrimental to our development. Within the context of moving away from an Industrialist's approach to the world, we must first examine how much of our sense of self comes from our work. Again, there is a healthy understanding and appreciation of the work you do in the world. But for many who struggle with moving toward a four-day workweek, this hustle narrative is rooted in an overdeveloped sense of worth derived from work.

This manifests in inflated ego, obsession with projects, high focus on achievement, devastation when failure occurs, avoiding risks so as not to fail, or beating up one's self when something is done incorrectly.

In short, if you succeed or fail in work, what happens to your emotions?

Again, there is a healthy frustration when something goes wrong. All of us would feel frustrated if we spent time on something important, only to see it launch differently than expected. But what happens when there is an overdevelopment of worth is overwork. Instead of having a hard stop for your workday, you may check emails after hours, return client texts, or fit in just a few more small tasks.

You may say, "Joe, I just have so much work. It's like fifty hours of work in forty hours and you want me to take another day off? That's now fifty hours in thirty-two hours—that's unreasonable!"

But the issue is not the workload, it is the value you put on the work. Yes, there are jobs that make unreasonable demands, but you are still choosing that job. Yes, you may have built a business that heavily relies on you as the owner to do fifty-plus hours a week, but you created that job for yourself. When I dig in with clients, almost always it comes down to an overdeveloped worth coming from work.

I don't want to be seen as a failure.

I want my boss to know I'm a good worker.

My business needs my guidance.

No one can do it like me.

I'm too important not to work fifty hours.

Yet, at some point, you do call it quits. You end at some point. If you're working a fifty-hour workweek, why not a fifty-one-hour workweek? If you work five days a week, why not work a little bit on Saturday? You already have a point when you say, "I just can't do anymore this week."

Remember, we made this all up! The Babylonians made up the seven-day week. It's only because Henry Ford saw it as an economic benefit that people work forty-hour workweeks. It just as easily could have been an eight-day week like the Egyptians or a ten-day week like the Romans. Ford could have done seven-hour days and we'd have a thirty-five-hour work-week. Humans made this up. You already aren't completing everything, so why not back that up a bit?

Stepping back from your work often allows you to see things differently. I often do a sudoku when I fly. Inevitably there's a stuck spot. I'll sit and ponder. Then I'll get up to use the restroom, and nearly every time I see an answer right away. The Industrialists want you to think that the forty-plus-hour workweek is the answer to success, but it's not. You'll actually work faster and more efficiently when you move away from the overdevelopment of worth and take more time away. But there are two more tractor beams of the Industrialists' Death Star trying to suck you back to the old way.

What if the three-day weekend was the new status symbol of choice?

The underdevelopment of fun is the second reason we are sucked back into the Industrialists' Death Star. If you've been assigning too much worth into your work, you have probably been neglecting socialization, hobbies, and adventure. Or at least it is undervalued compared to your work.

When you have underdeveloped fun, there's little to look forward to outside of work. The chemical release in the brain from working and getting things done is more valuable than the fun. Avoiding failure and feeling a sense of accomplishment (all part of the overdeveloped worth) feel better. It's like when I try to get my child off one of our iPads. If they don't have hobbies, toys, friends, or things to do outside, the iPad will feel like their only entertainment. But, if they have developed fun outside of the iPad, then they will transition away from technology.

Imagine if someone spent ten years working forty-five hours a week and then in the little free time they have outside of regular adulting chores, they find time for five hours a week of genuine fun. Over those ten years, taking two weeks off per year, that is 22,500 hours of work and 2,500 hours of fun (for the two weeks of vacation, I didn't include any fun or work time because people spend their vacations differently). Of the total 84,000 hours (24 hours a day, 7 days a week, 50 weeks in a year because I excluded the two vacation weeks), 26.79 percent is work and 3 percent is fun.

Based on these numbers, of course that time spent working will be justified as more important and the fun will be undervalued. We will mentally value that work time and overdevelop the worth associated with it. If we switched to a thirty-two-hour workweek and allocated all of the extra time to fun, self-development, and optimizing the brain, our new split would be 16,000 hours of work and 9,000 hours of fun. Work would be 19.05 percent of the time and fun would be 10.71 percent. Just by starting to have clear boundaries and focus on slowing down and building fun, the numbers start to line up.

Developing new hobbies, friends, and social engagements is often difficult for adults. We undervalue free time and look for an ROI on it. But free time for the sake of free time often leads to more productivity and creativity in the workplace without directly associating it.

The final reason we get sucked back into the Industrialists' tractor beam is the biochemical addiction. There are four chemicals in the brain worth noting: serotonin, dopamine, glutamate, and norepinephrine.

The brain communicates by sharing chemicals within the brain between neurons, nerves, and through other ways. There are two major types of chemicals: excitatory and inhibitory. Excitatory chemicals like glutamate stimulate the brain activity. Whereas, inhibitory chemicals like serotonin have a calming effort on the brain.

Serotonin works to help with sleep, depression, appetite, and mood. Researchers are finding that serotonin is stored in the intestine, and a growing body of research is looking at gut health being related to serotonin release and depression.

Dopamine helps with behavior, emotions, cognition, and communication with the frontal lobe. That is the part of your brain responsible for decision-making, rewards, and pleasure. It is a chemical that helps with motivation.

Glutamate is the most common excitatory neurotransmitter, found in your brain and spinal cord. It helps with early childhood brain development, learning, and memory.

Norepinephrine is key to your fight-flight-freeze response. It is both a chemical and a neurotransmitter. It is triggered during stress, and when this occurs over time, it pulls resources away from other parts of the body. A 2009 study researched the consequences of long-term stress on norepinephrine: "The consequences can include slowing of growth (in children), sleeplessness, loss of libido, gastrointestinal problems, impaired disease resistance, slower rates of injury healing, depression, and increased vulnerability to addiction."[4]

When you are working hard, maybe getting into a flow state, or even under stress, many of these feel-good chemicals are released. So, imagine you're working long hours and feeling some stress. This is the same thing that happens when you're feeling stress, worry, or fear at other times. The HPA (hypothalamus pituitary adrenal axis) activates a series of reactions. The primary one is that cortisol is released. Cortisol is a really helpful chemical for survival.[5]

When cortisol starts doing its thing during stress, sugars in the bloodstream increase, which helps the brain use glucose to make rapid decisions. The Mayo Clinic put it this way: "Cortisol also curbs functions that would be nonessential or detrimental in a fight-or-flight situation."[6] When released in an emergency or even within a flow state, cortisol and the waterfall of other chemicals can be extremely helpful for survival.

But, like anything, prolonged exposure leads to negative side effects. For example, learning and creativity weaken because of the chemical focus on survival. During a stressful emergency, you're focused on getting away safely, not self-actualization, so the brain de-prioritizes those functions. Also, over time, elevated cortisol levels lead to the brain reducing in size, lowering social interaction abilities, and reducing judgment. Fewer cells are made and memory decreases.

Studies in mice have shown that many of these stress traits can open genes that otherwise would not have been triggered (known as epigenetics). When this happens, stress and cortisol issues can get passed down through generations.

In addition to the cortisol issues, chemicals like serotonin, dopamine, and norepinephrine cause us to build a biological addiction to stress, overwork, and the chemical flood that often accompanies this work.

Further, this overworking is fueled by two of society's most prominently approved addictions: caffeine and alcohol. The workforce is kept in an underslept, stressed, hyper-cortisol state because of these two opposing chemicals. Stimulants help us to be alert when our body says we should still be sleeping. Alcohol depresses us to calm down, when we're still hyped up from work.

In Steven Kotler and Jamie Wheal's book, *Stealing Fire*, they say, "Consider three substances that sit squarely inside the state's pale: caffeine, nicotine, and alcohol. The coffee break, smoke break, and happy hour are the most culturally enshrined drug rituals in the modern era . . . an optimally attuned market economy needs alert employees who work as hard as possible for as long as possible. So dedicated time-outs for stimulant consumption that is the coffee break . . . are institutionally sanctioned and socially reinforced, which is where the cocktails come in . . . add in some booze from time to time and you have a cycle of stimulation, focus, decompression, that dovetails with broader economic goals."[7]

In short, the tractor beam of the Industrialists' Death Star is powerful because it triggers our biology, exploits our overvaluing and worth of work, and causes us to underdevelop fun. The hustle narrative is not serving you, it is not giving you a life to enjoy. But there is another factor we have to evaluate: why the most confident people are often the ones newest to the game.

These three tractor beams are the individual reasons why we get sucked into the hustle narrative, but there is one other phenomenon that researchers have observed. It is called the Dunning-Kruger effect. In 1999, two Cornell psychologists, David Dunning and Justin Kruger, were studying the logic, grammar, and sense of humor of a variety of subjects. They found that those with the lowest abilities had the most confidence.

In looking at an XY axis, with the X being skill and the Y being confidence, the Dunning-Kruger effect describes what happens when a person who begins with no skill in a particular subject and, consequently, no confidence, develops just a little bit of skill: confidence skyrockets. After that first burst, confidence diminishes and doesn't recover until much later.

Dunning and Kruger wrote, "Those with limited knowledge in a domain suffer a dual burden: Not only do they reach mistaken conclusions and make regrettable errors, but their incompetence robs them of the ability to realize it."[8] It is as if the same skills that are being acquired match those it takes to understand what is needed in a field. Early on, people have enough knowledge to be dangerous, but later they have enough knowledge to be grounded.

So, why does this matter in the context of the hustle narrative? Many of the loudest voices are those new to a cause. Those with amplified voices don't know what they don't know. Instead of following a hustle narrative, we should examine the science of the brain and explore what is actually emerging as best practices. The Dunning-Kruger effect shows us that when someone is new to a topic, they have elevated confidence in their understanding, but once they see the full complexity of the field, they are often deflated.

So let's examine these challenges and see how we can free ourselves of the tractor beam of the Industrialists.

SALARY VS. PROJECT-BASED MODELS

One of the biggest challenges we face in confronting the hustle narrative and the Industrialists' mentality is when looking at key performance indicator (KPI) models vs. salary models. A typical KPI model measures KPIs. This is a project-based approach instead of hourly- or salary-based. Most of the world works on a salary or hourly model.

First, let me tell you what I'm not going to do in this section. I am not going to give you the answer. I know as an author, I'm supposed to say, "Here is the exact model that will work every time." But that's just not the reality. There are some jobs and roles where an hourly or salary position makes the most sense, whereas others are better for a KPI model.

For example, if I am sick of folding laundry I may decide to outsource that. In negotiating payment, I really have two options: pay a specific amount per load or pay per hour. If I look at the pile of laundry and I say, "I think that is worth $50," then a certain dynamic emerges. Whoever is being paid now has an incentive to complete the task quickly. If they can fold the entire pile in an hour, even with those teeny tiny kids' socks that are a pain to match, that is $50 per hour. So there is an incentive to hurry and not make things perfect. But I may end up with laundry that is folded in a sloppy way.

If I pay hourly, that person may drag out the amount of time it takes them to complete a task. They may listen to a podcast and meticulously fold everything in a way that is nice, but not worth the extra cost.

In both of these situations, there are ways to improve on the flaws in each system. In the KPI model, I could have standards or expectations to make the folding count. With the hourly system, I could set a cap.

In moving away from the Industrialist system, we want to incorporate elements of allowing ourselves to slow down, build creativity, and optimize time while we are working. For example, this week we had a big push for the sale of Podcast Launch School. But the lady in charge of this had a wedding to go to. So she took off ten days. She set everything up. On the webinar for launch day, she started texting me. I texted back, "Aren't you on vacation? Stop worrying about this."

She wanted to make sure all the text worked correctly. I appreciate that attention to detail; that's why she's good at what she does. But if she can't relax with her family, then we're moving toward the Industrialists' mindset. She needed permission to step back and assurance that if things failed she wouldn't be blamed.

As the owner, I need to let go of having things run perfectly. For example, in an email campaign for this same launch, some links were not working. Earlier in the book, I talked about putting out immediate fires and figuring out systems to prevent them in the future. We'll do that same thing here: fix it now, examine what happened, and create a system to avoid that.

But things will happen. For example, in the webinar I said the price would go up by $100 at noon the next day. For some reason the automations were all set at 5:00 p.m. and the emails aligned with that. I had to say to myself, "It's not worth going through and redoing all this, especially when she's out of the office."

Next time, we'll talk and be clearer. Having the flexibility to see the organization as an organism is the key. These are people, not machines. This stands in contrast to what a recent marketing manager told me.

In the middle of the 2020 COVID-19 quarantine, the owner of a company told his marketing manager, "I don't care what's going on, we're paying for butts in chairs."

Butts in chairs, is that a KPI? What does that do for the bottom line of the company or for staff morale in a health crisis? It doesn't have to be this way. Even when you are later in your career, you can make a significant shift quickly.

TIM BROUGHT A CAKE TO A CONFERENCE

At a conference breakout session with about forty people at an oil and gas conference, Tim offered the team of mostly older white men a cake. He said, "This cake is for you. Soon this will be your retirement cake." They looked around not really understanding what he meant, so he continued.

"Soon, your legacy will be gone, and the next generation needs your knowledge."

Tim is a consulting engineer who focuses on prepared gas storage feasibility studies, inventory verification, tracer survey results, and expert testimony. He is known for environmentally friendly underground storage of gas. He came to me for counsel about adding new streams of revenue to his business.

At that point, much of his work was time- and project-based; he wanted something different.

As Tim and I started working together, we evaluated the value of knowledge about underground storage. Tim explained to me, "When gas prices go up and down, there's only so much capacity to move it. But if a company has underground reserves, they can take advantage of higher prices."

"What does this translate to financially?" I asked.

"Millions. If a company can position themselves and do this right, it can bring in millions," Tim replied.

We got to work identifying the pains that prevent companies contracting storage, replicating Tim's teachings, and, most importantly, identifying how Tim could stand out as a consultant.

Tim's first draft of his pitch almost put me to sleep. He was technical, long-winded, and very engineer-y.

I stopped Tim and said, "We have to think of this as a TED talk. What's the real story here?"

Tim started talking about how the field is getting older and older and knowledge isn't being passed on. We discussed how many of the older workers have a fear of being forgotten. They worry that their knowledge will just be lost and how they desire to make a greater impact and leave a legacy. By tapping into something deeper, Tim's focus was no longer on training gas guys, it was providing for a human need . . . to be remembered. To have lived a life that contributed to society.

At the conference, Tim captured their attention with a cake. "This cake is for you!" He flashed forward with each one to their retirement day. A lifetime of work and a cake. After he had their attention, he shared stats and figures about how many in the room would be retiring soon. The reality created a hush because, in five to ten years, more than half the people in the room would be out of the industry. Then he created an authentic sense of urgency to engage others to train the next generation. Tim created a pathway to resolve this tension. He invited them to join his Underground Natural Gas School. For $3,000, they could send their best young and emerging engineers to a three-day conference.

Tim sold out the first event and changed the direction of his life. Tim says, "I can't believe this is what I get to do now." As we enter the next chapter, we'll be discussing how you can continue to launch new projects that double and triple sales, but for now I want you to reflect on the core of Tim's story. It was all about meeting his potential clients' human needs. He saw their pain and offered them a transformation.

Tim wanted to examine the minimum viable product before he launched his Underground Natural Gas School. What was his investment? He flew to Texas, went to a conference, bought a cake, and printed some postcards to hand out for registration. As you'll see later, testing and pre-selling is the key to this kind of leveling up.

When I first started my website, PracticeofthePractice.com, I wanted to get content ideas before I started offering consulting, a membership community, and other services. So, I joined quite a few LinkedIn groups. Groups that are discussing topics that are relevant to your business are a great place to find content ideas.

The LinkedIn groups had rules against self-promotion. So I would look for posts where I could add value. There might be a question like, "Any tips on naming a private practice?"

Most people would just answer the question there. Instead, I wrote a blog post answering the question. Then I would take a paragraph and put it in the answer on LinkedIn. I'd say something like, "This is from a blog post I wrote about the topic; let me know if you want the link." More times than not, people would ask for the link, which was acceptable within the group rules.

The hustle narrative says to work harder. It values the 80/20 rule, where 20 percent of what you do gives 80 percent of the results. But if that's true, why don't we just work 20 percent of the time? The Industrialists argue that it takes the other 80 percent to find the 20 percent or that we don't know which 20 percent is giving those results. But I no longer buy that. With technological innovations, new apps, and an unspeakable number of new tracking devices, we can figure out what works.

We often imagine that we are starting from scratch and that's why we need so much time to discover what works. In reality, most innovative ideas are a repurposing and melding of other good ideas. Uber and Lyft melded smartphones and on-demand technology, even though both had been around for a while. Throughout the rest of this chapter, we'll be shifting into talking about techniques.

In part one we looked at your internal inclinations. This helped you to understand your baseline inclinations and how to develop habits and action. Then we looked at slowing down to optimize your brain. But now, what do you do with that optimized brain?

TRIGGERS: WE DO WHAT WE SEE

I put my insulin next to my toothbrush. I was diagnosed with Type 1 diabetes when I was thirty-two. It's sometimes called late onset, Type 3, or doctors just say, "Maybe a virus made your pancreas stop working." They don't really know why a relatively healthy guy all of a sudden got diabetes.

But even though I'm almost ten years into being diabetic, I sometimes forget to take my insulin. So I put it next to my toothbrush, and I never forget.

What we see, we do.

For the longest time, I pushed back against vision boards, journaling, or setting intentions. It seemed so woo-woo to me. Somehow, by cutting out a picture of a Hawaiian beach house and a MINI Cooper, you're all of a sudden going to own them. C'mon. I was further jaded when I met a woman in Missouri that had just read *The Secret*. She said, "This morning I woke up and set my intentions to the universe. For some reason I woke up wanting buffalo chicken wings. So I set an intention to the universe for chicken wings. I went to the nonprofit board I sit on for our monthly meeting. What were they serving for lunch? Chicken wings! The universe does provide."

To me, vision boards, journaling, and setting intentions felt a bit like Chicken Wing Lady, but recently I have changed. Now I think the important factor is that they keep you centered on your goal; they're triggers to keep your mind focused. Everyone's method may be different, but the goal is the same: stop getting distracted from things that matter.

Imagine I have a vision board featuring a Hawaiian beach house and a MINI Cooper. I'm probably going to start researching how much a house like that would cost; how I could make enough money to buy it; what I need to do today that will move me toward that goal.

If I journal to build gratitude or evaluate my goals, that will help me stay focused. Setting intentions, writing things on a mirror, or having a whiteboard with next steps, they are all just triggers.

What we see, we do.

These can be small things like putting out running shoes the night before, blocking out a schedule, or putting insulin next to the toothbrush. Or they can be bigger things like setting aside weekly time to work on bigger projects that don't move the needle forward but double and triple profits. So let's look at a few of these techniques.

It starts with our internal world, because it's what really moves things forward in my consulting work. Clients will often start with goals like, "What social media formats should I be participating on? Should we rebrand? How do I triple profits this coming year?" These are all questions that we might label as the "how" of the conversation. But our path to success starts much earlier than the "how" of things. Instead, we need to start with the right posture and orientation toward success; then a process can actually take you somewhere.

So, what is the process that I have developed over the years and seen work with thousands of clients who have enjoyed rapid and sustainable business growth and success? The process that I have repeated in my life and imparted to my consulting clients? Before we can get to the actual framework in the next chapter, the following concepts will make the soil more fertile. In the same way we optimized the brain by slowing down, these actions will optimize your business growth before we build the framework. Just remember the acronym FIRST.

Here's some of what I teach:

- **Fruit | Low-hanging fruit:** Identify what's already working and how we can effectively and rapidly enhance those systems.
- **Inflect | Act as if . . . :** By inflecting in a direction you seek, you're magnifying and pushing yourself to play bigger. To be clear, you are not lying, saying you are an expert when you are not, or

falsifying anything. I teach actions that build a brand and image that stand out quickly and are built on acting as if you are an expert (because you already are). It will also press you to grow your knowledge base, stories, and behavior faster while utilizing undervalued skills and expertise you already possess.

- **Reinvest | Make the business stronger:** This part of the approach trains you to quickly take off hats and know the real ROI on your time. My signature breakdown of how you value your time is one of the life changers in my process.
- **Specialize | Stand out and micro-niching:** Pick a market you can really stand out in as an expert. I teach how to get very specific and how to both recognize and attract your particular ideal client. Many are so worried that if they specialize, they will miss their market as they scoop up everyone. But serving too broad a market can be draining and you already know which part of the market excites and satisfies you best, but you may not yet be willing to admit it or embrace it. My process helps you find each other!
- **Time-limited | Six- and twelve-month goals:** Forget five-year plans and goals; we'll set up triggers and planning in really short timespans. You will begin to recognize triggers that call out for action.

One final guiding mindset before we dive into this: fall in love with the pain and the people before you pitch a product.

Most companies will spend a significant amount of time developing new products, without doing the testing needed. Building an audience of loyal customers, who feel you are helping them to overcome a pain and transform them into something new, is the essential ingredient to all of this.

Fruit: Low-hanging fruit

This first step in the process helps you decide how you want to scale. Most counselors, coaches, consultants, and small business owners already have some traction. They may have one-on-one clients, be known in their community, or even have an employee or two. But here is what I really need you to understand: they've given themselves a job, not a business. That's right. Maybe they dreamed of more flexibility than they had in previous employment, or they couldn't find the dream job they wanted. But they have just given themselves another job. To grow, you have to be able to step back from the one-on-one work. This phase is all about reducing hours and increasing revenue.

Typical low-hanging fruit includes raising prices; adding additional clinicians, agents, consultants, or other appropriate colleagues; or creating added value like an e-course that puts what you do well in front of others who can then share your knowledge without sharing your time.

The Low-Hanging Fruit phase is all about optimizing whatever is already working through:

1. Increasing profits.
2. Increasing engagement.
3. Decreasing your time on the work that brings in revenue.

Here are questions that help to get to the low-hanging fruit:

- If someone can't afford our current core service, what is the downsell?
- If someone wants a more high-touch or concierge service, what is the upsell?
- How can we automate all or most of our process in a self-guided course or service?
- What are our clients asking for that we don't provide?
- What do we refer out that we don't provide; is there a new offering there?
- If the owner took three months off, what would we need to automate or systematize?
- After clients go through our product offering, what is their natural next step? Do we offer that?
- How long do clients stay with us; how could we double that? Why do they leave?

Inflect | Act as if . . .

Step two in this process is to begin to build expertise. The word "inflect" means "to bend; turn from a direct line or course" or to "alter or adapt." When you move away from your typical course, it magnifies what you're doing. We're not talking about representing yourself as something you are not. But to push yourself to expand. When you start to act as if you are moving in a stronger direction, others join you.

We know from numerous research studies that your best work and peak performance will come when you are slightly outside of your full potential and offering. Stepping into work that stretches your ability will attract high-end clients, open you up to relationships and partnerships beyond your current offering, and force you to rapidly build your skill set.

Typical ways of doing this are to create offerings for services you have yet to develop, begin speaking on topics where you are a growing expert, or joining groups where you are not yet the leading expert. In doing this, you grow your skills and attract new clients.

The Inflect phase is all about stretching your skill set to:

1. Explore new waters for business development.
2. Attract a different set of clients.
3. Align with experts that are beyond your skill set.

Here are some questions to help you grow your Inflect phase:

- What skills do you have that are not top of mind?
- What experiences have given you more expertise?
- What groups or organizations align with your growing expertise?
- What new markets are you interested in?
- What emotional triggers do you need to work on to build your confidence?
- What daily mindsets need to change to convince yourself you have authority?
- What content could you create to build your own shift in expertise?

Reinvest | Make the business stronger

Mostly likely you are spending time on things that could be outsourced. Peter Drucker said, "Do what you do best and outsource the rest." Reinvestment is in people, processes, and systems. As a business leader (whatever your phase), your time needs to be as lean as possible. That frees up your creativity and ability to go after the big game-changing ideas instead of the daily fires within a business. Reinvestment is a way to free up your time. It can be small things like personally paying someone to mow your lawn, do your laundry, or clean your house. Or it could be to hire someone to interact more directly with clients, build a dashboard of essential reports, or oversee specific aspects of your role. When evaluating your own time, you have to ask, "Why am I spending time on this?"

The Reinvest phase is all about:

1. Freeing up your time to optimize your brain.
2. Working on the best projects and ideas for massive growth.
3. Building systems to expand beyond you.

Here are some questions to help you grow your Reinvest phase:

- If you had only fifteen hours a week to work, what would be the core things you would spend time on?
- If you were going on a six-week sabbatical where your staff and clients could not reach you, what systems would need to be in place?
- If you were allowed only fifteen minutes per day on email, what would an assistant need to know if they were overseeing your email?
- What activities do you dread? Is your participation essential?
- What is your hour worth?
- If you only needed to work on projects that had the potential to grow the business by 200 to 300 percent in the next year, what would you work on?

Specialize | Standing out and micro-niching

Are you micro-niching? Customers will assume a specialist is a generalist, but they won't assume a generalist is a specialist. When you hyper-specialize, you give yourself the ability to charge more, have stronger offerings, and work with only your favorite clients.

Typical ways of micro-niching are to look at your clients and determine who has spent the most money and has been the easiest to work with. Refine your offerings into the most specific and most profitable services or products. Lastly, evaluate emerging markets and look into what training and marketing could be done in that area.

The Specialize phase is all about:

1. Refining your customer base to those you most enjoy.
2. Increasing the overall customer value.
3. Increasing specialization to level up quicker than competitors.

Here are some questions to help you grow your Specialize phase:

- Which customers do you love working with?
- What type of customer has brought in the most revenue for the company?
- What work, direction, or services are you sick of offering as a company?
- What are you personally interested in? Is there a market for that?
- If you had to maintain the same revenue with only 10 percent of your current clients, how would you do that?
- In your industry, where are people being served already; is there a refined and specialized version of that since there is already a market?
- In your industry, where are people being underserved; is there a specialization there?

Time Limited | Six- to twelve-month goals

Five-year goals suck. Did you set a goal for yourself five years ago? How accurate was your prediction? Be honest. I had a general direction, but there's no way I could have anticipated the growth, new connections, or technological advances of the last five years. I hate five-year goals. A general direction is fine, like, "I'd like a lake house," or "I want to care less financially," but having a goal is much different than a direction.

Forget five-year plans and goals; we'll set up triggers and planning in really short timespans. You will begin to recognize triggers that call out for action. Realistically, we have no idea what the market dynamics, technology, or life circumstances will be that define our decisionmaking in five years. Modern living is rapid-fire, so instead of spending energy on longer-term goals, we focus on six- to twelve-month goals, which is a time period that sets a pace of urgency and forward motion and within which you can see real change.

The Time-Limited phase is all about:

1. Setting short-term goals and sprints to get more done.
2. Adjusting to your customer base quickly.
3. Being agile enough to change directions as your business changes.

Here are some questions to help you grow your Time-Limited phase:

- How do you want the company to be different in six months?
- What steps do you need to take this month to achieve those goals?
- If a six-month goal was to be completed this month, what would need to happen?
- How do you want your personal life, time, and slowing down to look in six months?
- What needs to shift off your plate to work on the big goals?
- Where are you wasting time now?
- What if you spent half as much time planning and twice as much time implementing; what would that look like?

- Are you focusing too much on accuracy and perfection instead of implementation and speed?
- If you were ahead of schedule on everything, how would that feel?

Now that we have laid out FIRST, it's time to really dive into how we Kill It in business!

9

KILLIN' IT IS THE YIN

TO SLOW DOWN'S YANG

Do what you do best, and outsource the rest.
—Peter Drucker

Ted Forester is the Auto Technologies Operations Manager at Kalamazoo Valley Community College in southwest Michigan. He's a professor working with students in the area of auto technology. But he's a bit of a legend on campus. In October 2009, he made a presentation to the KVCC board of trustees that would change the workweek for the entire college. But it didn't start in 2009. Four years earlier, Ted was put in charge of observing energy within the HVAC systems at the college.

Ted explained what he saw as the energy manager: "At your house when you need air-conditioning, you have a thermostat. When it hits that set point, it shuts down. That's not the way it is in these larger buildings. These larger buildings are designed to run twenty-four hours a day, seven days a week. It is an energy monster. Imagine running a furnace to heat up your house in the summer. For a large business or school system, the HVAC system runs completely different from home."

Ted began to implement innovative solutions in the summer. He determined when the buildings were occupied and started to move away from running the HVAC system 24/7. He changed the model to turn off the system in the evenings and over the weekend. By doing this, he saved the college $3 million over four years. In October 2009, the board wanted to know more about how the energy program was working, but three months earlier, Ted had the foresight to start taking pictures.

On Fridays in July, Ted would take pictures of the KVCC parking lot. He'd walk through typically populated areas and photograph them. They were nearly empty. He started collecting data from computer labs and other services. "How many people are you servicing a day on Fridays in the summer?" Usually it was only a handful. He quietly gathered data and put together a presentation without his boss or the vice president knowing about it. He kept the presentation on his key chain in case the opportunity arose.

Honestly, it's such a ninja move. Ted, an HVAC energy guy with a specialty in automotive technology, was a guerrilla warrior quietly planning an attack on the Industrialists.

Then the moment came. He was asked to present to the board of trustees, the elected officials that oversee the college. They are the college president's bosses. He presented on the economic impact of shutting down the system for evenings and weekends. It had saved $3 million. After his presentation was completed, he anticipated the final follow-up question, "How can we save more money?"

"Well, I've put together a short presentation. It will take about five minutes; would you like to see it?"

"I'd love to hear it," President Marilyn Schlack said.

Just stop for a second to think about the guts it took for Ted to do this. His boss had no idea he had this presentation. He's now in front of the president of the college and the board of trustees sharing his covert mission.

The board agreed to hear his presentation. Ted's focus was on the difference between July Fridays and October Fridays. The parking lot, hallways, and communal areas were all but empty. Computer labs were not in use and Fridays were often needless for students. He completed the presentation.

"What was the reaction by the board and the president when they heard this?" I asked him.

"Crickets. A lot of head shaking but not a word said. What they decided to do with it is on them. If they didn't like it, I wouldn't do it. But I had to present it to them."

The next summer, 2010, KVCC implemented a four-day workweek for summer. Employees worked thirty-six hours over four days, and HR "gifted" the other four. Ted calculated the numbers, savings, and challenges of the first years.[1] Initial projections were that the project would save $100,000 to $500,000 per summer depending on how many extreme heat days fell on Fridays.

By 2020, KVCC had saved over $2.5 million by not working on Fridays in the summer. Now, when the board of trustees votes annually, the money isn't even the driving factor; it's the staff engagement and quality of life.

Ted said, "People love it and I'll tell you why. Giving people Friday off gives people family time . . . it builds a stronger, happier family. It gives you some time, especially in the summer, to spend with the family. We live such busy lives nowadays; our families are being destroyed because we don't have any time."

As I talked with Ted, it became apparent that the slowing down of the three-day weekend at KVCC made working more efficient Monday through Thursday. He spoke about a dynamic that is typical in prepping for a working Friday. People will save their easy tasks for Friday to make it a lighter day. But what has now happened is that people will integrate those tasks and get everything done faster. Slow down and then kill it.

We see the same thing at Slow Down School. Remember Michael Glavin, the guy who skipped the "unskippable" stone? When he did that, it was his second year at Slow Down School. In year one, he was struggling through capturing, creating, and launching a process to help couples and relationship therapists.

Michael had been in my Mastermind group, focusing on his big idea for several months. He wasn't feeling motivated and there were numerous obstacles to formulating his ideas. He second-guessed himself because of an early-career supervisor who was harsh and verbally abusive to supervisees. For Michael, Slow Down School broke open the opportunity to come out of his shell and see himself as the amazing professional the rest of us already saw.

That year, we did a silent disco party (where you play music through headphones, then you can chat without screaming). Michael reluctantly joined in and got mad props from other dancers. We did some improv on the beach and he had one of the funniest improv skits I have ever seen (mind you, none of us had skills or experience in improv).[2]

From Sunday to Wednesday morning, the pressure valve is building. Despite slowing down, participants get excited about working. They want to sprint! We often hear, "I don't know if I'm more excited to slow down or to sprint!"

Yes, that's the point! Most authors, influencers, and teachers take one side or the other. Hustle harder! Or meditate more!

But that's why this works; we absolutely love the slowing down and we absolutely love the killin' it! Back to Michael. So it's Wednesday morning. I outlined our Sprint Structure™ that I'll share later in the book. Michael has the framework and goes off for a twenty-minute sprint. I'm floating around helping people. Inside the library, soft music plays with soft lights on. Other people go outside for their sprint.

Michael is sitting on the grass. We talk through his book, ideas, and planning. His first sprint was mostly about framing out the sprints. Sometimes that is what you have to do: think about what you're going to think about. Even writing this chapter, I felt stuck as I started. So I changed the music, then turned it off. I stepped back. Then I asked, "What are the questions or pushbacks for killin' it?" I brainstormed on my whiteboard. Then it started to come together.

Sometimes you have to take time to plan your plan. That's what Michael needed. Then the timer buzzed and I forced everyone to come inside the library.

"But I'm in a flow!"

"I want to keep working."

"Do I have to?"

You would have thought it was an elementary school. "Yes, you have to."

I was building the tension and pressure to want to work faster and harder. We did a quick five-minute standing debrief. "What worked? What do you need for the next sprint? Where do you need help?"

In the next twenty-minute sprint, Michael sketched out seven chapters with five to seven bullet points under each. "I got months of brainstorming done in twenty minutes; this actually works!" he said.

Welcome to my approach where I challenge conventional ideas. You see, I view the heavy lifting in my process as giving yourself over to slowing down. This allows for your creativity and all your vitality to set the path for what you truly desire. Killin' It is important for sure, but in this part of the rhythm you enlist and enact what you know needs to get done, only to return to your charging station of slowing down for the next round. It is the ideal orbit!

In this chapter, we're going to look at tools and mindsets that determine the orbital path for how these two interact and support each other. When the orbital path works, there is an almost automatic, yet totally vibrant, rhythm and frequency between the two.

Here is a good exercise to get us started:

1. How do I take ownership of my baggage, shortcomings, and frustrations and have a happier life?
2. What is the unhealthy behavior others see when you're not at your best?
3. What is the situation that fuels this?
4. What actions should you take?

Then:

1. What will get in the way of these actions?
2. What would life look like if you did these actions on a regular basis?

This chapter is jam-packed with the exact actions and processes I use to help people have shorter workweeks and level up. First, we'll look at what type of sprinter you will be. Once you identify your Sprinter Type™ we will examine the macro flow of sprinting in a week. These include identifying bolts and levels, single best, and focused sprint. In this section, we will examine what works (and how to amplify that), time blocking, and flow research. Next, we will reexamine the Three Questions to Launch™, and other practical shifts (you'll see why I call them "shifts" in a minute) to get the most out of your sprints. Lastly, we will look at practical case studies in a variety of environments such as solopreneurs, small teams, and organizations/agencies.

WHICH TYPE OF SPRINTER ARE YOU?

Einstein said, "Life is like riding a bicycle. To keep your balance you must keep moving." But he also said, "He who can no longer pause to wonder and stand rapt in awe is as good as dead; his eyes are closed." So which is it? Do we keep moving or pause?

I would argue (although I'm not sure I would actually try to argue with Einstein) that when Einstein speaks of "balance coming from moving" he does not say that movement needs to be work. Movement can come from learning, understanding, experiences, or just plain lack of stagnation. In other words, be someone different today than you were last week, a year ago, or a decade ago. Stagnation, not rest, is the enemy.

I bring this up because, when people hear my admiration of the hare over the tortoise, they often disagree; they push back. The way that people sprint can be very different. Deep inside of me, I have been a hard-core sprinter and a hard-core rester. Earlier, I mentioned my college schedule. I wanted to jam-pack all my credits in four days and know that I had nothing scheduled for three days. Even the semester that I took twenty-one credit hours, it was over a four-day workweek.

That's me. Your schedule will look different. But there are three guiding principles before we look at your sprinter-type.

1. **Do your very best work first.** By doing this, you allow yourself to perform your work with severe boundaries. This exposes what work is most likely to level you up.
2. **Be uncompromising about your boundaries.** Do not let emails, texts, and work slowly creep in. If you know that you must work on a Friday, schedule a limited time for it. Don't let it creep in or your overvalued work and underdeveloped fun will continue.
3. **Give yourself less time.** When you keep pulling in the time you take to complete tasks and deadlines, you may do work that is less than perfect, but remember that speed is greater than accuracy (unless you're my surgeon, then spend all the time you need). This builds the muscle of productivity when it's time to work.

There are four primary types of sprinters with two differences on each axis. There is the use of time within the day and there is the use of time within the week.

1. **Time-Block Sprinter** will set aside a minimum of one hour and a maximum of four hours at a time to work on one specific task, outcome, or project. This person tends to stay highly focused during this time and takes minor breaks.
2. **Task-Switch Sprinter** intentionally switches tasks every twenty minutes or so. They set a timer and determine each sprint's purpose. For example, they may work on copy for a blog post for twenty minutes, then do a call with a client lead; next, they check email, walk outside during a call, and then approve a project's final stage.

So, which are you? Do you tend to focus on one project for a longer period of time and batch it, or do you tend to strategically switch tasks? Most people think they are doing one or the other but are distracted during a time block or all over the place when they are task-switching.

Next, how do you plan your sprints?

1. **Automated Sprinter** sets a schedule to repeat, usually weekly. For example, on Thursdays I do most of my writing for the week. My consulting, podcasting, and other projects are complete, and Thursday is more of a creative day. I block out the whole day, but usually do four hours or so in the morning. This repeats in my schedule weekly.
2. **Intensive Sprinter** schedules a multi-day intensive or retreat with a specific sprint purpose over that time. It could be reading, thinking, planning, or working on a specific project or set of tasks. This is similar to Dr. Jeremy Sharp's practice of retreating for several days to sprint toward a project, gain ideas, and level up.

So, which are you? Do you see yourself setting aside time weekly and automating that? Or do you see yourself having a scheduled intensive every month or quarter?

Let's mix these all together now:

1. **The Time-Block + Automated Sprinter:** This is me. I prefer to have a very specific task, like writing, podcasting, or working

on a webinar for one to four hours. I have specific projects to work on scheduled in my calendar weekly. I can look ahead months and see the big projects and sprints I will be tackling. The Time-Block + Automated Sprinter often takes big bites out of projects over time but can also overthink deadlines since the end is not always clear.

2. **The Time-Block + Intensive Sprinter** works on one major task, but instead of working on it weekly, they get away and spend a few days doing it all at once. During a retreat, for example, this sprinter may write, film, and launch an e-course, webinar promotion, and set up all the Facebook Ads. At the end of the intensive period, everything is done. This sprinter gets a significant amount of work done in a short period of time but may miss the feedback needed when a project lasts longer.

3. **The Task-Switch + Automated Sprinter** values variety. They will have weekly time blocked out and rotate between several aspects of leveling up, keeping all the plates spinning. They often get more feedback from a variety of areas, but are also more likely to be distracted into meaningless work that has very little ROI.

4. **The Task-Switch + Intensive Sprinter** plans several days to complete a variety of projects and tasks. They pre-plan to get the most important items completed quickly and leave feeling relieved. They usually finish a load of tasks quickly, but may accidentally spend time checking things off a list, rather than having the sprint focus on really big projects that will help them level up.

All four of these Sprinter Types™ have pros and cons. The biggest thing is to remember the original three principles:

1. Do your very best work first.
2. Be uncompromising about your boundaries.
3. Give yourself less time.

There are times that different projects and tasks require you to adjust. Even if your tendency is one type of sprint, know that you can integrate all four types.

GET THE BOLTS AND LEVELS RIGHT

Next, I'll describe a macro process that will allow you to get the most out of these sprints. Here are the steps:

1. Identify bolts and levels.
2. Determine the single best use of your time.
3. Plan a focused sprint.

If you have ever owned anything constructed with a bolt, you have probably noticed that over time that bolt loosens. Maybe it's the bike brakes, the lawn mower casing, or a wobbly table leg. We need to examine the bolts in our business, too, the things that loosen over time. Things wear down, and past levels of performance aren't what they were. Levels can refer to those areas that are no longer straight or levels that need to be pulled. Where are there new processes and areas of improvement within the business? Bolts and levels are the things in a business that need to keep moving to keep revenue coming in and to stay true to the original mission. They may not be the most exciting, but they create a stronger structure for the entire business.

For example, I originally began my blog and podcast, *Practice of the Practice*, to help counselors, social workers, and psychologists to start a private practice. Over time, more people wanted training to open group practices and expand. I've become known as the guy that can help you grow your practice. We need to stay true to that *Practice of the Practice* audience or slowly pivot. Otherwise, we lose people and income.

Our bolts and levels are the measures we examine to make sure we are still doing what has worked in the past. We keep our membership community, Next Level Practice, going. We continue with consulting and Mastermind groups while serving through the podcast. Before I look to try something new, I need to tighten the bolts and examine the levels.

Since my goal is never to work more hours long term, if things aren't cleaned up before we start a new project, there will be more on my plate (or my team's plate). If it starts messy, growth will only expand that mess.

That's why we start with bolts and levels. Typical bolts to examine are systems, sales acquisition, items that can be outsourced, and what is frustrating clients. How can everything run as smoothly and cleanly as possible, while also not falling prey to overthinking?

When we examine typical levels, we'll want to populate the dashboard with KPIs. How will we know if the business is still on track? Typically, markers include revenue, people served, satisfaction, and our costs per hour. A leader in the company will want monthly access to three to five quick numbers that give a quick idea of the levels, freeing up time and energy for its best use.

To determine the single best use of your time, we need to examine the biggest ROI on your time. After rolling out complementary advertising campaigns, for example, you would probably run A/B tests to figure out which campaign brought in the most revenue for the least amount of money. In the same way, we want to A/B your time expenditures. ROI on time can come in a variety of forms:

- Direct sales
- Networking with others who become referral sources
- Expanding services and innovation
- Increasing systems and productivity
- Working on risky and unknown outcomes that could have a large impact on the bottom line
- Training someone else to do a task to free up your time

When examining the single best use of your time, think about what would be a huge level-up for you? We're not looking for 5 percent growth; we're looking for 100 to 200 percent. What has that looked like for me?

While I was working at the community college full-time, I was charging $125 per counseling session in my private practice. I knew if I added five more clients at $175 per session, that would be a huge level-up. So everything I did went through that filter. The next year, as my practice consulting grew, I knew I needed at least five clients paying me $500 per month to level up.

After that, I was able to leave the college. Next, I focused on building Mastermind groups, where I had six people in a group, meeting twice per month for at least $500 per person. That year I launched five groups. By the end of the year, I was charging $795 per month times 6 people = $4,770 for two hours of work per month. I also added in a weeklong conference and a few laser coaching sessions.

After that, I launched a membership community where we offer thirty-plus courses, live events, access to experts, logos, and other tools to grow a practice. Earlier, I showed how I created a community using the Three Questions to Launch™ formula and was able to charge more. Now we have more than four hundred people in the group. The earliest access cohort is paying $55 per month while new customers pay $99 per month. That brings in around $30,000 per month and takes me about three hours of work per month. After that, my goal was to get a traditionally published book deal. I knew that would grow my network, expand the audience for my message, and reveal other potential ways to level up.

See how I focused on the single best use of my time at each phase?

Will this get me more clients at the $175 rate?

Will this get me more consulting clients at the $500 per month level?

Will this get me people into my Mastermind group?

Will this grow my membership community?

Will this get me a book deal?

For you it may be much different but will still follow that pattern. Determine the single best use of your time, make it a priority, and see your work through that lens.

At every step, I asked if something was the single best use of my time. Other authors frame this in similar ways. Let's revisit how Gary Keller and Jay Papasan frame this idea in their book *The ONE Thing*: "What is the one thing I can do, such that by doing it everything else will be easier or unnecessary?"[3]

After tightening bolts and determining levels, and evaluating the single best use of your time, then begin focused sprints. Even if you are a Time-Block Sprinter who is planning to work on one topic or project for four hours, breaking up sprints into sections helps the brain to avoid vigilance decrement (vigilance = how well you pay attention, decrement = decreasing over time).

Here's the typical format for our Sprint Structures (see Figure 1):

1. **Pre-sprint:** Set aside at least twenty minutes for the sprint. Put your phone on airplane mode to avoid any interruptions. Think

for one minute about what you want to achieve in this sprint and what you need for this sprint (passwords, a cup of coffee, notepad, data, etc.). Maybe change the setting through music or lighting. Decide: "During this sprint, I will achieve _____."
Examples are:

Structuring a blog post
Writing a blog post
Scheduling social media posts
Emailing potential podcast guests
Evaluating particular systems in your business (bolts and levels)

2. **Sprint:** Set a timer for at least twenty minutes and focus on completing the task at hand. Do not stop, do not edit, do not evaluate, just keep working. You can have an editing sprint later, but the focus of the sprint is to get three to four times more done than usual. When the timer goes off, stop immediately. You will want to work; you'll feel in flow. But, when you first start doing this, it is important to stop. This builds the tension and excitement for the next sprint, so you get more done then too.

3. **Post-sprint:** Reflect on what worked during that sprint; what do you need for the next one? How could you work even faster?

— SPRINT STRUCTURE —

A SPRINT IS A 20 MINUTE FULL TILT RUN TOWARD A GOAL.	THINK FOR ONE MINUTE ABOUT WHAT YOU NEED FOR THIS SPRINT, THIS COULD BE:
Put your phone on airplane mode	DATA / NOTEPAD PASSWORD / CUP OF COFFEE
YOUR SPRINT ACHIEVEMENT SHOULD BE A QUICK WIN, EXAMPLES ARE:	DURING THIS SPRINT, I WILL ACHIEVE:
• STRUCTURING A BLOG POST • WRITING A BLOG POST • SCHEDULING 5 SOCIAL MEDIA POSTS • EMAILING POTENTIAL PODCAST GUESTS • EVALUATING A SYSTEM IN YOUR BUSINESS	Now, let's kill it!

— SPRINT REFLECTION —

1. WHAT DID YOU TOTALLY ROCK OUT DURING THIS SPRINT? _____

2. WHAT TOOLS, RESOURCES, OR INFORMATION DO YOU NEED FOR THE NEXT SPRINT? _____

FIGURE 1: PRINTABLE DOWNLOAD AT WWW.JOESANOK.COM/RESOURCES

Why do sprints work so well? When we do this at Slow Down School, participants routinely say, "In those five sprints, I got more done than I get done in months of work!" Five twenty-minute sprints or one hundred minutes is greater than months of work?! Really? Really.

When we slow down, it allows our brains to get excited about work. This is work that makes a difference in the world. We know it helps us level up. It taps into a feeling of "I was made for this." These feelings and emotions cause a biochemical reaction that lead to what researchers call "flow."

The Flow Genome Project's statement of purpose declares, "We are an interdisciplinary, global organization committed to research-based training of ultimate human performance."[4] On their website, they bring together research from a variety of disciplines. They cite a McKinsey & Company study that showed that a flow state increases productivity by 500 percent. *Harvard Business Review* says it this way: "In a ten-year study conducted by McKinsey, top executives reported being five times more productive in flow. Think about that for a moment. This means, if you can spend Monday in flow, you'll get as much done as your steady-state peers do in a week. In fact, according to these same McKinsey researchers, if we could increase the time we spend in flow by 15–20 percent, overall workplace productivity would almost double."[5] Further, DARPA (Defense Advanced Research Projects Agency) has done research on flow states, and found a 490 percent improvement in learning during flow states.[6]

It's not just entrepreneurs and businesses that are employing these tactics; the military is as well.[7] DARPA has publicly reported these projects—funded by US taxpayers—to examine brain optimization:

- An Arizona State University team is targeting trigeminal nerve stimulation to promote synaptic plasticity in the brain's sensorimotor and visual systems.
- A Johns Hopkins University–Maryland team focuses on brain regions involved in speech and hearing to understand plasticity's effects on language learning.
- A University of Florida team is identifying which brain neural pathways VNS activates.
- A University of Maryland team is studying the impact of VNS on foreign language learning.

- A University of Texas–Dallas team is identifying stimulation parameters to maximize plasticity, and comparing the effects of invasive versus non-invasive stimulation in people with tinnitus as they perform complex learning tasks such as acquiring a foreign language.
- A University of Wisconsin team is using state-of-the-art optical imaging, electrophysiology, and neurochemical sensing techniques in animal models to measure the influence of vagal and trigeminal nerve stimulation on boosting neuromodulatory neuron activity in the brain.

Collectively, these studies hope to help with the following areas: "intelligence, surveillance and reconnaissance and another practicing marksmanship and decisionmaking . . . ability to discriminate phonemes—sounds that distinguish one word from another—learn words and grammar, and produce unique sounds used in some foreign languages . . . perception, executive function, decisionmaking and spatial navigation . . . decisionmaking regions in the prefrontal cortex, and optimize VNS parameters in this circuitry . . . neural function during speech perception, vocabulary and grammar training . . . learning tasks such as acquiring a foreign language . . . vagal and trigeminal nerve stimulation on boosting neuromodulatory neuron activity in the brain."[8]

So there it is, the macro plan for your next steps:

1. Identify bolts and levels.
2. Determine the single best use of your time.
3. Do focused sprints.

That's the macro flow of how you can implement these best practices. Now we are going to examine individual shifts that can be part of the menu of actions you will take.

PRACTICAL SHIFTS

I prefer "shifts" to the words "tools" or "actions."[9] For most people, a "shift" feels delicate, easy, just a slight tilt. In most self-help books, the psychology of habits and change isn't usually considered. Instead, the reader is handed a to-do list, which may feel like a monumental assignment, and which often leaves the poor reader feeling guilty and unaccomplished.

If we're going to optimize the brain, it will happen in shifts in thinking and action. So view these shifts as another menu to draw from, not an all-inclusive list. These shifts fall into three major categories: mindset shifts, planning shifts, and action shifts. I'm going to give a few practical examples, but, again, this section is far from inclusive. However, the concepts should be applicable within almost any business environment.

Mindset Shift #1: Pain + People = Product

With Mindset Shifts we adjust how we think about our business, customer engagement, and leveling up. First, the core of the plan: "Fall in love with the pain and the people before you ever pitch a product." I mentioned this when we looked at your Curiosity Assessment and also in the Triggers section. But it is worth revisiting. As I train podcasters, they frequently have ideas about e-courses, membership communities, or other products. But they have no clue how their audience or current customers will respond.

Most people will agree on the surface. "Yes, of course I want to know my clients' pain!" they will say to me. Then they will talk about how they have sketched out the perfect solution. Yet they have not done market research, focus groups, calls, or tests.

Mindset Shift #2: Pain to Transformation

Next, we always want to go back to the Pain to Transformation Formula™. In everything you do, you are diagnosing the pain that you mean to address and the transformation you are promoting. This should be true in meetings, emails, website copy, and products. For example, maybe a team is creating a landing page for a webinar that will provide great content and then have an offer that will sell a product. Start with the audience's pain. Why are they spending time on this webinar? What transformation will they undergo without ever giving us a dime? How will they be changed for the good as a result of this time together?

Mindset Shift #3: Give Up the Control

Another Mindset Shift focuses on giving up control of the "how" in team development. To move away from the Industrialist mindset, one clear shift is having the "how" be worked out by the team. Earlier, we discussed how you need to examine what only you can do, what you love doing but shouldn't do, and what you hate doing. I go through that process regularly. With a team, it's important to have members change roles, level up, and learn.

Recently, our Organization Guru (that was her official title) told me she just wanted to focus on helping podcasters launch. So we looked at all she wanted off her plate and asked the team who wanted those items. If no one had wanted them, we would have hired another person. The Director of Details (that is her official title) liked leveling up her skills. I said to the two of them: "Spend some time discussing the transition; let me know the timeline and what you need from me."

They co-create the handoff, own the process, and have pure ownership of the tasks and outcomes. I save a ton in training time. Even the old model of hiring for a role is outdated (but that's for another book). If we see our business as an organism that is changing, improving, and adapting, instead of a stagnant machine, of course we wouldn't hire for a role and keep someone there indefinitely.

Mindset Shift #4: Experiment vs. Failure

Remember our curiosity inclination quiz? There is real value in viewing almost everything as an experiment. Results for most things you're engaged in are not pass/fail but can just be part of the data for the experiment. Think like a scientist who examines the variables that influence an outcome.

Thinking about things as pass/fail can paralyze or delay you. If you approach projects and ideas as an experiment, it relieves the pressure and allows you to try new things without the fear of failure because, in an experiment, "failure" is just more valuable data. Success is a process, not an arrival point. Experiment, gather data, consider the variables, tweak, and move forward.

Mindset Shift #5: We > Me

Having consulted one-on-one with hundreds of practice owners, run numerous Mastermind groups, and hosted several conferences, I see the same struggle when people move from the Growth Phase to the Scaling Phase.

In the Growth Phase you're still wearing numerous hats. You're hovering in the high five-figure and low six-figure range of income. But you start to realize that you're turning people away and you need to add more staff, more professionals, or more employees. But your systems aren't quite there to support that. You might need to hire a virtual assistant to answer the phones, an accountant and bookkeeper, an on-call IT company, or someone to start cleaning your office.

The Scaling Phase Switch is one of the hardest, because it is about letting go. But it's not really letting go; it's systematizing. How can someone else sound like you? Or think like you? Most practice and business owners don't think about what it is they do. They just do it. That's why they are successful; a lot of it is innate. But that innate ability does not automatically transfer to their staff. I'll include tested tools, tips, and checks that accelerate this phase and ease stress during this critical transition.

Success requires you to understand that "we" is greater than "me" when you begin and continue to scale outside what you alone can accomplish.

Mindset Shift #6: You're Okay

Realize that you're okay. Achievement and growth should be about becoming the best version of yourself while creating the best environment within which to thrive. Thriving extends beyond you. Demand from yourself that the ways in which you spend your time working are fun and exciting, not exhausting and constantly stress-inducing. Success has to come from a place of your own personal brilliance, not from a place of exhaustion, lack, or constantly proving yourself.

So let's talk about Planning Shifts. Mindset Shifts are all about the switches that need to change to enact that macro plan of bolts and levels, best use of your time, and sprinting. Planning Shifts are about moving from the right mindset to the right plan.

Planning Shift #1: 1:1 vs. 1:Many

Remember what I said earlier about giving yourself a job? The Industrialist mindset often traps you in an hourly-rate framework. You've just given yourself a job, not a business. Even if you are within a business, your job should not just be a job. Here's what often happens with some of my practical clients:

A counseling practice owner, let's call her Maria, accepts insurance and gets an average of $105.65 per session. At 20 sessions per week = $2,113/week.

To increase income, Maria hires three new clinicians and adds an office (or telehealth when a pandemic is happening); she gets 50 percent of what the clinicians bring in. Say they each see 15 clients at $105.65. Then 3 clinicians = $4,754.25 and 50 percent = $2,377.13/week. Maria has equaled her income by hiring others. That's great! This is where the We > Me Mindset comes in.

But let's say half of those sessions are on parenting. Maria notices that they are mostly seeing parents of middle school and high school students. The best question Maria needs to ask herself at this point is: "How do I go from 1:1 to 1:Many?"

Her exploration of this (based on her internal inclinations) might lead her to put together a video course, a monthly webinar, or a private Facebook Group for middle and high school parents.

Maria decides to offer a monthly webinar that is transcribed into an eBook each month. She sells it on Amazon to get extra exposure. She gets on one podcast interview per month to get the word out beyond her clients and connects with Mommy Bloggers. She figures it will take her three hours per month to build all this after the startup phase of the idea.

Once Maria launches her new initiative, she charges $29/month to participate and 40 percent of her practice clients join. That's 26 sets of parents x $29 = $754/month, and since she's spending three hours per month on it, that's $251.33 per hour she's now making, or 238 percent more than the insurance pays for her sessions! You can see how she was stuck when she couldn't see past her dependence on insurance payments.

Now imagine the podcast interviews pay off and she gets 10 new people to join per month that aren't from her practice and 10 new people per month from her practice. After a year, that's 240 people plus the original 26 for a total of 266. Say she loses 20 percent through the year, bringing her down to 213 sets of parents x $29/month = $6,177/month. If she's putting in extra time, say six hours a month instead of three, she's now making $1,029.50 per hour.

Can you see how moving from 1:1 to 1:Many can help you level up quickly? Maria made a shift from giving herself a job to growth to scaling. That's what making some strategic effort toward attracting ideal clients and creating services that go beyond what will keep the doors open and the lights on will do: it lets life in and moves you out of the struggle to a larger, more impactful play. You always want to be adding something of value that actually helps people have a better outcome. To get to these big ideas, you have to get into that rhythm between killin' it and slowing down.

Planning Shift #2: Life Blocking

The twin questions that I am most often asked as professionals begin to dedicate themselves to fighting the Industrialist mindset are:

"How do I actually get to the next level?"

"How do I get more done?"

The thought process that is called for here is to:

1. First understand how you define your life.
2. Then decide how you want to spend your time.

This is a topic that my friend Pete Kirkwood and I have explored together on the *Happitalist Podcast*. Pete has spent a ton of time exploring the research about well-being. The quick overview of Pete's macro research is that after our basic needs are met, every dollar provides less and less happiness. Our basic needs can usually be met with between $80,000 and $120,000. Each dollar above that will give less happiness than spending time on other things. Meaningful work, volunteering, learning a new skill, or spending time in nature will all give you a better ROI on your time than just making more money. The absolute best way to make progress on your goals is to commit time to them and block them out in your schedule.

We just saw how to do this as you explored your Sprinter Type.

Life-blocking is the action to take here. Whatever is most important needs to be put in your schedule first. Here's how it looks:

1. **What is most important for your life?** Think through socialization; time to be a partner/parent/personal time. Think through your innovation, influence, and impact. This is where we move from the underdeveloped fun to putting those things into your schedule strategically before work takes their place.

2. **Run the numbers.** How much time and money do you need to make this happen? For example, if you need to take home an average of $10,000 per month to serve your family, then maybe you need to bring in $15,000 per month, which is $180,000 per year. If you know the actual numbers, it's easier to take time for the life plans! If your commitment is to eat better and exercise more, what would the schedule for that look like? Maybe it means leaving your desk at lunch and taking a full hour. Perhaps it means scheduling a prep day to allow more access to better meals. Or, on the cost side, it could mean hiring a nutritionist or ordering healthy, prepared meals that are delivered directly. There is a time commitment and a dollar amount associated with your goal or desire.

3. **Block these time commitments out in your schedule.** For example, if you want more lunches with friends, put "Lunch with friends" in your calendar every Tuesday. If you want to work out, look ahead a few months and put the time on repeat. If you want to spend time with family, block out a time each week to be home by 3:00 p.m. on a weeknight. Block out the ideal, not the minimum, then if something comes up, you're still close to your target.

Show up for yourself in the same way you'd show up for a client, customer, or referral source. It's like an important meeting or a doctor's appointment. Schedule yourself first!

Planning Shift #3: Live Your Sprint Type

What type of sprinter are you? Get that in your calendar now. Train your team to follow it. Many people struggled with working from home during COVID-19 in early 2020. I heard friends talk about how kids were interrupting them, they couldn't focus, and that for a while they felt less productive. Of course, when the brain is under stress, numerous issues can be magnified. But, outside of that, setting clear expectations with those around you will ensure success.

For me, that is having clear boundaries with my family when I am working. I say, "I'm headed to work," I hug them, shut the door, and never respond when I hear kids freaking out.

I've mentioned how I did an experiment to take Fridays off in the summer. Experiment with your team to try to sprint more and work fewer hours. Remember, we made this entire five-day workweek up—actually, Henry Ford did. This model isn't even a hundred years old!

All right, we hit on the Mindset and Planning Shifts, now we'll cover practical Action Shifts that will help move things away from the Industrialists.

Action Shift #1: Repeat What Works

Steve Jobs often said, "Good artists borrow, great artists steal." This quote was stolen and slightly misquoted from Pablo Picasso who had said, "Lesser artists borrow; great artists steal." But Picasso stole this phrase and changed T. S. Elliot's phrase, "Immature poets imitate; mature poets steal; bad poets deface what they take, and good poets make it into something better, or at least something different. The good poet welds his theft into a whole of feeling which is unique, utterly different than that from which it is torn."[10]

In *Frozen II* there is a siren song that Elsa keeps hearing. No one else can hear it. It is like an invisible character pulling her "into the unknown" as the title song says. My daughters would walk around the house humming that Gb, F, Gb, Eb sequence. While looking up how to play it on the piano (I learn Disney songs mostly to impress my daughters), I discovered an interview with the writers of the song.

In New York, Kristen Anderson-Lopez and Robert Lopez explained the tune at a Deadline's event. "We made the voice sing the 'Dies Irae,' which is a Gregorian chant from the eleventh century. Composers from Sondheim to Berlioz to John Williams, it's in *Home Alone*, it's in *Star Wars*, it's in everything. It means death or danger." Anderson-Lopez said you can hear "Dies Irae" in *The Shining* too.[11] This riff from the eleventh century has been in over thirty films.[12]

The story of how the original *Frozen* was so bad they scrapped it and cobbled together a film made from the best parts of other films has become lore. Now in *Frozen II* they used a time-tested melody that worms its way into your subconscious and dreams.

Frequently, entrepreneurs believe they have to be original. But successful products, apps, and businesses often repeat what works. Smartphones + GPS = Uber/Lyft. That same type of technology was just reapplied to Airbnb. Birds and Nest scooters do it too. That's just one technology that has been applied to a variety of forms.

When you're looking for innovation, don't look for something new, look for a new application of something that is already working. I once heard a podcaster say, "When you find a unicorn, make tiny unicorns."[13]

About a year into my blog, I was doing research and found I had accidentally started ranking #1 in Google for the phrase "how to name a counseling practice?" It was bringing in a few hundred extra visitors a month. At the time, that was significant. I wrote a follow-up article, did a podcast, and created resources, all about how to name a private practice. Then I wrote articles for other types of businesses on how to name them. I found a unicorn and made mini-unicorns.

Action Shift #2: Information < Implementation

A common question I get when consulting with businesses and individuals is, "Isn't the market saturated?" Behind the question is often uncertainty over worth, offerings, and wanting a good ROI on consulting and staff time. No one wants to launch something only to say, "Wow, there's a lot of people in this space." Books like *Blue Ocean Strategy* talk through specifically how to stand out in competitive markets.

But key to understanding our new post-Industrialist schedule is to know that the Information Age is over. There is more than enough information in the world right now. In the last two years, nearly 90 percent of the world's data has been created![14] My wife fixed our washer and saved us $300 with a YouTube video and a $30 part. You can build, design, or launch just about anything if you have the time to search out information.

But the next phase is absolutely the Implementation Age. Apps, businesses, and technology that can aggregate the massive amounts of data and information into something usable will own this next phase. So, when someone asks about market saturation of information, yes, they are correct: there is more information than anyone needs. But when someone can shortcut the information acquisition process, that is where the money is right now.

Action Shift #3: Work on What's in Front of You

The last shift is a personal one. When you are sitting or standing (sitting is the new smoking, I hear) while you work, are you sprinting toward "what's the task at hand?" Is there extreme focus, flow, and fluidity? If not, change it. Otherwise, this entire system breaks down. If you work less and don't achieve more, you will go back to the life the Industrialists designed for you: that of being a machine. Don't check texts. Don't have pop-up reminders for email. Design a tunnel with clear boundaries for optimum productivity. Then slow down afterward.

HOW THIS LOOKS IN BUSINESSES

How This Looks for Solopreneurs

For solopreneurs, side-hustlers, and individuals in a service-based industry (counseling, law, chiropractor, etc.), this model can feel disruptive. Typical mindsets that block solopreneurs:

- I need to work to make money.
- Only I can do it best.
- I need to have eyes on the quality.

- Slowing down will make me lose my edge.
- Yes, I can do the billable work, but how will the rest get done?

When I consult with solopreneurs, we almost always look at their lifestyle first. For example, I have a client who is working thirty-five clinical hours per week. She is almost an archetype of so many clients I have met. Her thirty-five clinical hours translate into about fifty hours a week of actual work. Outsourcing, hiring, or creating systems could ease some of the tension, but she has resisted those solutions.

So what have we done? We have compared her needs to her income. Like many people, she can't take an economic cut. But she's in the trap of only getting paid when she works—she has a job, not a business. Ideally, she would work twenty-five clinical hours. Since each clinical hour also has about forty-five minutes of paperwork, marketing, and other items tied to it, reducing clients is key.

First, we establish the goal of total hours and total income. Then we examine raising prices for new clients. Remember earlier how I told the story about how I raised my prices? I was busy and didn't want to see anyone new, so I kept pushing up the price. That's exactly what we do. So this client raised her prices from $175 per session to $300 per session. She realized that with her waiting list and stress load, she couldn't build anything new without making a huge jump.

Now, she's positioned to explore a few income strategies that aren't tied to direct client work. So we examine her skill set and think about how it applies to the general public and how it applies to other professionals. People like Dr. Jeremy Sharp take their skills of testing psychologists and teach those skills to other professionals. Jessica Tappana took her SEO skills and helped other therapists. Whereas one of my consulting clients, Veronica Cisneros, took her skill set of helping women clinically and launched the *Empowered and Unapologetic Podcast*.[15] She helps women through retreats, courses, and a membership community.

So back to the fifty-plus-hour-a-week lady: We look at her skill set and examine where the general public needs help and where professionals need help. From there, it's just a matter of determining the single best use of time. Is it a podcast, being interviewed on podcasts, creating a course, eBook, or membership community? For most people it doesn't take a lot to replace ten hours of income.

To work ten hours less, she needed to replace the income of seven clients: 7 x $175 = $1,225 x 48 weeks a year = $58,800 or $4,900 per month. For the general population, this might be a parenting course that sells for $297. She'd need to sell 16.5 per month. At 5 percent conversion on a webinar, that means she needs to have 330 people on a webinar once per month. With a solid ad campaign, podcast, or affiliate connections, she could do this in about half the time it takes to see clients. Remember, she's replacing ten hours per week, so if it takes less than forty hours per month, she's ahead.

Another option is higher-end coaching with add-ons like group calls. To replace $4,900, she could have ten people who pay $490 that meet in weekly group coaching calls. That'd be four hours a month compared to forty.

In the first few months, this may take the full forty hours, but then the system is set up. With this solopreneur, I'd most likely have her take these steps and set aside time to determine one specialty area for the general public and one for professionals.

1. In online communities, research the main pain points for each of these groups.
2. Guest blog and be a guest on podcasts to build connections.
3. Create an email course (not a newsletter) that walks that population through the pain and transformation.
4. Do the Three Questions to Launch™ exercise once you have a hundred people on your email list.
5. Launch an early opt-in with the proposed product and price. This is an interest group that wants first access.
6. Set a date for opening access; limit the number of people in this first group.
7. Open for sales on that date.
8. Create the product after you sell it. Make sure you tell people ahead of time you are doing that.
9. Deliver an awesome product, course, or group or individual consultation. Get testimonials.

10. Create a webinar outlining the pain: the typical way people approach it, why that's wrong, and a few solutions. Give bonuses that aren't available during regular sales such as a live Q&A, lifetime access, or bonus downloads. Outline your program and give a discounted price for the next hour after the webinar. This should be 50 percent of the usual price. After that hour, go up to 70 percent of the original price for twenty-four hours, then go up to 80 percent for the next twenty-four hours. Then close the cart.

11. Deliver the product and refine, get feedback, and add free bonuses to keep people happy.

12. Rinse and repeat.

This is the exact step-by-step formula we have used to launch Podcast Launch School™, our e-course on podcasting and our membership community for professionals, Next Level Practice.

How This Looks for Small Businesses

Steve Glaveski is a small business owner and writer. In his *Harvard Business Review* article, "The Case for the 6-Hour Workday,"[16] he discusses a two-week experiment he did with his team. He says, "I conducted a two-week, six-hour workday experiment with my team. . . . The shorter workday forced the team to prioritize effectively, limit interruptions, and operate at a much more deliberate level for the first few hours of the day. The team maintained, and in some cases increased, its quantity and quality of work, with people reporting an improved mental state, and that they had more time for rest, family, friends, and other endeavors."

For small- and medium-sized businesses, experiments are typically the best approach to enacting these modalities. There is a tendency in the business-book world to have a perfect solution that fits for every team. Those books purport to capture exactly what every team should do. But more often than not, a top leader makes the decision without his team's buy-in and enacts his "solution" only to abandon it in favor of the next business-book fad. Instead of having a prescription, I want you to have a system for creating dialogue for experiments.

With small- and medium-sized businesses, experiments are the best approach to find what works for your particular team, business, and culture. Imagine you've been the only one reading this book and you're ready to make some changes. First, remember that we are moving away from the Industrialist approach. Industrialists think of a business and its people as a machine that can be perfected, optimized, and the end result is to set it and forget it.

Our approach views teams and businesses as organisms that are adapting, changing, evolving, and improving. So how does that look? First, start with a small team of six to twelve people. Anything larger than that gets messy. The boss, leader, or point person for an organization should not be the leader of the team, but a participant. Here are the three phases to enact the experiment:

1. Phase 1: Team brainstorm with bolts and levels
2. Phase 2: Experiment enacted
3. Phase 3: Assessment of experiment

In Phase 1, the team should gather for ninety minutes in a multi-use, non-boardroom setting where people can stand, break into small discussion groups, come back, and move. Pick a time when your team is well rested, not drained, and their brains are optimized. Consider allowing them to come in late on that day or meet off-site. Here are some questions to be considered (think of this as a menu to get to the goal of establishing an experiment):

- What rules do we need to enact in this meeting to help everyone feel safe to openly explore a creative experiment?
- What tasks are this team responsible for? Is this an effective use of our time? How do we track whether what we do helps the business?
- If we were to stop doing everything and leave for a month as a team, what would be the three biggest impacts to the company? What would be felt immediately?
- What do we hate doing that we would love to outsource? If you had that additional time, how would you spend it?
- If we worked thirty-two hours a week or shifted our schedules to be

more flexible, what would that mean for you personally?

- What have you been dying to learn, explore, or create that you would want to work on?
- What is the single best use of your time right now; what do you love doing but shouldn't be doing; what do you hate and wish you could pass off to someone else?
- Does anyone love doing what someone else hates doing?
- What type of experiments do you think we could do? How would we measure success, creativity, productivity, and whether or not this should be more than an experiment?

After the team establishes the experiment, how it will be measured, and, most importantly, boundaries to protect it, move into Phase 2 of enacting the experiment. Here are examples of experiments:[17]

- Take every Friday off for a month or summer.
- Outsource everyone's "I hate this" list for one quarter.
- Create a flexible schedule where the team is 100 percent in charge of when they come and go, meetings they attend, and the best use of their time.
- Cancel all meetings for a month or limit them to fifteen minutes each.

In Phase 3, the goal is to look backward and forward. Backward, how did this go? What worked? What are we onto? What didn't work? We gave it our best shot, then we realized that our culture here is this way. This experimentation process often reveals barriers that were unknown. Maybe it is a particular staff member, tendencies, feelings of inadequacy, or that the Industrialist mindset goes deeper than expected. Now, do it all over again.

How This Looks in Big Business

The German company Siemens is huge with over 380,000 employees. Their incoming CEO, Roland Busch, just announced this in a tweet:

The basis for this forward-looking working model is further development [of] our corporate culture. These changes will also be associated with a different leadership style, one that focuses on out-comes rather than on time spent at the office. We trust our employees and empower them to shape their work themselves so that they can achieve the best possible results. With the new way of working, we're motivating our employees while improving the company's perfor-mance capabilities and sharpening Siemens' profile as a flexible and attractive employer.[18]

In other words, in the world of COVID-19, things are rapidly changing. Hours in the seat should not be the KPI. Instead, projects completed and total value should be a measure. The truth about the forty-hour week is that Henry Ford pushed for it, so it happened. Before that, people worked six or seven days a week.

In May 2020, Gallup did a poll of worker engagement. This was in the midst of the COVID-19 pandemic when most people were working from home, juggling childcare, and worrying about disease. Unemployment was on the rise and there was uncertainty about the elections in late 2020, an economic downturn, and the future of work. There was a lot to be worried about.

But "Gallup found that in early May, the percentage of 'engaged' work-ers in the U.S.—those who are highly involved in, enthusiastic about, and committed to their work and workplace—reached 38 percent. This is the highest since Gallup began tracking the metric in 2000."[19]

Wait . . . in the middle of all this, engagement was up? And it was still only 38 percent! Maybe those who were disengaged were more likely to be laid off. Maybe in social isolation from quarantine, people wanted the connections and distraction. Maybe, finally, staff could make their own schedules and get the same results.

Instead of having to be in an office, after commuting an hour each way, they were spending more time with their families, trying new hobbies, baking bread, and juggling work and life. One of the remarkable positive consequences of this worldwide lockdown was that it was an experiment in working from home and making our own schedules.

The year 2020 was a year of turmoil, uncertainty, and anxiety; no one disputes that. But I believe that, as in May 1886 when the Haymarket Square protests changed the trajectory of work and May 1926 when

Henry Ford created the forty-hour workweek, May 2020 will come to be recognized as the birth of Thursday as the new Friday. It is the death of the Industrialists' machine way of thinking and a shift into organism thinking.

This shift is most difficult for larger businesses. Much like small and medium businesses, larger businesses need to think of teams as organs in a body that are evolving. As each person becomes healthier, works less, is more creative, and aligns their work with their strengths, exploration, and passion, the overall business will shift.

Like many movements, this is messy, usually coming from the bottom up, but needing the support of the top. There is deconstruction, testing, experiments, and revolution. When CEOs ask me what they can do, I suggest they get a diverse team of leaders together in the company. Gather a couple of C-suite people, mid-managers, creatives, and aspiring leaders. Get a group that is less than twelve. Together, run an experiment and see what it does for each person.

Focus less on the team and more on the personal. If the CEO and a handful of leaders experience a shift personally, they'll want to adopt some of the exercises of small/medium businesses.

In the final chapter, we'll be bringing all of this together into one plan for your life. Here we go!

10

YOUR BIG, SUCCESSFUL, HAPPY LIFE

Nature does not hurry, yet everything is accomplished.

—Lao Tzu

History has been leading to this moment. Hunter-gatherers and farmers didn't take major breaks or weekends. Spiritual traditions had long advocated a day of rest each week; this broke with the tradition of nonstop work. Until the late 1800s, the idea of a weekend wasn't a part of the human experience. In the 1920s, when Henry Ford pushed for a forty-hour workweek, we saw a shift toward a five-day workweek. Then the COVID-19 pandemic hit in early 2020. Globally a work-life experiment occurred. Families engaged in online school, remote work, and a different work schedule.

Many people found during that time that they could complete their "full-time" workweek in twenty-six to thirty hours.

But as is often the case, humans return to what they know. I was on a Zoom call with friends recently. Their employers are having them return to the physical workspace to make them work remotely there. One friend said, "It's like they want to train us to come back in again."

We laughed at the ridiculousness of their employers trying to have people come in physically despite it being completely unnecessary. It is the siren song of the Industrialists. Those employers fear their workers aren't working, assume they can't be trusted, and want to have butts in the seats.

Instead, they could examine appropriate outcomes, KPIs, and worker creativity. But, alas, evolution takes time. More often than not, humans return to what they know rather than exploring something new.

But this evolutionary process won't be complete. That is what needs more exploration. This is not my method and evolution; it is ours. You are a part of this. You will find new and creative ways to apply these principles and even to outgrow them. Your work, implementation, and advocacy will move us past the Industrialists and into a world of work, life, and play that allows us to slow down, not at the expense of productivity and creativity, but in support of it.

In this final chapter, we will recap the key principles of this book, examine the idea of starting from scratch, and create a plan for your life.

THE ESSENTIAL DNA OF THIS NEW ORGANISM

Throughout this book, we've deconstructed the Industrialist mentality. We have acknowledged that it was a step forward in its time and led to improvements in worker experiences, safety, and quality of life. But we've also found that the Industrialist legacy is outmoded.

In the old way of thinking, if you slow down or seek to be less productive, you're lazy. The Protestant Work Ethic is the pronouncement that a divine being wants you to use your talents in a way that leaves you too tired to do anything sinful in the world. The Industrialists see you as part of a machine; you can't stop. If your gear isn't there, the whole machine breaks down, so you are both essential and replaceable.

This approach values polarized thinking, black and white thinking, and magnification: what cognitive behaviorists call "thought distortions."

In the old way, you're tired. You can't give yourself permission to take time off without feeling guilty, and you intuitively know that something is way off.

Compare that to what Jesus is quoted as saying: "So why do you worry about clothing? Consider the lilies of the field, how they grow: they neither toil nor spin; and yet I say to you that even Solomon in all his glory was not arrayed like one of these. Now if God so clothes the grass of the field, which today is, and tomorrow is thrown into the oven, *will He* not much more *clothe* you, O you of little faith?"[1]

We're okay. The anxiety, worry, and stress can be replaced with slowing down and creating a contribution to the world that is creative and productive.

Let's look at the Ten Tenets of *Thursday Is the New Friday*:

1. **Internal Inclinations:** Before you run out into the world and move into a four-day workweek, know yourself first. Is it natural

or developing for you to have curiosity, have an Outsider Approach, and Move on It?

2. **Parkinson's Law:** Remember that work expands to the time given to it. In this section, we discussed whether you more frequently value accuracy over speed. Seek to move quickly; don't overthink or get paralyzed by perfection.

3. **Three Questions to Launch™:** The three questions that will make all the difference: What has that been like? (Diagnoses the pain). What is something I could create that would alleviate the pain? (Leads to the product.) How much would you pay for that? (Leads to the price.) Your customers explain their pain and the transformation they seek, so if your product authentically helps to relieve that pain, a purchase is the natural next step.

4. **Slow Down:** Most people will run full tilt until they are burned out, have blown out their nervous system, and wreck relationships. Flip it. Start by slowing down and then the work you do will be more exciting. Time off won't be a break from work but a refocusing on life. From that life, pull all that creativity and energy back into the work you do. We know that when we need a breakthrough, we need to get away, step back, and let our brains work through slowing down.

5. **Stop, Eliminate, Reduce:** If you slow down and then just start adding creative projects to your plate, you'll just get more stressed. Instead, work to minimize your current work environment tasks. Stop doing them, eliminate them, or reduce them. Have another person or system take over the non-essential. This will make room for new, more creative work.

6. **Growth Over Reaction:** Keep moving forward and proceed until apprehended. Encourage your team to try new things, gather information, and look up the river if there is a fire. In this approach, things will get screwed up. If everyone expects that, they can work more creatively, find work they enjoy, and pass off work that isn't aligned with their personalities. Remember, we're building an organism, not a machine.

7. **Boundaries and Breaks:** As you start to implement the slowing down and speeding up, it can be easy to fall back into

old patterns. Setting firm and clear boundaries allows you to know when work is done and slowing down is beginning. Having clear breaks will optimize your productivity and creativity.

8. **Triggers and the FIRST Model:** Whether it's a vision board, journal, writing on your mirror, or a sticky note, it's all the same in the brain; it's a trigger. We do what we see. That's why putting out clothes the night before saves time and protects your brain. Put that new medicine by your toothbrush. If we see it, we are more likely to do it. Remember the acronym FIRST: Fruit, Inflect, Reinvest, Specialize, and Time-Limited. You're going to optimize what's working, act as if to stretch your skill set, reinvest to free up time, specialize to refine your client base, and have time-limited goals to focus on what's happening right now.

9. **Bolts and Levels:** As you get into the pattern of slowing down and killin' it, you'll need to return to the bolts of the business that need to be tightened. Phase 1: Team brainstorm with bolts and levels, Phase 2: Experiment enacted, and then, Phase 3: Assessment of experiment. As you enact and refine this model, reconfigure who does what, how they do it, and when. Set your KPIs to measure the experiment, do it, and assess what worked and what needs to change.

10. **Find Your Sprint Type™:** Do you prefer to have a specific sprint time blocked each week or take lengthier retreats away? In your sprints, is it one topic area or multiple? Know your Sprint Type™ and have that time and work be a nonnegotiable with your team.

Remember that this is an organism. It's not just you but your team. It shifts, evolves, and changes. That's true of your market and customers as well. They personally change and so do their pains and desired transformations.

THROW IT ALL OUT

Why are you doing any of this? Seriously. Why do you have your job, business, or side gig at all?

One of the most important things to think through is the idea of starting from scratch. Knowing what you know, would you do it all over again? The next five, ten, or thirty years of your life may be spent in this work. Statistically, a third of your life will be spent working.[2]

So why spend it doing this? In this section, I want to go super macro and challenge you to think about why you do what you do, then we will go super micro and examine a plan for your workweek.

If you started your business/career from scratch, would you do it this way? Here are some questions to look at your overall direction:

- When do you get lost in a project? When do you experience a flow state?
- What are you curious about? Does that line up with your current work tasks?
- When are you happiest in work?
- When are you happiest outside of work?
- Say your business dissolved and that industry disappeared: What new type of business would you create or join if you knew it would be successful?
- If you were starting from scratch, what would you not do in the first three years that you are currently doing?
- If you were to start from scratch, what would you start doing earlier in the life of the business?
- What is taking up mental energy that needs to be left behind?
- What do you wish took up more mental energy?
- If your business and life never progressed past this point, how would you stay happy?
- What activities build your happiness that you are doing?
- What activities build your happiness that you are not doing?
- Is this the life you want?

Next, it's time to run some experiments. Pick one area in life or business and view it as if you are starting from scratch. It could be a system, relationship, product, or customer group. What if you were building from scratch without any of your systems, investment, or emotional baggage:

- Would you still serve that type of client?
- Would you still be connected with that person?
- Would that be the system you choose?

Now you can compare your current model with the experiment. For example, we use an email system that is not what I would choose if I started over. But, for the added benefits of some other systems, it's not worth losing current clients, rebuilding the system, or trying a new product that might not be around in a year. There are times you stick with what you know and it's good enough. I know taking on a new project like that is not the single best use of my time, or my team's time. But there are other times that we may pivot and start from scratch despite previous investments of time and money.

YOUR WEEKLY SCHEDULE: SLOW DOWN + SPRINTING

Pull out your schedule. Look ahead and block out time for your first sprint. Maybe it's next Tuesday morning for thirty minutes. Maybe it's an hour Thursday afternoon. It could be in a few weeks. Put it in.

Now, look ahead and block out some time that can repeat. Schedule some boundaries to slow down. Here are some Slow Down Boundary ideas:[3]

- Schedule thirty minutes each morning to walk or work out.
- Sign up for a weekly workout class.
- Block out one Friday a month from work.
- Schedule all your medical appointments in one month.
- Block out lunch on Wednesday and commit to having a non-business lunch with a friend or someone important.
- Listen to a podcast that fills you up spiritually.[4]
- Meditate more than you do now.
- Set time aside to go into nature.
- Do a five-sense exercise where you focus on one sense at a time.
- Take time on Friday afternoons to do all your errands for the weekend so you can have fun.

- Plan things on the weekend that are fun, not just getting things done.
- Don't catch up on work email or texts after work hours.

Think through all that you need to remove from your plate in the coming weeks to try an experiment.

There will be no typical week, but here is a potential schedule:

Monday–Thursday: Seek to work no more than eight hours. Identify your body's needs for food, breaks, and movement. Try to double up phone calls and a walk so you are meeting needs during this time. Frequently think about the single best use of your time.

Friday–Sunday: Move toward working less. This might start with being done by 3:00 p.m. Then move it to noon. Then once a month take a full Friday off. We're looking for progress, not perfection. Push yourself to get as much done in four days as possible. For a while spend Friday getting life things done so that you have two full days of fun and adventure over the weekend. Don't look at your next week's schedule until Sunday after dinner.

WE NEED REVOLUTIONARIES LIKE YOU

The Industrialists want your life. But it is not theirs to take. Sure, your situation may feel like these topics are unmovable for you (good for you getting to this point if that's you). The movement toward a four-day workweek is humanity's natural next step in evolution. This is the time for us to do this.

Throughout this book, you've seen that science overwhelmingly shows that through slowing down our creativity and productivity expand exponentially. We need the new Henry Fords to make clear and authoritative statements about the next step of human potential as we move away from a five-day workweek.

Dream with me. Imagine a world where our brains feel calm with less anxiety and coordinate with nature. Imagine we spend time with friends, family, and have time alone from the world. Then, when it's time to work, we are so excited, creative, and productive that we leave work wanting more.

Imagine we're so in the zone or in flow that what we do doesn't drain us but instead makes us feel more alive.

Imagine being in a flow between slowing down and killin' it in work that feels like anything else in nature. Instead of a 5:2 ratio of workdays:rest, we move toward 4:3, and then who knows where we go from there?

You are needed to make Thursday the new Friday.

THE THURSDAY IS
THE NEW FRIDAY MANIFESTO

To download a printable copy to frame, hang up, or put anywhere, go to www.joesanok.com/manifesto.

This life is ours.

We believe that we are made for slowing down and doing creative and impactful work, that weekends are not enough, and that our best work comes after we slow down.

We believe that the mechanical system created by the Industrialists was a step forward for the time but is no longer what is best for humans or the world. Our human potential is being limited by mindless and useless work instead of the impactful work that sits quietly inside of us.

We believe that slowing down is the way to release this creativity into the world. Our best work comes when we are centered, de-stressed, and able to breathe. We will contribute in disruptive and world-changing ways only when our body is centered and has slowed down.

We believe that we are a changing organism that is allowed to switch interests, experiment with ideas, and fail. Failure and experimenting are linchpins to allowing ourselves to expand. Gone are the days of being paralyzed by perfection. Instead we will live with a posture of pushing the limits to find what we and society are made of.

We believe that we are re-creating our world in a way that will expand our potential, open us up to better living, and create the most meaningful work we could imagine.

We believe that Thursday is the new Friday.

Get coaching for yourself or your team or apply for our waitlist to become a certified Thursday Is the New Friday coach at www.joesanok.com/coach.

ACKNOWLEDGMENTS

Every book takes a team of people who support, dream, and push the author to do better. First, my family. Rick and MaryEllen Sanok, you've been such amazing parents who gave me so many opportunities and hugs to feel grounded in the world. Lydia and Pete Sanok, thank you for all your sibling love and ideas. Lucia and Laken Sanok, you're the whole reason I slow down, so we can play, be silly, and have adventures. Penelope, Paige, Hadley, and Fin, you make being an uncle so fun! Christina, thank you for the years together and your support. Paul and Diane Kolak, your book feedback, friendship, and game nights have been so helpful. To Taylor Nash, Jeremy Blaha, Chris Stroven, Chris Barrett, and Aaron VanHeest, you are guys who show up, you're amazing. Greg Ray (my agent) and Nancy Hancock (my writing coach), how could I have done this without you?! Tim Burgard and the whole HarperCollins team, Cave Henricks, and Interview Valet, thanks for getting this vision out to the world. *Practice of the Practice* team, you have been so supportive: Jess Ross, Whitney Owens, Alison Pidgeon, LaToya Smith, Sam Carvalho, Sam Rudowski, Adrienne Kruger, Niranda Hoctor, and Dana Barber. Kelly Higdon, Dr. Jeremy Sharp, and Dr. Julie Schwartz-Gottman, thank you for your friendships and ideas. Dr. Megan Warner, for your research help. To all the consulting clients, *Practice of the Practice Podcast* listeners, Next Level Practice members, Group Practice Boss members, Podcast Launch Schoolers, Killin'It Camp participants, and Slow Down Schoolers, you make all of this so fun! Thanks also to my fellow HarperCollins authors John Lee Dumas, Allie Casazza, and Angie Morgan. Pat Flynn, you've been such an inspiration and help. Lastly, to all the revolutionaries who don't accept the world as we see it, the Haymarket protesters, and those who will make Thursday the New Friday, this is for all of you!

NOTES

1. WORKING LESS IS DANGEROUS

1. Witold Rybczynski, "Waiting for the Weekend," *Atlantic*, August 1991, https://www.theatlantic.com/magazine/archive/1991/08/waiting-for-the -weekend/376343/.
2. Kristin Heineman, Colorado State University, "Why Are There Seven Days in a Week?" *Discover*, January 15, 2020, https://www.discovermagazine.com /planet-earth/why-are-there-seven-days-in-a-week.
3. Elisabeth Achelis, *Journal of Calendar Reform*, 1954, http://myweb.ecu.edu /mccartyr/Russia.html.
4. Natasha Frost, "For 11 Years the Soviet Union Had No Weekends," History.com, May 25, 2018, https://www.history.com/news/soviet-union-stalin-weekend-labor-policy.
5. Willam J. Adleman, "The Haymarket Affair," Illinois Labor History Society, http:// www.illinoislaborhistory.org/the-haymarket-affair.
6. Philip Sopher, "Where the Five-Day Workweek Came From," *Atlantic*, August 21, 2014, https://www.theatlantic.com/business/archive/2014/08 /where-the-five-day-workweek-came-from/378870/.
7. History.com Editors, "Ford Factory Workers Get 40-hour Week," https://www .history.com/this-day-in-history/ford-factory-workers-get-40-hour-week.
8. History.com Editors, "Ford Factory Workers Get 40-hour Week."
9. Brian D. Ray, "Research Facts on Homeschooling," National Home Education Research Institute, March 23, 2020, https://www.nheri.org/research-facts -on-homeschooling/.
10. Manuel Moerbach, "Remote Work is Here to Stay," Newsweek, April 30, 2020, https://apple.news/A3ZtybwYPSf2mE5pvs-S2Rg.
11. Sometimes revolutions take a while to stick and need a rich advocate that sees how it makes business sense to listen to those in less powerful positions.
12. Allard E. Dembe and Xiaoxi Yao, "Chronic Disease Risks from Exposure to Long-Hour Work Schedules Over a 32-Year Period," *Journal of Occupational and Environmental Medicine* 58, no. 9 (2016): 861–867, https://journals.lww.com/joem/Abstract/2016/09000/Chronic_Disease _Risks_From_Exposure_to_Long_Hour.2.aspx.
13. Sophie Jackman, "Japan Says Four-Day Work Week Boosted Productivity 40%," Bloomberg, November 4, 2019, https://www.bloomberg.com/news/articles /2019-11-04/microsoft-japan-says-four-day-work-week-boosted-productivity-40.

14. Juliana Wolfsberger and Jutta Lena Rübelmann, "The 30-hour Workweek - A Promising Alternative for Knowledge Workers?" Master thesis, Lund University, 2017, https://lup.lub.lu.se/student-papers/search/publication/8919921.

15. Matthijs Baas, Carsten K. W. De Dreu, and Bernard A. Nijstad, (2008). "A meta-analysis of 25 years of mood-creativity research," *Psychological Bulletin* 134, no. 6 (2008): 779–806, https://doi.apa.org/doiLanding?doi=10,1037%2Fa0012815.

16. Courtney Connley, "Why the CEO of Basecamp Only Allows Employees to Work 32 Hours a Week," CNBC Make It, August 4, 2017, https://www.cnbc.com/2017/08/03/the-ceo-of-basecamp-only-allows-employees-to-put-in-a-32-hour-workweek.html.

17. Sam Harris, "194: The New Future of Work," March 24, 2020, in *Making Sense*, podcast, https://podcasts.apple.com/us/podcast/making-sense-with-sam-harris/id733163012?i=1000469417564.

18. Jerry M. Flint, "G. M. Strike Impact Begins to Spread," *New York Times*, October 3, 1970, .https://www.nytimes.com/1970/10/03/archives/gm-strike-impact-begins-to-spread.html.

19. Gloria Mark, Daniela Gudith, and Ulrich Klocke, "The Cost of Interrupted Work: More Speed and Stress," *Proceedings of the SIGCHI Conference on Human Factors in Computing Systems* (2008), https://www.researchgate.net/publication/221518077_The_cost_of_interrupted_work_More_speed_and_stress.

2. INTERNAL INCLINATIONS

1. Julie A. Mennella, Coren P. Jagnow, and Gary K. Beauchamp, "Prenatal and Postnatal Flavor Learning by Human Infants," *Pediatrics* 107, no. 6, E88 (June, 2001), https://pediatrics.aappublications.org/content/107/6/e88.

2. Karen M. Dyer and Jacqueline Carothers, *The Intuitive Principal: A Guide to Leadership* (Thousand Oaks, CA: Corwin Press, 2000), 7.

3. From the Ricky Gervais Netflix stand-up special, *Humanity*. Ricky has a politically incorrect view of the world, so please don't take this as a full endorsement; he just makes an awesome point about intuition I could not ignore . . . and it's just plain funny.

4. "intueri." WordSense.eu online dictionary (2021), https://www.wordsense.eu/intueri/.

5. "intuition." Dictionary.com (2021), https://www.dictionary.com/browse/intuition?s=t.

3. CURIOSITY

1. A. Jones, H. J. Wilkinson, and I. Braden, "Information Deprivation as A Motivational Variable," *Journal of Experimental Psychology* 62, no. 2 (1961), 126–37.

2. Referenced in George Loewenstein, "The Psychology of Curiosity," *Psychological Bulletin* 116, no. 1 (1994): 75–98, http://www.andrew.cmu.edu/user/gl20/GeorgeLoewenstein/Papers_files/pdf/PsychofCuriosity.pdf.

3. Loewenstein, "The Psychology of Curiosity," 81.

4. Want to launch a podcast? We can help by doing it for you at www.practiceofthepractice .com/apply to apply for done-for-you podcast services or sign up for the course at www.podcastlaunchschool.com.

5. Ainsley Arment, *Call of the Wild and Free*, read by Piper Goodeve (New York: HarperAudio, 2019), 8:45:00.

6. Jillian D'Onfro, "The Truth About Google's Famous '20% Time' Policy," Business Insider.com, April 17, 2015, https://www.businessinsider.com /google-20-percent-time-policy-2015-4.

7. Read *The ONE Thing*. You won't regret it.

8. "Udemy in Depth: 2018 Workplace Distraction Report," https://research.udemy. com/wp-content/uploads/2018/03/FINAL-Udemy_2018_Workplace_Distraction _Report.pdf.

4. OUTSIDER APPROACH

1. Malcolm Gladwell, "Lost in the Middle," *Washington Post*, May 17, 1998, https:// www.washingtonpost.com/wp-srv/national/longterm/middleground/gladwell2.htm.

2. From the documentary *Jane*, dir. Brett Morgen (2017, Washington, DC: National Geographic Studios).

3. E. D. Wesselmann, J. S Nairne, and K. D. Williams, "An Evolutionary Social Psychological Approach to Studying the Effects of Ostracism," *Journal of Social, Evolutionary, and Cultural Psychology* 6, no. 3 (2013), 308–27, http://dx.doi .org/10.1037/h0099249.

4. Marwa Azab, "Is Social Pain Real Pain?" *Psychology Today*, April 25, 2017, https://www.psychologytoday.com/us/blog/neuroscience-in-everyday-life/201704 /is-social-pain-real-pain.

5. Brian McCollum, "New Crop of Motown Artists Get Inspired by Hitsville in Detroit Visit," *Detroit Free Press*, December 11, 2018, https://www.freep.com/story /entertainment/music/brian-mccollum/2018/12/11/motown-artists-hitsville-detroit -visit/2264461002/.

6. Motown Museum, https://www.motownmuseum.org/story/motown/.

7. My brother Pete Sanok pushed me on this early in my career and I still use this technique to this day.

8. Center on the Developing Child, Harvard University, "Take the ACE Quiz—and Learn What It Does and Doesn't Mean," https://developingchild.harvard.edu /media-coverage/take-the-ace-quiz-and-learn-what-it-does-and-doesnt-mean/.

9. "Got Your ACE Score?" *ACEs Too High News* (blog), https://acestoohigh.com /got-your-ace-score/.

10. Slutsky, et al., "Mindfulness Training Improves Employee Well-Being: A Ran-domized Controlled Trial," *Journal of Occupational Health Psychology* 24, no.1, (2019): 139–149, https://www.apa.org/pubs/highlights/spotlight/issue-126.

11. Lindsay, et al., "Mindfulness Training Reduces Loneliness and Increases Social Contact in a Randomized Controlled Trial," *Proceedings of the National Academy of Sciences* 116, no. 9 (2019): 3488–93, https://www.pnas.org/content/116/9/3488.

12. Slutsky et al., "Mindfulness Training Improves Employee Well-Being," 139–49.

13. Joseph Sparks, "Minority Influence—Consistency and Commitment," tutor2u .net, https://www.tutor2u.net/psychology/reference/minority-influence-consistency -and-commitment; and S. Moscovici and M. Zavalloni, "The group as a polarizer of attitudes," *Journal of Personality and Ssocial Psychology* 12 (1969): 125–35.

14. C. J. Nemeth, "The Differential Contributions of Majority and Minority Influence." *Psychological Review* 93 (1986): 23–32.

5. MOVE ON IT

1. C. Northcote Parkinson, "Parkinson's Law," *Economist*, November 19, 1955, https://www.economist.com/news/1955/11/19/parkinsons-law.

2. C. Northcote Parkinson, "Parkinson's Law."

3. Pauline Rose Clance, "Impostor Phenomenon," paulineroseclance.com, https:// www.paulineroseclance.com/impostor_phenomenon.html.

4. Cowie et al., "Perfectionism and Academic Difficulties in Graduate Students," *Personality and Individual Differences* 123 (March, 2018): 223–28, https://www .sciencedirect.com/science/article/abs/pii/S0191886917306840?via%3Dihub.

5. It's crazy that principals still take away recess from the kids that need it most. Classes like gym, art, and music all stimulate the brain in a way to make learning easier in other areas. Even education still has the Industrialists' fingerprints all over it.

6. Wiklund et al., "ADHD, Impulsivity and Entrepreneurship," *Journal of Business Venturing* 32, no. 6 (November 2017): 627–56, https://www.sciencedirect.com /science/article/abs/pii/S0883902616302348.

7. McMullen and Shepherd, 2006; Paulus, 2007.

8. Hugh Molotsi, "There's an MVP for That," Lean Startup Co., https://leanstartup .co/5026-2/.

9. Interested? Read more at www.practiceofthepractice.com/plan and www .practiceofthepractice.com/apply.

6. SLOW DOWN

1. Sam Harris, "205: The Failure of Meritocracy," May 22, 2020, in *Making Sense*, podcast, approx. 11:00, https://podcasts.apple.com/us/podcast /making-sense-with-sam-harris/id733163012?i=1000475455398.

2. A. Ariga, and A. Lleras, "Brief and Rare Mental 'Breaks' Keep You Focused," *Cognition* 118, no.3 (2011): 439–43.

3. Tim McMahon, "Long Term U.S. Inflation," InflationData.com, April 1, 2014, https://inflationdata.com/Inflation/Inflation_Rate/Long_Term_Inflation .asp#:~:text=As%20we%20saw%20the%20Average,since%20they%20 began%20keeping%20records.

4. To hear much more about this, listen to me and Pete Kirkwood on *The Happitalist Podcast*, http://happitalist.com/.

5. Olga Khazan, "Thomas Edison and the Cult of Sleep Deprivation," *Atlantic*, May 14, 2014, https://www.theatlantic.com/health/archive/2014/05 /thomas-edison-and-the-cult-of-sleep-deprivation/370824/.

6. Centers for Disease Control and Prevention, "Sleep and Sleep Disorders: Data and Statistics," https://www.cdc.gov/sleep/data_statistics.html.

7. Robert Klara, "Sleep Deprivation Is Quietly Draining Revenue from Brands in the COVID-19 Era," *Adweek*, April, 22, 2020, https://www.adweek.com/brand-marketing/sleep-deprivation-draining-revenues-covid-19/.

8. "U.S. Shows Widening Disconnect with Nature, and Potential Solutions," *Yale Environment* 360, April 27, 2017, https://e360.yale.edu/digest/u-s-study-shows-widening-disconnect-with-nature-and-potential-solutions.

9. Christopher Ingraham, "Americans Are Getting More Miserable, and There's Data to Prove It," *Washington Post*, March, 22, 2019, https://www.washingtonpost.com/business/2019/03/22/americans-are-getting-more-miserable-theres-data-prove-it/.

10. R. Sturm and D. A. Cohen, "Free Time and Physical Activity Among Americans 15 Years or Older: Cross-Sectional Analysis of the American Time Use Survey," *Preventing Chronic Disease* 16 (2019): 190017, https://www.cdc.gov/pcd/issues/2019/19_0017.htm.

11. Twenge et al., "Age, Period, and Cohort Trends in Mood Disorder Indicators and Suicide-Related Outcomes in a Nationally Representative Dataset, 2005–2017," *Journal of Abnormal Psychology* 128, no. 3 (2019): 185–199, doi: 10.1037/abn0000410.

12. Jeremy Campbell, *Winston Churchill's Afternoon Nap: A Wide-Awake Inquiry into the Human Nature of Time* (New York: Simon & Schuster,1987).

13. Walter Isaacson, *Steve Jobs* (New York: Simon & Schuster, 2011).

14. From the documentary *Jane*, dir. Brett Morgen (2017, Washington, DC: National Geographic Studios).

15. Walter Isaacson, *Einstein* (New York: Simon & Schuster, 2007).

16. Gloria Mark, Daniela Gudith, and Ulrich Klocke, "The Cost of Interrupted Work: More Speed and Stress," *Proceedings of the SIGCHI Conference on Human Factors in Computing Systems* (2008), https://www.researchgate.net/publication/221518077_The_cost_of_interrupted_work_More_speed_and_stress, https://www.ics.uci.edu/~gmark/chi08-mark.pdf.

17. http://sleep.org/.

18. https://www.givingwhatwecan.org/ is one of many websites where you can enter your information and data to see where you line up in the world. It's often shocking how affluent we are, without making an extra dime per year. It really puts our monetary goals in perspective.

19. The Bill Gates documentary, *Inside Bill's Brain*, on Netflix is an awesome insight into how Bill thinks, understands, and absorbs information. I do think that his model of reading and diving in may get a bit obsessive and isn't applicable to every person, but we need people like him who dive deep and don't come up for air. I wonder if he took more time to slow down, would he have even bigger ideas? https://www.netflix.com/title/80184771.

20. Drake Baer "The Scientific Reason Why Barack Obama and Mark Zuckerberg Wear the Same Outfit Every Day," *Business Insider*, April 28, 2015.

21. Jeremy pulls from Gary Keller and Jay Papasan's work in *The ONE Thing.* I highly recommend this book to help you with focus and ROI on your time.

22. Chin et al., "Mindfulness Training Reduces Stress at Work: a Randomized Controlled Trial," *Mindfulness* 10 (2019): 627–38, https://www.researchgate .net/profile/Brian_Chin6/publication/327223752_Mindfulness_Training _Reduces_Stress_At_Work_A_Randomized_Controlled_Trial /links/5b816589299bf1d5a727076f/Mindfulness-Training-Reduces-Stress-At -Work-A-Randomized-Controlled-Trial.pdf.

23. Christopher Ingraham, "People Who Spend More Time Outdoors Lead More Fulfilling Lives, New Research Shows," *Washington Post*, June 19, 2019, https:// www.washingtonpost.com/business/2019/06/19/people-who-spend-more-time -outdoors-lead-more-fulfilling-lives-new-research-shows/; and White et al., "Spending at Least 120 Minutes a Week in Nature Is Associated with Good Health and Wellbeing," *Scientific Reports* 9, 7730 (2019), https://www.nature.com/articles /s41598-019-44097-3.

24. Luders et al., "The unique brain anatomy of meditation practitioners: alterations in cortical gyrification" *Frontiers in Human Neuroscience* 6, 34 (2012), https://doi .org/10.3389/fnhum.2012.00034.

25. Lindsay et al., "Mindfulness training reduces loneliness," https://www.pnas.org /content/116/9/3488.

7. HOW TO SLOW DOWN

1. American Psychological Association, "Americans Stay Connected to Work on Weekends, Vacation and Even When Out Sick," press release, (2013), https://www .apa.org/news/press/releases/2013/09/connected-work.

2. B. Jiang, R. Schmillen, and W. Sullivan, "How to Waste a Break: Electronic Devices Substantially Counteracts Attention Enhancements Effects of Green Spaces," *Environment and Behavior* 51, no. 9–10 (2019): 1133–60.

3. Mastercard News, MasterCard TV Commercial #OneMoreDay, YouTube video, 0:32, September 22, 2014, https://youtu.be/snT9McxPAeI.

4. R. Sturm and D. A. Cohen, "Free Time and Physical Activity Among Americans 15 Years or Older," https://www.cdc.gov/pcd/issues/2019/19_0017.htm.

5. Claudia Dewane, "The ABCs of ACT—Acceptance and Commitment Therapy," *Social Work Today* 8, no. 5 (2008): 34, https://www.socialworktoday.com /archive/090208p36.shtml.

6. Steven Hayes, "The Six Core Processes of ACT," Association for Contextual Behavioral Science, https://contextualscience.org/the_six_core_processes_of_act.

7. Steven Hayes, "The Six Core Processes of ACT."

8. David DiSalvo, "Forget Survival of the Fittest: It Is Kindness That Counts," *Scientific American*, September 1, 2009, https://www.scientificamerican.com /article/forget-survival-of-the-fittest/#:~:text=People%20who%20have%20 high%20vagus,%2C%20gratitude%2C%20love%20and%20happiness.

9. Home of Dr. Stephen Porges, https://www.stephenporges.com/.

10. Chispa Motivation, "Work Every Waking Hour: Elon Musk," YouTube video, 1:23, November 29, 2019, https://youtu.be/unU9vpLjHRk.

11. R. H. Matsuoka, "Student performance and high school landscapes: Examining the links," *Landscape and Urban Planning* 97, no. 4 (2010): 273–82, https://www.sciencedirect.com/science/article/abs/pii/S0169204610001465?via%3Dihub.

12. My best research has determined that Kurt Vonnegut said this first.

13. Since this is not legal in the United States, except with limited FDA approved trials, such experiments happen outside of the United States. Do so at your own risk, do your own research, and work with your doctor.

14. Bruce Tuckman created this model in 1965.

8. YOUR HUSTLE NARRATIVE

1. Chispa Motivation, "Work Every Waking Hour: Elon Musk," https://youtu.be/unU9vpLjHRk.

2. Isaacson, *Steve Jobs*, 118.

3. Isaacson, *Steve Jobs*, 119.

4. G. P. Chrousos, "Stress and disorders of the stress system," *Nature Reviews Endocrinology* 5, no.7 (2009): 374–81, https://pubmed.ncbi.nlm.nih.gov/19488073/.

5. This is a great TED Ed video all about how cortisol changes the brain when under stress, TED-ED, "How stress affects your brain—Madhumita Murgia," YouTube video, 4:15, November 9, 2015, https://youtu.be/WuyPuH9ojCE.

6. Mayo Clinic Staff, "Chronic stress puts your health at risk," MayoClinic.org, March 19, 2019, https://www.mayoclinic.org/healthy-lifestyle/stress-management/in-depth/stress/art-20046037#:~:text=Cortisol%2C%20the%20primary%20stress%20hormone,fight%2Dor%2Dflight%20situation.

7. S. Kotler and J. Wheal, *Stealing Fire*, read by Fred Sanders (New York: HarperAudio, 2017) audiobook, 2:30:00.

8. J. Kruger and D. Dunning, "Unskilled and Unaware of It: How Difficulties in Recognizing One's Own Incompetence Lead to Inflated Self-Assessments," *Journal of Personality and Social Psychology* 77, no. 6 (Dec. 1999): 1121–1134. PMID: 10626367.

9. KILLIN' IT IS THE YIN TO SLOW DOWN'S YANG

1. To hear the entire interview with Ted Forester, go to joesanok.com/interviews.

2. That year at Slow Down School we had more activities during the "slow down" period, because the group seemed more engaged in that way. In other years, we just watch sunsets. So, if doing improv or silent disco freaks you out, don't rule out Slow Down School. We look at each year's participants, goals, and potential outcomes. Also, we keep a similar structure, but change it to make it interesting for returning Slow Down Schoolers. www.SlowDownSchool.com for more info.

3. Read *The ONE Thing*. You won't regret it.

4. Flow Genome Project, https://www.flowgenomeproject.com/.

5. Steven Kotler, "Create a Work Environment That Fosters Flow," *Harvard Business Review*, May 6, 2014, https://hbr.org/2014/05/create-a-work-environment-that-fosters-flow#:~:text=In%20a%2010%2Dyear%20study,times%20more%20productive%20in%20flow.&text=In%20fact%2C%20according%20to%20these,workplace%20productivity%20would%20almost%20double.

6. Cheryl Pellerin, "DARPA Funds Brain-Stimulation Research to Speed Learning," US Department of Defense, April 27, 2017, https://www.defense.gov/Explore/News/Article/Article/1164793/darpa-funds-brain-stimulation-research-to-speed-up-learning/.

7. If you are interested in going deep into flow, you've got to check out Kotler's book *Stealing Fire*; it's amazing!

8. Here is the rabbit hole of government-funded brain research. Consider yourself warned; you might lose a weekend diving into this: Pellerin, "DARPA Funds Brain-Stimulation Research," https://www.defense.gov/Explore/News/Article/Article/1164793/darpa-funds-brain-stimulation-research-to-speed-up-learning/.

9. *The Full of Shift Podcast* is a great resource for making small changes on an ongoing basis. Kate's interviews and approach are awesome!

10. T. S. Elliot, *The Sacred Wood* (New York, Alfred A. Knopf, 1921).

11. Fred Topel, "'*Frozen 2*' Songwriters Reveal Where You've Heard That Siren Call Before," Deadline.com, December 19, 2019, https://deadline.com/video/frozen-2-into-the-unknown-song-kristen-anderson-lopez-robert-lopez-interview-oscar-contenders/.

12. For an amazing discussion of the "four notes of death," check this article out: Jason Kottke, "The Four Notes of Death," Kottke.org, (blog), September 17, 2019, https://kottke.org/19/09/the-four-notes-of-death.

13. I have looked high and low for who said this and can't seem to find it. If you know, I'll give you credit on the website www.joesanok.com/resources.

14. Domo, "Data Never Sleeps 5.0," Domo.com, https://www.domo.com/learn/data-never-sleeps-5?aid=ogsm072517_1&sf100871281=1; and Bernard Marr, "How Much Data Do We Create Every Day?" Forbes.com, May 21, 2018, https://www.forbes.com/sites/bernardmarr/2018/05/21/how-much-data-do-we-create-every-day-the-mind-blowing-stats-everyone-should-read/#1cce544a60ba.

15. For a list of the podcasts we have helped launch that help the world to be better, go to practiceofthepractice.com/network. Shows like: *The After the First Marriage Podcast*, *Behind the Bite Podcast*, *Beta Male Revolution Podcast*, *Imperfect Thriving Podcast*, *Bomb Mom Podcast*, *Full of Shift Podcast*, and *Eating Recovery Academy Podcast*.

16. Steve Glaveski, "The Case for the 6-Hour Workday," *Harvard Business Review*, December 11, 2018, https://hbr.org/2018/12/the-case-for-the-6-hour-workday.

17. If you have great examples of experiments that you have undertaken, will you submit them for possible inclusion on my site? www.joesanok.com/experiments.

18. Roland Busch, @BuschRo, Twitter, https://twitter.com/BuschRo?ref_src=twsrc%5Etfw%7Ctwcamp%5Etweetembed%7Ctwterm%5E12836888153

62703361%7Ctwgr%5E&ref_url=https%3A%2F%2Fwww.siliconrepublic
.com%2Fcareers%2Fsiemens-remote-working-plan.

19. Jim Harter, "Employee Engagement Continues Historic Rise Amid Coronavirus,"
Gallup.com (blog), May 29, 2020, https://www.gallup.com/workplace/311561
/employee-engagement-continues-historic-rise-amid-coronavirus.aspx.

10. YOUR BIG, SUCCESSFUL, HAPPY LIFE

1. Matthew 6:28–30 NKJV.
2. World Health Organization, https://www.who.int/occupational_health/publications
/globstrategy/en/index2.html.
3. Find more resources, webinars, and tools at joesanok.com/resources.
4. Some I enjoy are Rob Bell's *Robcast*, Sam Harris's *Making Sense Podcast, The
Ram Dass Podcast, Heart Wisdom Podcast with Jack Cornfield, Armchair Expert
with Dax Shepard*, and *Fulfillment Stories*.

INDEX

ABOUT THE AUTHOR

Joe **Sanok**, MA, LPC, LLP, NCC, is a business consultant, keynote speaker, and author of *Thursday is the New Friday*. Joe has the #1 podcast for counselors and coaches, *The Practice of the Practice*, with one hundred thousand listens per month. As well, Joe's work with www .PracticeofthePractice.com helps private practice owners to start, grow, and scale to offer more mental health services in communities around the world. Joe is trained and licensed as a counselor and psychologist. He has consulted with and trained thousands of businesses to help them make the greatest impact on the world. As a passionate revolutionary around the four-day workweek, Joe enjoys finding innovative solutions to build creativity and productivity with companies and entrepreneurs.

Joe is also the founder of two annual events, Slow Down School and Killin'It Camp. These events help entrepreneurs and business owners to slow down to spark innovation.

Because Joe seeks to live what he teaches, he pushes himself to find adventure in stand-up paddle boarding, road trips with his two daughters, Lucia and Laken, painting, music, and improv. For more resources, events, and to work with Joe, go to www.joesanok.com.

RESOURCES

- Starting a practice: www.practiceofthepractice.com/start
- Growing a practice: www.practiceofthepractice.com/grow
- *Practice of the Practice* podcast network: www.practiceofthepractice .com/network
- Joe's membership communities: www.practiceofthepractice.com/invite
- Joe's speaking and thought leadership: www.JoeSanok.com